Mary's Way

A Memoir of the Life of
Mary Cooper Back

Compiled and narrated by
Ruth Mary Lamb

Mary's Way: a Memoir of the Life of Mary Cooper Back

First Edition 1999

Cover design by Ruth Mary Lamb & Kris Wendtland
Cover art: *Wyoming Earth* oil painting by Mary Back
Illustrations by Mary Back

ISBN 0-9671734-0-X

Prepared for printing by
FuturePrep Corporation
427 E. Birch   PO Box 4141
Glenrock, Wyo. 82637   Casper, Wyo. 82604

Grateful acknowledgement is made to the following for permission to reprint previously published material.

Coverage of Mary Back when she was honored with the Governors Award for Service to the Arts, *Dubois Frontier*, Feb. 26, 1987. Reprinted with permission from the *Dubois Frontier*.

Excerpt from *Seven Half Miles from Home, Notes of a Wind River Naturalist* by Mary Back, Copyright Johnson Books 1985. Reprinted with permission from Johnson Books.

Sketches by Mary Back and excerpts from articles published by the *High Country News*, Jan. 26, 1979 and Dec. 12, 1980 editions. Reprinted with permission from the *High Country News*.

Berea College Year Book
1927

Mary Waters Cooper
Major: Ancient Language
Thesis: The relation of Greek literature and art to modern art
Yearbook Editor

She is nature's child. When she speeds over the hills the squirrels chatter to her and the trees, in sympathetic kinship, hold out their branches. When she laughs the golden moon beams are shot with silver.

When she speaks, words of wisdom fall from her lips. Her play with nature's children has given her courage and self-reliance. Her communion with mother earth has bestowed upon her a strong body, a keen mind and a magnificent spirit. She is one who says, "I will lift up mine eyes unto the hills, from whence cometh my help."

❖ ❖ Acknowledgements ❖ ❖

This book would not have happened
without the following wonderful people:

Mary, who lived the life of love
Mary's brothers and sisters who saved the letters

My husband Sandy, critic and supporter extraordinaire
My children - Bonnie, Glenn and Bruce - patient, caring commentators
Mary's cousin Mary Ellen Lindley - faithful reader, critic, and supporter

Mary's good friend Twila Blakeman - a very busy lady who opened many
        doors for me and kept me focused
Mary's Dubois neighbors, especially - Lindy Duff, Jeannine Nelson, Mary
        Ellen Honsaker, Sylvia Crouter, Betty Wendtland, Stan Blakeman, Vic
        Lemmon, and Robin Waldron - who helped in countless ways

Family readers, advisors and providers of memorabilia: Carolyn Morris,
        Malcolm McGawn, Janet Bozidarevic, Laura Merrick, Mary Schwarz,
        Ed Lyon, Jane Larsh, Joanna Spence, Ellen Hudak, Wilson and Nancy
        Cooper, Bill Larsen, Chuck Larsen, John Larsen, Eleanor Brigham, Ric
        van der Schalie, Marilyn Anderson

Other readers, especially - Jane Caldwell, Lee Cadwallader, Doug and Jan
        Spencer, Margaret Whitaker, Helen Stern, Patti Barrett, Berta Collins,
        Mark Merrill, Arline Chase

Mary Hennen of the Chicago Academy of Sciences who scoured Academy
        records finding references to Mary Cooper and her contributions
Kris Wendtland of FuturePrep Corporation who thoughtfully transformed
        my manuscript into a book

The many folks who shared memories and photographs

Contents

Sketches

Photographs

Introduction

Candlelight shines on my paper, faintly illuminating our white collie, Lady, just composed to slumber on a chair. The glow is reflected from a washtub on the stove and from the tall tower of two cans soldered together that are used for a flour bin, and makes just visible the rough log walls (lit only by contrast with the black holes of the windows). Outside I can hear Joe's ax as he gets wood ready for breakfast. Lava Creek murmurs over stones. The wind makes music in the pines. Except for these things there is a great silence, punctuated by the occasional hooting of a horned owl.

It's half a mile to the quiet highway, quiet for many a mile before it comes to any bustle of life…. You might think there'd be some loneliness, but it's not so. The log walls, the purring fire, the little gentle loyal dog, the finest man in the world, makes a combination that means home. This is our ranch.

Mary Cooper Back had just arrived in the Wind River valley of Wyoming in 1935 with her new husband when she wrote this. Flushed with the excitement of reaching for a dream and beginning to fulfill it, she sparkled with delight. Pausing in her writing, she touched the braid circling her head and frowned a little. She and Joe were going to become Wyoming artists, she told herself, but first they had to get themselves established in this beautiful wild country, so strange to Mary but as familiar as an old shoe to Joe.

It was going to be hard work, but they would do it.

As she straightened up, she glanced out the window where the early morning glow sharply etched the mountain silhouettes. She recalled how she had worried as a college student in Berea, Kentucky that she would never fulfill her great desire to become a mountain adventurer. And now here she was, close to the loves of her life: Joe and mountains. What more could she ask?

Putting aside her pen to call Joe to breakfast, she realized there <u>was</u> one big drawback. Her family... they were so far away. She tried to picture them - sisters Miriam in the Nebraska Sand Hills; Dorothy in Illinois; Frances and their dad sharing a house near Chicago; while brothers Ed and Milton (my father) were far away in Maine. How she wished she could share this new life with them. Well, at least she could send letters.

And she did. Writing at odd moments, her thoughts traveled thousands of miles over the years and were savored by her siblings. Many letters were saved. Using these treasures, I have found it possible to develop a portrait of Mary, mostly based in her own words. Since I grew up in Delaware, I came to know my aunt Mary first through my father's eyes. I learned early from him that she was a unique individual, worthy of all his love and admiration. Her adventurous, unquenchable spirit shone like a beacon from Wyoming where she lived a life very different from ours.

My father kept in touch with her and the other Cooper siblings through a round-robin letter that circulated cross continent. When it came to us, we read the latest from all the others, removed our old letter and added a new one. The old letters were carefully saved over the years until today, in 1999, 66 years of family recollections are stashed safely away. Mary's Robin letters really caught my attention. After my dad died, I found other family letters he had collected, stashed in dusty boxes. As I read through them, I discovered many from Mary written from her college dorm room. Following Mary's death, another stash of letters surfaced, along with smoke-damaged journals. Her youngest sister, Frances, corresponded faithfully with Mary and of course, saved all Mary's replies which came to me.

Reading her journals and letters after her death in 1991, I became convinced her story needed telling.

As a start, let me take you back to the year she was born, 1906.

Prologue: Minnesota

1906 was an unforgettable year for the C.P. Cooper family. It had not seemed that unusual when Charlie (C.P.) and his wife Juliet celebrated the new year in their comfortable Minneapolis home. He was satisfied with his work at the Creamery Packaging Corporation and pleased to have a house brimming with young children: Miriam (11), Milton (5), Dorothy (3), Horace (2) and Theodore (6 months). He still marveled at his good fortune in finding Juliet and convincing her to marry him after his first wife, Ada, died of tuberculosis leaving him with their infant daughter Miriam. Juliet, a devoted mother, basked in the lively children and looked forward to having an even larger family, God willing. It was also a joy to share her home with her younger sister Fannie, who filled the third floor of the house with youngsters who came to frolic and sing in her kindergarten there.

Then came June when C.P. turned a Seattle business trip into a family adventure. Juliet and the two oldest children joined him traveling by train, and exploring along the way. Life seemed very rich indeed when they returned to the little ones and Fannie to settle into Minnesota summertime. Within a few weeks, however, illness struck. The two babies were very sick and became the center of everyone's attention and concern. Juliet, five months pregnant, nearly worried herself sick as the two boys struggled to breathe and refused to eat. Suffering severely from the effects of whooping cough, their small bodies just couldn't cope. On August 14 Horace died, followed sixteen days later by his brother Theodore.

Juliet regretted the June trip, and could hardly be consoled. It helped to know another baby was on the way, and she clung to her Christian faith. Friends from the Linden Hills Congregational Church (which C.P., Juliet, and Fannie had helped form) gathered round with loving support. Fannie had plans to wed in October, so Juliet must have thrust her grief aside to busy herself with those arrangements. The simple wedding included Miriam and Dorothy as attendants. And then Fannie departed, another hole in the household. Charlie's feelings, while intense, were probably not shared easily, for he hid inner turmoil behind an easygoing, quiet exterior. When his boss spoke to him about a new position in Rutland, Vermont at a woodworking plant producing icebox refrigerators, he jumped at the opportunity. This would give the family a new start.

On December 3, before the move could get under way, the new baby was born: Mary Waters Cooper. Grateful for this new life

Mary as a toddler, with her sister Dorothy and her mother Juliet.

 Mary's Way

Juliet held the baby close, ever so aware of her fragility. Humming a lullaby, she cuddled Mary, knowing she replaced the two lost children. Even in her eighties, Mary Cooper Back remembered how she felt destined to fill the shoes of those two children. It was a big responsibility that she took seriously.

Mary's Way

Rutland

❁ ❁ ❁ ❁ ❁

After their move to Vermont in 1907, the Green Mountains near Rutland became the lifeblood of the Coopers. Both Juliet and C.P. loved the outdoors and walked the countryside and mountain slopes whenever possible. They immersed their children early in nature's wild world. Mary felt equally at home with frogs and rag dolls; every bird and animal she met intrigued her fancy. When the family kept chickens, Mary enthusiastically became a care giver, even naming the hens. When the chickens began to appear on the dinner table, she found it impossible to eat her friends, and ran off in tears.

While Mary didn't consider herself an artist as a child, her artistic bent was first seen at the age of 4, when she wrapped grass around a stick and created the picture of a green tree by rubbing the grass on paper. Juliet, who also loved to draw, supplied her daughter with crayons after observing this. Doodling and sketching became second nature to Mary after she entered school. Books and papers were festooned with drawings that her brain and busy fingers just had to create.

In Rutland the family kept expanding, with Ed born in 1908 and Frances in 1911. The children felt a close kinship, even though Miriam was so much older. She became known as "Yummy" - an indication of how popular she was with her half-brothers and sisters. Juliet marveled at Mary's gusto for life, reporting in a Christmas letter in 1915, "Mary's paper dolls made her shriek with delight (and you know what her shrieks are like!)." She adored her older brother Milton, whose mountain lore and camping skills she greatly admired. She called him Bones, as she recalled in a letter to him written in college. *"I'm thinking about one time when I was 11 or 12 and sick with flu or grippe or measles or something and I called you that. You gave me some learned discourse on bonus melior optimus. I got tired of calling you anything so complimentary and changed it to Bones. Then you called me Maggots, remember? Everyone else in the family was disgusted."*

The Cooper children emulated their father when it came to the mountains. He was hooked on the range just east of Rutland, providing a ridge of peaks from the Massachusetts border all the way

From upper left, the Cooper children, Milton, Miriam, Dorothy, Mary, Ed and Frances

to Canada. The idea to create a trail - a Long Trail - that hikers could take across these Green Mountains became his passion. He became an early president of the newly formed Green Mountain Club and involved his children in trail work as they were growing up. Many a weekend Mary and her sisters and brothers accompanied him along a trail section to undertake needed work. Her forte was brush cutting.

When Mary was 14, her twelve-year-old cousin Mary Ellen came to spend the summer. For Mary Ellen, the best part was going out with Uncle Charlie on Long Trail work hikes for the Green Mountain Club. One time they took the train to the trailhead for the Clarendon shelter where porcupines had destroyed most of the roof. At night they lay on fragrant bough mattresses and looked up at the stars through the open roof.

Mary Ellen remembers Mary with much affection. The two girls became close companions, collaborating in all sorts of imaginative play. Thrilled with stories she had read about Montcalm and Wolfe, generals in the French and Indian War, Mary enticed Mary Ellen to help dramatize their death scene, using suitcases for horses. Mary loved Vermont and its mountains and had memorized a multitude of facts about the state that she shared enthusiastically.

The Cooper home was a big house with a lively household spilling all over it. The atmosphere was upbeat and free, against a background of order and firmness. Creative play led to imaginative high jinks, that Mary Ellen still remembers.

"One thing we did was to see who could hold his
breath the longest under water, plunging one's face into
a basin of water while someone else counted time. It
was an exciting competition. Then we tried seeing who
could stay in a cold shower the longest. That stunt came
to an abrupt end when Aunt Juliet discovered why the
water was always running."

The Evergreen Avenue neighborhood was a close knit one and the Cooper house attracted youngsters from up and down the street. Every summer Ed and Mary organized some big shindig to make use of all the child-driven energy. That year a track meet spurred excited practice of all sorts of imaginative events.

On a visit three years later the girls of the family created a mock wedding with Dorothy as bride, Mary the groom and Mary Ellen best man. Mary and her cousin had great fun creating the men's costumes. Scrambles into the mountains were led by Mary and Ed who had learned much from their father. Often they headed for the new clubhouse of the Green Mountain Club built just off the Long Trail where it descended from Pico Peak to cross Sherburne Pass. They enjoyed riding bicycles there, along the steep gravel mountain road, knowing that the Club President's family was always especially welcome at the rustic lodge. One trip nearly turned into a disaster for Mary, who fell off her bike after skidding on gravel, while Mary Ellen looked on in horror.

"Suddenly she was lying motionless in the middle of the road. I yelled to Ed and we got to her as fast as we could. She was bleeding from a cut in the head and in shock. The first car that came along drove us home at such breakneck speed that I was almost as much afraid of the ride as worried about Mary sitting like a zombie beside me. Ed stayed back to retrieve the bicycles. It was a scary time, but Mary's head was tough and, aside from the bandage that long decorated her forehead, she was soon as good as new."

The clubhouse (which burned down many years later in

Mary Cooper
Rutland High School student

Mary's Way

1969) held a special place in Mary's heart. She had her first job there when she waitressed in its restaurant. She discreetly watched doctors from the County Medical Association get tipsy at their annual meeting and marveled at the chef's lightning speed when slicing roast beef and lettuce. She fell in love for the first time there and, more importantly, met her first wild cat on the Long Trail one evening.

Mary's love of mountains continued after she graduated from high school at the age of 16 and followed her sister Dorothy to college in the Kentucky mountains at Berea. Her feelings for the wild landscape of Vermont and her growing spiritual hunger are reflected in two poems she wrote, probably around this time, as she traded Vermont mountains for those of Kentucky.

❈ ❈ Poem I ❈ ❈

*Today I have grown taller from walking
with the trees
The seven sister poplars who go
softly in a line
And I think my heart is white for
its parlay with a star
That trembled out at night and
hung above the pine.*

❈ ❈ Poem II ❈ ❈

*The call note of a redbird from the
cedars in the dusk
Woke his happy note within me
I answer free and fine
And a sudden angel beckoned from
a column of blue smoke
Lord, who am I that they should
stoop - those holy folk of thine?*

Mary's Way

Berea College Days

The Cooper family took church-going seriously. They were active members of the Congregational Church in Rutland and Miriam attended the Chicago Theological Seminary where she majored in religious education. After Dorothy graduated from high school she went to Castleton Normal School and then taught for several years. While working at a church mission in the South one summer she learned about Berea College from a Berea teacher. His description of the school piqued her interest. This Christian, non-denominational institution sought particularly to educate children from Kentucky mountain families. They did, however, accept students from other states too. Students paid no tuition, but worked at various jobs at the college along with taking a demanding schedule of classes. Wanting more education than she had gotten at Castleton, Dorothy, with the help of this new friend, enrolled in Berea.

She loved the college and encouraged Mary to join her there, which Mary did in September, 1923. (Ed and Frances followed in later years, so that going to Berea became quite a Cooper tradition). Mary arrived accompanied by Peter Pan, her pet blazing blue-eyed racer snake, who ended up in a biology lab after demoralizing the other residents of her dormitory. As Mary settled in happily she kept her family posted on college life through almost-weekly letters that included frequent requests for more allowance. The only hint of homesickness came with pleas to send more maple sugar soon. On her mother's birthday, Mary drew a handsome illustration to head her letter and sent a description of a typical freshman's day.

> *Mad rush from geology to dinner, to which I was late; mad rush from dinner to my room to study history; mad rush to history, late; mad rush to tennis class, excused; mad rush to dancing practice...; mad rush up three flights of stairs and down again to Greek class, seven minutes late, didn't know a solitary thing; mad rush to work, putting books away in the biggest hurry you ever saw....*

As one of the youngest students, Mary had little interest in boys and preferred to go on outings with just girls to avoid all the necessary chaperons. She had her long hair bobbed and yearned to get her hair cut as short as a boy's. Her irrepressible spirit finally got her into trouble in her sophomore year. Milton received an alarming letter from her warning that she and her roommate were about to be expelled. They had sat in their dorm window one October evening with their legs hanging outside while fraternity brothers serenaded below. While the college could not condone such goings on, the girls were finally just reprimanded and penalized *"rank privileges until Thanksgiving"*.

At Mary's insistence, Milton wrote Juliet about the episode, allowing, "Poor Mary - always in hot water!" Before Thanksgiving could arrive, more trouble erupted which Mary described in another letter.

> *Did you hear about the rolled sock episode? Mary no sooner gets out of one thing than she gets into another. Miss Welsh asked in chapel how many thought rolled socks were all right.... A couple of people in the back row put their hands up a little ways, and Mary Cooper in the front row put her hand up as high as it would go. You should have seen MEW's face....*
>
> *'Well you are greatly in the minority!' And that afternoon before Greek class she attacked me. She said how disappointed she was, and how shocked and grieved and that I was getting depraved...and what did I have to say for myself, and so I said considerable and the debate grew quite heated...*

In early December Mary's roommate spoke with Miss Welsh

who told her that she had very high respect for them but they were much too adventuresome and impatient. Mary was sensitive about this tendency of hers to get into trouble. She compared herself unfavorably to the rest of her family in one letter to Milton.

> *I declare it's awful to have such handsome and talented big brothers and sisters - and little ones too, for that matter…. People who know Frank (Frances) expect me to have a way with children. At the clubhouse everyone expected me to be a great joker and fun-maker like Ed. Down at school I am supposed to be intellectual like Dot…. I tell you, it's awful how I have to carry the burden of all my family's successes. Please feel sorry for me. I can't help it if I'm a black sheep among the white ones, and a dark spot in my family's sun.*

Mary's religious beliefs, based in her love of God's natural world, put her at odds with some of Berea's rules and regulations. She, in fact, found them very foolish and loathsome. After attending a revival meeting, she complained loudly:

> *I most certainly did not get converted. It just made me feel wicked. I decided I would like to take a car ride (a cardinal sin…), go to the movies (for which six boys were expelled…last week), go into the restaurant (another scarlet crime),…and eat a huge meal…I would rather do that than be dragged into salvation by the hair of my head.*

While Mary fretted about these rules made in the name of religion, she must have been growing spiritually at Berea where she basked in the college's insistence that "God has made of one blood all peoples of the earth". Even at this age, she expanded this notion to include not just humans but all life. Many years later she remembered -

> *Biology classes…showed more and more clearly how closely we are related to all life. The embryology and comparative anatomy classes showed it clearly. So did historical geology. The astonishing thing was botany, where I learned that there is no final criterion of difference between plants and animals, and that the stuff of life is basically the same in both: that plants and animals share the same primal urges - hunger, sex, growth, death.*

Her enthusiasm for nature, even when it misbehaved, came

across in her letters. She examined the world around her through a rainbow lens, with an artist's eye.

This is the most wonderful day! There is a great wind sweeping down from the hills, roaring around the corners of the hall and blowing all the gorgeous leaves round and round in whirlwinds. And if you could see the birches!...

The leaves are pure gold, and the wind blows them round like sheer gold, spangled draperies.... They are so graceful and happy looking as if they were just on their toes to dance....

(After a bad rainstorm and flood) Oh it is so fresh and pretty out in spite of the rain. Or perhaps because of it. It's not at all cold, and during the night the winter wheat has turned green all over the gardens - a bright vivid brilliant green. And the leaves on the oaks don't look brown any more - but orange -burnt orange- rather; and the hill slopes are yellows and purples and grays. I'm just sighing for a pair of rubber boots and a rubber hat. I'd go for a hike.

Whenever she got the chance, Mary trekked the mountains. On one October jaunt to a bungalow that allowed miles of mountain hiking, she and two other girls killed a belligerent rattlesnake without many qualms, slept outside on a rock ledge only to get rained on, and cooked meals over an open fire. They hiked to North Pinnacle:

About two miles over as rough mountain terrain as I've ever seen, where there was almost no trail, and that one never cleared. We climbed cliffs and fell over rocks and hauled ourselves up by grapevines, and climbed trees after bittersweet and had a glorious time.... You came out from a thicket of laurel and sawbrier right onto the edge of the world. You can see for miles and miles right over the blue-grass on one side and over the pinnacled mountains on the other three.... I'm most ready to transfer my allegiance from Vermont to Kentucky. It's so wonderful here.

I did tear myself up pretty badly (on sawbrier).... It runs along the ground and over bushes. It is lovely to look upon with its long graceful trailing stems, berries of soft blue and deep russet crimson pointed leaves. But once you get into it - oh my!...My legs are raw from top to bottom and one touch will set me dancing….

The cliffs here run for miles and miles…. If your arms are strong you can follow the cliffs for miles, stepping on one of these ledges and holding onto the one above you. It sure was thrilling although we didn't go more than two or three hundred feet that way….

Mary Cooper
Berea College senior

Mary's interest in art continued unabated, with sketches adorning her class work. Since the college had no drawing and painting courses, she sought other ways to use her talents: as decorator, poster maker and finally as yearbook art editor. She made a small income painting Easter cards and drawing illustrations for a story written by a professor. By pinching pennies, she came up with $47 so she could enroll in summer courses at the Art Institute of Chicago. She bubbled at the prospect of taking figure construction and elementary design. She could hardly wait to ride the elevated train the half hour trip from the Cooper's Maywood house (where Juliet, C.P. and Frances had recently moved) to downtown Chicago and then walking twenty minutes to the school.

By her senior year in 1927 she had tasted much of what Berea had to offer. Her jobs had included cleaning toilets, waiting on tables, working in the library, assisting a dean and serving as illustrator for the biology department.

It's rather fun but not extremely appetizing…. I know all about tapeworms now, from their scolex down through all their proglottides. Also, I believe I could pass an examination on the internal structure of angle worms. Kind of interesting to get a whole zoology course without having to study - and getting paid for it too.

She was determined to do well in her classes and received mostly As and some Bs. Although her studies focused on ancient languages (Latin and Greek) and the relationship of Greek literature and art to the modern world, she got very excited about geology and history. In one class she visited an ancient archeological site in a nearby mountain ravine where her imagination soared:

So Leata, Rufus and I started an exciting story about a bright-eyed…Neolith girl and a lusty Neolith brave. They had all sorts of thrilling adventures with their degenerate foe, and lived and loved and were separated and finally at the end were reunited and clasped in each others' arms!… We … are now contemplating writing the Great Berea Novel!

She had become an ardent booster for the college and could scarcely contain herself when the basketball team won the state tournament.

To have Berea with its poor equipment and poverty-stricken students rake off a victory over all the wealthy schools of the bluegrass! It's great! Just great! Every member of the college…feels that he had a … part in the victory - lots more so than usual. You know, the boys haven't had a special training table. They've eaten the same old boarding hall messes with the rest of us…. Well, at the beginning of the season, the boys lost one game after another. We couldn't understand it. They would play in great form, run up a big lead and keep it, easy, until the last quarter….Then they would give way, all of a sudden, and the other team would run up on them. That happened a dozen times….

Suddenly someone got an inspiration. Bacon and eggs! If they could only have an extra breakfast like that, it might give them the endurance that they lacked. But the Boarding Hall couldn't afford it. You know we pay only about nine cents a meal and nearly half goes to pay overhead.

And the boys couldn't afford to pay for their own. So one time when they were away we cooked it up. We each contributed a nickel. I happened to have a whole dime….So my last dime went to the team…. And I guess that did the business! For the team didn't play any better…than they had during a season of failure. But they played to the end! So the whole school feels a real share in the victory, you see.

As her days at Berea came to an end, Mary wondered about the future. Her growing confidence in her artistic talents boosted her courage to think about applying to the Art Institute of Chicago.

She confessed to her brother, a bit tentatively:

> *I almost think I'm going to the Art Institute .... Isn't that -isn't it - well, thrilling or exciting, or great aren't just the words. Wonderful!... If I can only go, it will be the biggest thing that ever happened to me. It would be a beginning toward the art education I'm going to have. That I'm GOING TO HAVE....*

Mary's graduation in June 1927 was a major family event. Her proud mother wrote afterwards: "I can place myself beside Mrs. Lindbergh, for while my children have not yet done anything to gain the plaudits of an admiring world (they may, who knows), they are filling useful places and commending themselves to those above them and with whom they work... If my heart were not so full of Thanksgiving to God for this great happiness and satisfaction in my children, I should be puffed up with pride in them. But I do expect much from you all - the utmost you can give to help the world to progress a little in your realm of work - and in understanding and sympathy among men."

Mary did indeed have a lot to live up to.

Chicago Reflections and The Art Institute

During Mary's college years, the Coopers moved to Chicago where C.P. now traveled widely for the Creamery Packaging Corporation. When Mary left Berea she joined her parents and Frances at their Maywood home, in the suburbs of Chicago and awaited word from the Art Institute of Chicago. The day the bulky envelope arrived, Mary's hands shook as she opened it; followed by a scream that brought Juliet at a run. Not only was she accepted, she had also received a scholarship! To attend her art classes at the Art Institute she took the L (elevated train) from Maywood. Train time became daily sketching and letter writing time, as she shared her excitement about art school and the city itself. The mountain girl fell in love with the windy city. She observed its many moods, and wrote enthusiastically about them.

The thermometer hit zero again last night. This morning it's so cold everything squeaks…. The air seems a little taut…. As we make each stop, the folks come in surrounded by a sort of aura of steam and smoking like a furnace, or a locomotive. But it's a beautiful day for all that, all blue and white and yellow. The sky is so soft and green a blue that it looks like a mild spring day. It's hard to believe when you look at it, that it is stretched over a whole world of quivering cold.

It's the absolute beauty of a day like today, when the place is all wrapped up in cottony mists, bluish over the city, greenish over the lake; when, of all the towers on the city's skyline, you can only see one or two, and those just the nearest...and they are like fairy castles, with no bases, and only a soft grey-silver outline round their turrets; when the inner breakwater is no more than a dusky line, and the outer breakwater just isn't; when to the ordinary noises of the city - the chug and puff of freight-engines and the rattle of boxcars, and the constant swish of motor cars on wet pavements - comes the rhythmic raspy groan of a foghorn; when the nearby lampposts and elm saplings are surprisingly, almost crudely distinct against the general blurriness. Gee, it's great! Our city is really beautiful at times.

Grant Park is a great invention, too. In a place that is so aggressively both a city and a lake port you feel sort of like a disembodied soul, to be able to stand on territory that is neither, and look at both. I get to do it often, for I have a class in the Field Museum....

The lake is up tonight. Last night when I came down to the shore, it was warm and summery, with a clear orange sunset behind the skyscrapers and soft amber fading into the blue to the east across the hazy water. Only the barest ripples splashed over the embankment. There was the feeling of great silence around, for the soft roar of the city is so steady as almost to go below consciousness. A white yacht far out near the edge of visibility was like a resting gull.

But tonight! A chill, damp breeze from the north has clouded the skies and moved the waters. Instead of ripples, the embankments are awash with the waters of noisy waves. The great silence has given way to the rhythmic, pleasant, complex deep splash of the water. In another day there may be breakers! Today, though, it's delicious enough to drink in the air, taste the mists on my lips, glory in the brilliant pearl-ringed lights, tingle with all my senses to the touch of the autumn night.

And in a poem Mary wrote -

> On my way to the city each day
> I pass a vista -
> Fields there are, and brambles,
> and brown and purple grasses,

The blue and yellow and gray of dug up earth.
And crooked elm trees, and a river.
But it is all cut up with heads of people,
Great, lumpish heads of people in the car.
People who never even see my vista,
And I long to push them away -
Elbow them -
Knock them off -
Wipe them out -
So that I may have the clear view
And feel the fresh spring breeze
And see the patterned gray sky -
Is it these other folks who are self-centered -
Or I?

Wherever Mary went - on the train or walking around the city - she 'collected' people: folks she observed very carefully, writing down a detailed description of what she saw. Perhaps she planned to draw them at a later time.

On my way home from night school…I've had Hoyne Avenue to look at…. You can't imagine how beautiful he looks! His name isn't really Hoyne Avenue, of course. That's where he gets off the L, that's all. We come home on the same train every night-school night. He goes to night school some-where else…and I always try to figure to sit where I can see him. Gee, he's good-looking! So tall he has to stoop to get in the door, with black hair and eyes, wide brows, clean sweep-ing planes of cheek and chin. He's a joy to the eye….I'd like to sculpt him. I'd like to paint him.

And wouldn't I like to date him! …. (See Sketch 1)

A well-dressed man out-side the theater door, young, with remarkable nose and tem-ples, feet rather wide apart, a cigarette between lips curved with a whimsical and cynical humor….

Sketch One
Hoyne Avenue

Faithful old horse hitched to a delivery cart, just the trace of a twinkle in a … drowsy eye, standing on one rear foot, the other cocked at a…rakish angle….

Trim looking man in a derby, carrying a little bag, crosses the street ahead of me - head a little low, coat a little shabby, eyes a little shifty. Hardly enough to convict him on. Wonder what he would have done if I'd said, 'Hey! What you got in that bag?' Wonder if he would have opened it and shown me a half-eaten sandwich and a cup dirty with old coffee grounds….

How different the University from the Loop! It seems like spring in the Midway, the earth all soft and the trees taking a preliminary yawn and stretch before waking up. And the University people! Crowds of gay, well-dressed girls, filling the sidewalks in clumps of three, or four or five. One girl alone, a little thin, pale golden hair pulled back in a simple knot, slipping …out of the library, briefcase under arm. A thin, elderly professor, with hair in a gray curl round a pink center, head sunk between his shoulders, crosses with long and silent strides….

I forgot to mention the small but commanding old man who blustered all unknowing into my net on the Avenue. A red faced, opinionated old man with bushy white eyebrows and a little curling white mustache to decorate his red face. He stepped along with his chin up, though he carried a cane and walked with the short step of old age. A black derby he wore, and a strange looking, well-fitting black topcoat, that fastened snugly under his chin with a single button….

Not the way a man stands is so much a key to his character-but the little things he does. That stolid, solid youngish suburbanite tonight on the L platform, for instance. If I draw his stance alone, it would express complacency, all right. But his own personality lay in his little actions, and to get him on paper I would have to suggest those. The little chewing sidewise motion he made as he talked, as if he had a half-chewed cigar in the corner of his mouth - but he hadn't. The grip of his pudgy fingers on his newspaper. The quick, efficient, perfectly unconscious gesture of folding the paper double….

Mary delighted in her classes, although from time to time she doubted her abilities.

> *My work is nothing to go upstairs and shout down about. I am beginning to think it will be my fate always to do good things but not superb things, work that you might say was 'nice' or 'had its fine points' but that you would never notice unless it was called to your attention....*

> *Well I'm sort of glad I wrote you that. I guess I nearly ditched that bogey by the very act of writing him down on paper. If I can do nice, careful, thoughtful work, that's fine, even if it isn't striking; and built on a solid foundation even if it isn't superficially clever - isn't that enough? Unfortunately it isn't, commercially speaking, but if it's enough to get along on, if not get rich on, I'm satisfied.*

Along with art school, Mary worked as an intern at the Field Museum of Natural History. She particularly enjoyed her research class on animal structure at the Field Museum and shared her delight in a letter to Milton.

> *Oh Milt, that class in the Field Museum is the joy of my life. It's a research class on animal structure, and the use of animals in illustration. I want to be an animal illustrator and work for a museum. It's my latest ambition, but it has sort of hung around in my mind for years. It crystallized suddenly last Sunday when I met Charles R. Knight, the great animal painter on the staff of the American Museum in New York. He is generally acknowledged to be the greatest in the world - and he stopped in the zoo where a boy from my class and I were sketching, and criticized our work. He sketched, and recommended things, and told us the important things to look for, and suggested what was ahead of us!...*

> *Now I work on animals just as often and as hard as I can. It's a great field, and one that sure appeals to me. Today I worked for three hours comparing hind legs of animals. It's awfully interesting. I finished a plate of fifteen different types of bone and muscle structure.... Mr. Wilkins, our instructor, said if I would work it up a little more carefully next time, he'd like to have it to reproduce for his next book. So who knows, I might break into photogravure yet.*

Wanting some live animal models, Mary obtained a pair of white mice that came to live with the Coopers. She created a home for them from a shallow pan, two window panes and two pieces of tin. Everyone soon succumbed to their charms, even Juliet and C.P. "Mary's mice ….run all over our persons when we permit it," wrote C.P. to Milton. "From pocket to coat collar and back in rapid succession and sometimes inside sleeve or collar until routed out." Juliet told how the mice escaped from their cage one day and everyone undertook a massive search; until they turned up on the porch. Mary's sketches of the mice soon caught the attention of the Art School faculty. Then Mary shared with Milton news of great import!

You can't imagine the exciting thing that happened to us yesterday. We acquired a brand new addition to the family! In fact, we acquired three of them. They belong to one of the white mice - three brand new little squirming younglings - just the size and shape of peanuts, sunburn red in color, no fur, eyes, ears, or conspicuous details of any kind, except four very tiny legs apiece… (later)

You should see how those babies are growing! Already they look more like mice than peanuts or shrimp. Their legs, which when they were born looked like nothing so much as crooked red threads, are strong enough to do some good now. They kick and push like anything with them. You can see their little mouths - I actually caught one yawning yesterday! And the bumps where their eyes will be, and the rudiments of their ears. It even looks as if there were a hint of white down on their naked little bodies. And every time you look at them they look bigger than last time.

Their mother devotes all her time to them. She and the babies live in a jelly glass in a cage all their own, with water and milk to drink, and oranges and bread and lilac twigs to eat. Little mother has made a grand nest in the jelly glass, in which the three babies squirm gaily, and she sits on top of them, apparently brooding them like an old mother hen. The babies don't seem to mind a bit being walked all over. They may even like it. Don't you think this business of having them live in glass houses is fine? We can see what they do all the time then. And they chose it themselves. They were

Mary's Way

living in a nice, warm, dark, comfortable cardboard box when Dad put a half pint bottle in the cage. And what do you know! They deserted their box and all three went to sleep in the bottle.

(A month later)

The mice are getting tamer every day. Now I have only to put my hand near the door for all five of them to be there on the inside, gripping the wire netting with all twenty paws, tails hanging straight down, wriggling their little noses like mad. You should see their excitement when the cage is cleaned out. They love to be clean and hate to be dirty, spend half their lives scrubbing themselves, so they acquire redoubled vivacity and energy when put in a clean cage. They can't run around fast enough. It looks as if I might soon be able to add rabbits to the bunch.

There are two who belong to the Art Institute, bought for the Saturday classes, and when they get through using them something will have to be done with them. Rabbits aren't nearly as interesting as mice, though. They can't do so much and aren't anything like as lively.

When Mary carried another live model the three miles from the Academy of Science (a natural history and science museum), to the Art Institute, she created quite a stir. She wrapped Horace, a bull snake, around her coat sleeve and walked along observing the reactions of those who approached her. When Horace began to unwind and loop a bit for exercise, she discovered that everyone she met rushed to get out of the way. One cold winter day she boarded the L with another snake tucked securely away, planning to study and draw him at home that night. Suddenly she realized the snake was gone! The car was crowded and she shuddered to think what would happen if the people around her saw that snake! Feeling cautiously under her coat, she breathed a sigh of relief when she found the snake curled around her waist, seeking more warmth.

Mary's overriding interest in animal structure provoked her to set traps at the Art Institute to catch the wild gray mice who infiltrated the supply room.

I want to skin one successfully, to study the superficial muscles. And I don't know a blessed thing about skinning mice. I've done one already, but I made such a mess of it I couldn't even use him afterward. I don't believe a mouse was ever worse skinned. I know you've done it, Milton, often - I mean skinned animals. Would you tell me how to go about it? Still, perhaps you'd better not bother, since it's tomorrow night I plan to do it again.

(Later)

You know, I'm just awfully anxious to work for a taxidermist. I think that would be the only accurate way to get real knowledge of animal structure. All the same it will be just terribly hard for me to get a job like that, for the simple reason that it's the sort of thing girls don't do. But why in the world shouldn't they? You don't happen to know any taxidermists do you? Anybody who would hire an honest, earnest, industrious individual who wanted to begin at the bottom?...

Then she discovered a talented taxidermist, Earl Wright, who worked at the Academy of Sciences. When he learned of her interest he hired her as a part-time technician. Mary practiced enthusiastically, even bringing a live turkey home on the L. In the interest of science she found she could kill it and remove the skin so she could stuff the hide, while the flesh was roasted.

Mary enjoyed the Academy Director, Alfred Bailey, who modeled many of her interests, including bird study and photography. She put in long hours learning more about animal anatomy and the skills and techniques used to preserve animals. In addition, she enjoyed the naturalists she met there, including Cap'n Charlie Brower, U.S. Commissioner from Point Barrow, Alaska who brought bird skins she proudly made up into museum specimens. Life was wonderful as she divided her fourteen-hour days between art school, Academy and Field Museum. She even took time in winter to soar across the ice in nearby Lincoln Park on newly purchased ice skates.

I am learning so much, and so fast. I'm painting, drawing, skinning, cleaning, casting, developing pictures, and playing with pets. Over the weekend I'm going trapping. I hope to have a job planning exhibits and doing taxidermy work for the Trailside Museum in the Forest Preserve....The Field Museum is such an exciting place to work. One is always so impressed by the fact that there's so much yet unknown. Someone is always discovering something. A few weeks ago our mammalogist discovered a brand new kind of pocket gopher right inside the area of greater Chicago....

And our pets - my, but they are fun. A boa constrictor, salamander, two freshwater turtles, a ground squirrel, two canaries and some fish. Our latest stunt with Jimmy (the ground squirrel) was to fill a square, shallow box with dirt, cover it with glass, cut a door in one end, turn it on its side and hitch it to his cage, for him to dig in. Does the boy enjoy it? He's frantically digging burrows all over the place. He built a nest and lined it with excelsior.... He's carefully built the corridors on the back side of that narrow box so we can't see in... This morning we removed the glass and opened the nest to view - a cozy, soft and very warm little nest. Wasn't Jimmy riled though! He chattered at us, he made faces. And soon, when the glass was replaced, he filled up the hole with promptness, asperity and his own plump striped back. He knew how to keep his place dark for a long nap.

Mary became quite serious about collecting animals for scientific study. Sometimes this meant killing them, and the Academy got her a federal permit to collect birds in Vermont. Excitedly, she wrote her brother Milton asking to borrow a hoped-for shotgun from him.

Now that I've got (the permit), I yearn to practice shooting, or the darn thing won't do me any good, except as something official looking to show folks to make me feel important. I'm learning a whole lot about guns from seeing them and listening to talk about them. I'm learning more about ammunition. I loaded all the cartridges for the Academy's spring expedition to Colorado. But I've not had a chance to shoot so far.

Vermont lured her. During her art school summers between 1927 and 1931 she had her fill of outdoor life and exposure to wildlife when she returned there each year to spend some weeks, first as camp counselor and then as explorer and collecting scientist. Doses of the mountains recharged her and she returned to Chicago ready to be captivated by the city again.

Vermont Adventuring – 1

Summer jobs as a camp counselor at two different Vermont girls' camps in Fairlee and Roxbury brought Mary much needed income and enjoyment. She exhilarated in these months outdoors, responsible for teaching campcraft to the girls under her care. Her aptitude for creating camp gear out of simple materials and then problem solving their use shines through in her letters to Milton as does her love of nature and enjoyment of teaching.

We have flying squirrels around here, and they cause more excitement … at times. They come in after the food the girls have … and race round and round the inside of the screens. Meanwhile the girls all scream and hide their heads under their blankets.… It's funny how scared some of these girls are.…

Woodcraft experience is surely coming to me by leaps and bounds. You never know how much you have to know until you get out with a bunch of tenderfeet and have to think for them all. And it is a grand and glorious feeling to get a crowd trained so they know something. I've got several expert cocoa cooks now and half a dozen expert firemakers and one girl who can chop wood as well as I. I see you smile at that last achievement, but honest, I'm much better now.… You'd really be surprised to see how nearly I can hit where I aim - and how often.

But I want to tell you about my last achievement … one

which I'm quite proud of. You know I never have put up any kind of tent.... And last week we were going on an overnight trip to the point, a little low strip of land jutting into the lake. But it was awfully gloomy overhead, with blackish clouds scudding across the sky ahead of a southeast wind that was whipping the lake into white caps.... Most of the point is open with deep wooded fringes.... The front end, which is way the nicest to camp on, being open and viewsome, caught the full force of the cold wind. We pondered the problem, and finally guyed up the extra ponchos into a...windbreak two ponchos long to accommodate the crowd, but we only roofed over half of it because there was thick foliage over the rest.... And it was all just as tight and firm as could be.... We had a nice tight shelter and the campfire's glow and the ripple of the lake pat-patting just behind our heads, and later a moon struggling through driving clouds , and the smell of balsam....

She fell in love with the second camp - Teela-wooket - where horseback riding was emphasized, and shared her joy enthusiastically (all the while sounding like the artist she had become).

It is certainly fine here.... I don't know why it is, what combination of factors is involved, but my dominant mood right now is satisfaction, deep-seated contentment. I sort of lean back against the country and luxuriate in it. I'm not nervous, or thrilled, or excited, or worried, or wondering, or full of serious plans, or hectically gay. I'm just satisfied. Days go along and along, and everything that happens seems right.... An elm lifts up in a great sweeping curve against the sky. It is just what that place needed to give it the fullness of perfection. Between the upthrust of two great firs I catch a sudden glimpse of a skyline miles away, where a high pasture is dotted with blue clumps of pine and fir and hemlock. It is all just what it ought to be - just right.

Excited about getting camping gear of her own so she could explore the mountains in longer jaunts, Mary wrote older brother Milton for advice. Not only did he know how to backpack, but also, as an engineer, he liked nothing better than solving problems, figuring out what made things work.

How much does your sleeping bag weigh? That's what's

puzzling me now - to get it small and light and still warm and comfortable as possible. Also I wish you'd send me another diagram of that pack arrangement of yours....

I've got my new blanket, and ...it is a peach. It's a wool batting comforter with a wool challis cover and quilted with yarn! So that everything about it is wool and warm.... It weighs only 4 1/2 pounds and it is the warmest thing! And what I particularly want to know is, what are the dimensions of the sack that goes with the bamboo frame of this pack of yours? And does it have gussets or is it just flat? I want to make a bag for foodstuffs that will fit in it. This is my idea. (Sketch 2)

Did I write you about my tarpaulin? I want to make one out of balloon silk, 6 feet by 8 feet, grommets at corners and in the middle of the side, and an extra strip inside with buttons on it you could button a poncho to. It would weigh practically nothing, and with it you could pitch a great one-person, weatherproof tent. I have to use the poncho ...because I have it, and can't afford anything else. (Sketch 3)

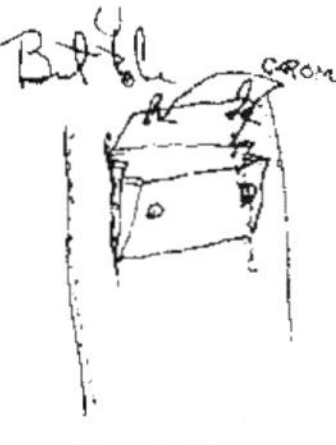

Sketch Two
Food Stuff Bag

And so her adventuring got underway. Her treks were challenging; not Sunday afternoon walks in the park. First she writes about a camping-hiking trip up Mt. Ascutney with another woman camp counselor Dot Emerson, using her car (nicknamed Delerium) to reach a seldom used trailhead.

The sun was very low indeed, and we had to find a place soon which boasted wood and water.... As we stood quiet a minute, just over the ridge from the car, up from the valley came an echo of children's voices, assuring us of a farm and drinking water not so far off.... We drove Delerium in and

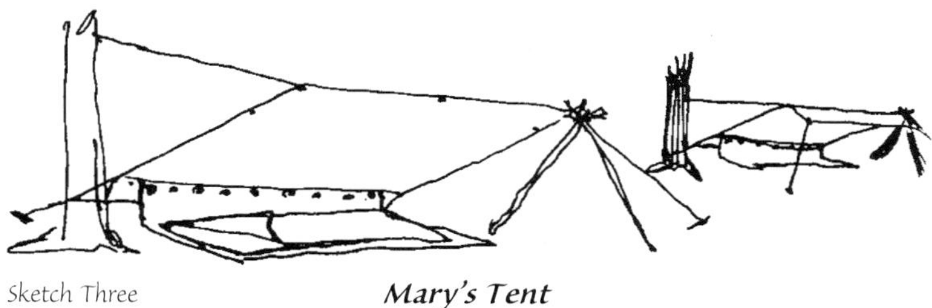

Sketch Three   **Mary's Tent**

parked her by our rock, grabbed our tin pail and started out through the gathering dusk.... The folks there made us welcome although they were sure I was Dot's little brother! They gave us water and permission to camp in their pasture and told us of a trail up that side of Ascutney. Most unenthusiastically, they described it. 'It's a poor trail.' We heard, 'But it's marked. You can go up that way.'

So we decided to tackle it next day. Meanwhile, we lugged our water up the long slope, built a fire and got supper.... We drank soup from our cups, then made cocoa in the soup kettle and drank it from our cups and ate fried biscuits.... The food was great, largely because the wood was so good. All in all, everything conspired to make it the most nearly perfect night camping I've ever spent...with the high old shoulders (of "Scutney") lifting up into the starlight, and the glory of the northern lights flashing overhead.

We climbed the mountain.... And the trail was just what was claimed for it - poor, but marked. Much of the way there wasn't even a footpath, and the blazes were very old.... It was through nasty old slash, such horrid stuff to get lost on.... Ascutney has a rather bad reputation...since the main mountain mass is divided off into so many high shoulders with deceptive peaks on them. So we thought we'd better keep to the trail if we could. Sometimes it took us as long as ten minutes to find our way from one blaze to the next one. It gave us a real thrill, though, to be out on top, having won it by so much effort.

Vermont Adventuring – II

Mary and younger sister Frances had planned a several day back pack on the Long Trail following her brother Milton's wedding in late June 1930. However, Frances got a summer job working at the Green Mountain Club Clubhouse at Sherburne Pass, so Mary decided she would just go ahead anyway and take a solo hike. She liked the idea of some time by herself to sort out her feelings about a new beau, Joe Back. His attentions pleased her but also made her wonder just how serious she wanted to get with him. She started where the Long Trail crossed the road at Sherburne Pass and planned to walk north for several days.

Monday

June 24, 1930

In the cold gray light of dawn when everything looks and feels its very low downdest, I glance around by way of …taking resumé of things, and, do you know, things aren't so bad at all. I slept lightly - oh so very lightly. I've a great flock of fly bites on the back of my neck and behind my ear. My collarbones are sore from the pack - but that's all I have to complain of. On the credit side, my tent is tight and firm and cozy, and big enough for two like me. My bed was warm and my fire lasted all night. I've firewood enough for break-fast. The smoke is rising merrily and so is the sun. It is a beautiful day, and the birds are singing.

To catch up my journal: I left the road at the top of the

pass at 3:45 p.m. Just before I left (Milton and his bride Marion who had dropped me off) commented on the coolness, way up here in the hills, but boy, I hadn't gone six steps on the climb before the perspiration began streaming like a shower when you turn on the faucet, better, like a wet towel when you wring it. That's what a pack does for you. It certainly takes the stuff out of you fast to start a climb like that under a 25-pound pack, when you are soft. I struck off the trail at the first ravine, aiming to camp where there was good water. Great heavens, no lack of water. The whole mountain side squished with it. But not collected; not streamy. I went down the east side of the range quite a way before I reached good water.

The timber has grown immensely since I saw Mt. Horrid last. It looks much better. Even so, due to my greenness …, and a bit of nervousness, it took an hour and a half to get my night's wood. …And I am getting hungry. The rest will have to come later.

Sucker Brook Lodge
Tuesday afternoon

You should see me now! Dressed in clean clothes, bathed, hair combed, I'm lying at my ease in bed, recuperating from the efforts of the last twenty-four hours. By which you are not to suppose that I have already repented my bargain and headed for civilization. Oh, dear, no! Sucker Brook Lodge is five miles from any road…much more than that from town, or any house at all. And it looks like this: (Sketch 4)

The guidebook says it accommodates eighteen people and has a fireplace. If eighteen people slept in here they'd have to sleep spoon fashion. The fireplace is a ring of stones outside where you may build a fire.

The place surely is porky (porcupine) ridden. The voracious brutes have chewed some of the logs nearly in two; and I had to scrub off the strip of corrugated iron that serves as a table before I would set my things on it. There are three pails, a kettle, and a frypan belonging to the lodge hung on nails six feet from the floor. They all have porcupine droppings in them! My first duty on arriving here was to inter a big specimen which was weltering in its blood by the front door. It was apparently killed by last night's occupant of the lodge, to judge by the freshness.

It was quite a problem to decide how to manage it. I scouted round and located a convenient hollow just the right size, then returned and picked up Porky by the very end of its tail, which has long stiff hairs on it, but no quills. That thing weighed almost as much as my pack.... I would carry him a ways, until I got tired; then I'd let him down and rest him on his nose, then up again. I put him in the hollow; and kicked enough dirt over him to cover him. I hope one doesn't come around tonight. I just don't like them.

To go back to where I left off this morning: After break-fast...consisting of prunes, two cups of milk (Klim mixed with water makes a very drinkable milk) and a biscuit loaf which turned out to be rather sad (Klephart quotes a saying 'Who has not tasted camp-made bread, molded by putty, and weighted with lead').

I noticed how suddenly and ominously the sky had clouded over. Brrr! My tent wasn't in a situation to stand off a continued rain, pitched as it was, practically in a mud pud-dle. I would have to get to Sucker Brook Lodge. And I was lost. I didn't even know where the Long Trail was. So I began to get a little panicky. I scolded myself, 'You goof, you were

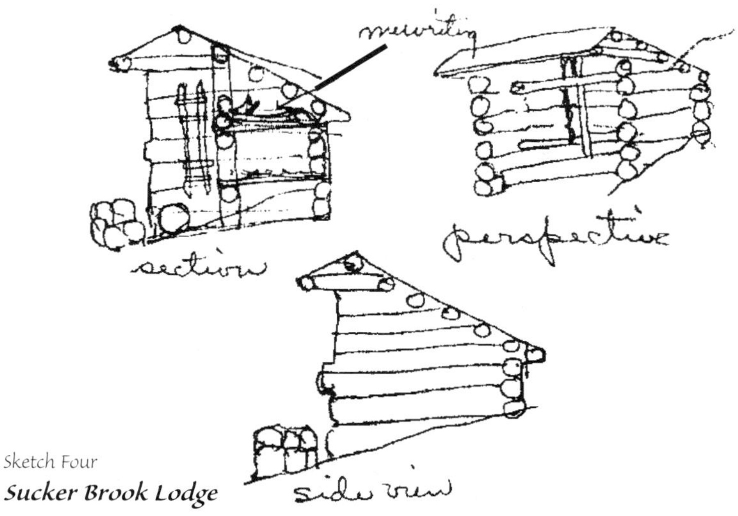

Sketch Four
Sucker Brook Lodge

out for an adventure and here's one. Can't you ever be satisfied?' But just the same, what with little sleep, little food, and a bit of panic, I was shaky…. When I got my pack all put together and tied up, it seemed as if I couldn't ever get it on, and go back <u>up</u> that hill, to where I figured the trail ought to be. I thought of going down instead, but the image of all those little bags of food rose in my mind, and I said, firm and determined like, 'No! Here I stay until they're et!'

And in time I did make the top of the ridge, and there, praise God, was the trail. I doubt if I have ever in my life been so pleased to see anything. 'Twas very inconspicuous. Ferns were arching over hip high on each side and completely concealing it. But you could see the white blazes on the trees. It was a way. It was going somewhere. I had an established footing. The Long Trail is delightfully casual. It ambles a few feet here, circles a few feet to avoid an old stump or a lady-slipper, changes its course permanently if a log falls across.

8:45 p.m.

Well, this is a funny situation and, no mistake. It begins to look as if I'm up for the night. Besieged. I never in my life saw such perseverance as those porkies are exhibiting…. I did sleep for an hour, and was wakened by the sound of chattering teeth. 'Hey you, git' cried I,…as I went for him with the axe. Missed him, worse luck, and now he is with me for the night. Once he shimmied right up the pole that supports my top bunk. I beat him down with the axe, but missed his nose - the vulnerable spot. How long will three candles last? Three of them below me now. They make such uncouth, horrid sounds - nasal grunts, squeals, and once, a grunty scream. (Sketch 5)

A great big beautiful polyphemus moth has come to my candle. I love to see him, but I hate to see him kill himself that way. A beautiful iridescent 'eye' in each wing. Lots of the big night moths are coming now…. I wish I knew more about them.

Wednesday 7:40 a.m.

Awake and just dressed. With their conversational gruntings and asthmatic wheezes and rattling of their quills and chattering of their teeth, the varmints kept me awake

Sketch Five
Porcupines

most of the time until daylight. Then they quieted down some…. And I slept the sleep of the dead from three until seven.

Wednesday 7:55 p.m.

By the shore of beautiful Lake Pleiad. I don't want to write. I want to look. It is after sunset, but still light. I am established for the night on top of a tall white rock which gives a grandstand view of the whole little sheet of water and the forested hills behind it. The register of the Lake Pleiad shelter…had example after example of folks…kept awake all night by the porkies. That lodge has four walls and you must choose between suffocation or porkies. So I locked up my food and came here.

Oh, the wildlife of this place! Deer apparently use all the trails, though I've not seen any yet. Bullfrogs of six or eight different inflections are all over the lake. Fish are jumping everywhere. A big gray rabbit with long ears and big feet (I imagine a varying hare) munched a paper bag in the door yard while I was getting supper. A little…richly colored chipmunk came right up to my nut bag as I was eating lunch. As something moved just outside the door this evening, I jumped only to grin as I saw 'twas the ears of a chunky little reddish cottontail sitting on the doorstep.

The timber is virgin, and huge, and wild. All day long I tramped through virgin timber. It is wonderful. But it's getting too dark to write. Besides, I <u>have</u> to look.

Thursday 6 a.m.

Still on the same rock. I eluded Porky all night and what an experience I had doing it. Such a calm night. Little wind, quite warm - in fact too warm in my big blanket, and too cold without it. It never got really dark here under the stars. I never knew there was so much starlight…. Chorus of bull-frogs, with its accompaniment of jumping fish, so steady that it passes notice. Suddenly in the woods beside me, and quite close, the strangest cry vibrated across the lake, and echoed from the cliff on the other side. My heart just stopped beat-ing, and then began racing until I was nearly suffocated. As near as it resembled anything human, it suggested a man blowing his nose suddenly and explosively…. It was repeated three times, then silence, except for the chorus of bull-frogs and fish. Later I heard a hare jumping around in that region, and associated with it the same sound, repeated so many times that I got all over being scared of it. Is it the love call of the varying hare?...

Later in the night, one lonely call came across the lake to me -a call that began like the me-ow of a cat, and ended like the howl of a dog. Was it a fox? The mosquitoes were rather bad so that I had to use citronella profusely. Just went down to the lake to wash. The water is lovely and cool, not cold. Three little frogs jumped off the rock I went to and went away swimming breast-stroke, using the frog kick I've learned so laboriously. One stayed nearby, so I could see him, his slick pale gray-yellow body, with its shining dark green splotches, his pop eyes, very serious, his beautifully hexago-nal cross section with all the angles very clearly marked by ridges. There were lots of lazy little water salamanders swimming round just under the surface, and a deer came down to drink just across the lake. Beautiful - lovely - per-fect.

> Thursday, 11:55 a.m.

...To catch up.... Hardly a mention of the weather any-where.... It was rainy and drizzly all day Tuesday, with the wind absolutely 'galeing' over the rock tops and through the bannered spruces of Cape Look-off and White Rocks Mountains. Yesterday was lovely, a perfect June day, and today is another one. ...Yesterday afternoon as I came out on Pleiad Lookout, I found two women enjoying the view. The first human souls I'd seen for 46 hours.... They brought me down to Bread Loaf Inn (in their car) where I sent some post-cards, and took me back again. It was nice to see someone again.

Just now as I was writing, three men came along from the road, the spokesman, Jules Whitney, of the Vermont Hydro Electric knew Dad more or less. ...He seemed amazed to think I was hiking alone, but he didn't exactly disapprove. The men say the funny noise I heard was a 'deer blowing' that it is quite characteristic.

Boyce Lodge, Thursday evening

Boyce is sort of all alone by itself …high practically at the top of the ridge and not far from timber line…. It's made of spruce logs with the bark on…and looks to the west, where a hole among the trees gives a gorgeous view over Lake Champlain and the Adirondacks. Numerous signs of porky having been killed are around, but the lodge itself isn't chewed up like Sucker Brook. We have at least an hour more of daylight than they have down in the valley, we are so high up. But being so high has meant an awful pull. The pack had seemed to be getting heavier instead of lighter, so tonight I went over it all. My trip's half over, and I had more than half of everything. So I threw away a lot of stuff, though it almost broke my Scotch heart. …My food's apparently a fairly good selection, except that I've not enough green stuff. I yearn unspeakably for the sight of a good red apple and a piece of lettuce. My idea of heaven right now is a grapefruit.

And next to fruit, I would like a little company…. Three nights by myself have convinced me that my longing is not because I am afraid, but simply that I am lonesome…. I am planning a forced march tomorrow, to pass two cabins, …in the hope that I may catch up with the person whose footprints have been so fresh in front of me ever since Mt. Horrid, and who wears the same size shoe that I do.

Top of Mt. Woodrow Wilson, 3700 feet
Friday, 10:20 a.m.

There is a lovely view…so I'll stay and write as long as I can for the black flies. Just as I quit writing last night a thin nervous pop-eyed gray hare, with thin, nervous, tense feet, and long, thin pink ears hopped up to me, put a front paw on my knee, twisted his head around to look at the map I had spread out, dropped down to take a tentative nibble of my shoe, and hopped off. Just like that!…

One porky came round last night and took, noisily, some more hunks out of the table. He tried hard enough to chew up my cup, which I had thoughtlessly left there, but with small success. However, I have tooth marks on the handle as a souvenir. A mouse chewed for a long time in the corner by my head. And either he or another mouse got into my pack.... He chewed quite a hole in the pack itself, and another in one of the little bags of dried corn. I don't blame him. The corn is good!

Do you remember when Seigfried wandered into the mist land and fought with the king of the dwarfs? I've been thinking of that all morning. When I woke I could hardly see the trees outside the door; but the fog soon lifted and became thinner fringes, more delicate, more like Seigfried's mist land.... For two solid hours I walked through timber-line country , a region of scattered, bent, gnarled, weathered spruces, tall luxuriant ferns, occasional towering rocks, and many mosses. And twining and twisting through everything were these fringes of mist, curling around your feet, brushing your cheeks and wetting your lips, slipping quietly off ahead of you, coming back and sitting on your hair! What a lonely feeling. From every lookout there was nothing to see but cottony space, with a nearby spruce top just poking into visibility.

But when I reached the top of Bread Loaf…and climbed the lookout of three old twisted trees piled together - behold, the mist broke up, patches of blue sky appeared, a vista opened - wider, wider, the clouds went galloping off trailing blue and white and gray fringes behind them. There was one wonderful view, north and east and south and west. And straightway they closed in again, and I was alone on a peak at the top of the world, clutching the only, whitened, weather-beaten stick left in existence. Forward!

Friday night

…It seems like a week since I made that entry this morning. I'd like to start…where I am now, but I guess I should take things in …order.... The individual wearing my size shoe seemed to have 'gone out' at Emily Proctor Lodge, for his or her footprints disappeared down that trail. The rest of the way, so far as I could see, I was the first person of the season. There were lots of deer tracks,…but not one human footprint. The trail had not yet been cleared or painted this season, and though the blazes were generally clear enough, there were some bad blowdowns to wangle through or around, and much of the footway was the sort you feel for with your feet rather than see with your eyes. I began to hope desperately that there'd be someone at Cooley Glen; someone coming through from the other direction. The guidebook, speaking of Cooley Glen, mentioned the fine stand of virgin spruce…and added 'beware of hedgehogs'…. I didn't want another night with porcupines all by myself….

The trail got worse and worse. Over Mt. Grover Cleveland it was unspeakable…wet, muddy, nettly, faint and finally, as I was going down the north slope, disappeared entirely, in a bunch of new slash. I was making…tentative forays …wondering what to do next, when I looked down a steep little slope…and there at the bottom was Cooley Glen Lodge. But what a pitiful sight. The virgin spruce is gone! All that wonderful south slope of Grant Mountain stripped to the limit, all scarred and gaunt and maimed…. The little lodge of peeled logs which had looked so very appropriate and fitting in its original setting, looked pitiful under the mocking light of the sun…. It was a sight to make one weep. It was nothing but a porky-ridden shanty, with a battered red tin roof…. Inside, the table was eaten almost completely away, so were the poles one sat on…. The little sheet iron stove had almost rusted away.

…It had been my original plan…to spend my last night in the wilderness at Cooley Glen, and to 'go out' from there, striking down the ravine in the direction of camp tomorrow, and spend tomorrow night at Warren either camping out… or staying at the hotel…. But now I didn't want to stay at Cooley Glen…. So I 'went out' then. I figured that by four o'clock I would be off the main range down where water was plentiful and the slopes not so frightfully steep. So I gave myself until four to find a camping ground.

You know it was fun, barging down the mountain side. I followed the ridge, rather than the ravine, and of course all the timber had fallen the same way I was going, and it was all downhill, so it was easy. I made all kinds of noise. If anyone heard me they must have thought all Barnum's elephants were loose. But pretty soon I came to some more slash.

Nasty stuff, that, but I knew it meant that there must be a road somewhere to take the logs out. After a bit I found it. Not a road but a log-slide. Anyhow, it was open, though very wet and steep and slippery. At the bottom I saw roofs. A lumber camp! Curses! I don't like lumber camps. But at any rate I must look my best if I am coming to civilization. So I stopped, dropped the pack, washed and drank, combed my hair and powdered my nose, adjusted my bandanna at its most rakish angle and moved to the conquest. The camp was deserted except for a porcupine who turned his rear-end to me and stuck his quills out so far you could see the dark pink skin between them.

On down the lumber road, through more maimed forest. I decided then and there that, unless I discovered a spot that simply said 'camp here', I'd go on to Warren. I'd probably get in at eight or nine, and they would take me at the hotel. But it wasn't long before the road, getting better, entered forest which had not been cut and it was rich and luscious.

Warren Post Office
Saturday, June 28

To take off the tale where I left off. The road crossed a brook on a corduroy bridge: a lovely, gurgling, splashing brook tumbling down over rocks in ripply cascades. On each side were tall straight spruce rising from high banks - well it said 'camp here'. I followed up one bank around a bend from the bridge, and there was the spot. An old, tall spruce with gray moss around the lower divisions of its trunk spread its roots out to enclose a little level place just big enough for my tent and fire, and carpeted thickly with needles and pink-striped wood sorrel. Right beside it the bank shelved down abruptly, a drop of fifteen feet to a little level space beside the stream, which was a succession of pools right there - ready-made bathtubs, cried my weary joints and my dirty hide!…Just over my tent place was a young moosewood, its big leaves clear yellow-green in the transmitted light of the sun, and all around the tall straight trunks of the spruces made a patterning of darks. It was as nearly perfect as I could ever dare to hope.

First, to get a fireplace. The humus was so rich and thick that I'd not dare light a fire on top of it. With the back of my axe I dug down to mineral earth - fully five or six inches of rich reddish mold, fragrant and crumbly.... There were plenty of flat rocks down by the brook to line the inside with. The finished fireplace was about a foot and a half square, with two sides and a back to enclose the fire and reflect it into the tent.

Then to get wood. How I love my little axe. More and more as I learn to know it better I appreciate it. My eye follows lovingly the sure, subtle curves of the handle, my hand thrills to the shaping of the steel. After a week of woodcutting I can handle it much better... and that is a source of deep satisfaction. I'd rounded up three or four good poles, and chopped out a couple of chunks of four-inch spruce ...when it began to rain. Grabbing my wood...I dashed over to my camping place, and...spread out the tent over everything, stretching it over as much ground as possible. By the time I had my poncho on, it was pouring. The woods were gray with rain. The great spruces were swaying, the little moosewood and the young maples were bowed to the ground.

Couldn't get firewood. Couldn't pitch tent. But there was no reason why I couldn't cut tent stakes and poles.... It was pretty hard finding just the right kind of forked sticks for shear poles, and the poncho kept swinging around to the wrong place. Somehow when I was building the fireplace I had managed to take a nick out of my axe's edge, but it kept me busy and warm during the deluge. Several times the rain slackened, but it was only to get a fresh grip and come down harder than ever. The song of the brook swelled to a paean....

About the time I finished getting my tent things, the rain really did slacken, so I decided that while it was stopping I'd take a bath. So my clothes came off ...and, armed with soap, toothbrush, and towel, I climbed down the mossy bank and plunged. Did it feel good! Cold and crisp and very fluid, deep and clean and refreshing. It made me laugh out loud. And by the time I was out and scrubbed dry it had quit rain-

Mary's Way

ing, the sky was blue, and the sunlight was sparkling on wet leaves. Dry clothes! You can bet I was thankful then that I'd carried them all those weary miles …even if they weren't anything more elaborate than a cotton shirt and a pair of cotton trousers.

After that for quite a time the sights you'd see at that campground would provoke an ascetic to mirth. Maiden barefoot, 'lightly clad', spurning the sorrel beneath her feet as she pitched tent, adjusted porch roof, stretched clothesline, built fire, dried poncho, buttoned poncho and ground cloth to tent roof, stretched out bed, hung other clothes to dry, arranged food, dishes, dry clothes, and miscellaneous in neat row on back side of tent, whetted axe, crept out carefully from beneath tent trying to avoid numerous ropes, hunted more wood, crept back cautiously into tent, got pail, crept cautiously out for water, got supper, spooning flour above one knee and below the other to hit proper receptacle, and at the same time spooning milk into another receptacle below the first knee. You see, the tent roof at the ridge is just high enough for my head as I sit, so I can't move around much, and have to have everything within reach.

It was just 6:30 as I ate supper - a simple, nourishing meal of cocoa, cornmeal griddle cakes fried in butter, nuts and raisins…. When supper was done, the dishes washed, the wipers hung up to dry on my private line, my own face and hands washed and my teeth cleaned, it was time to build up the fire with wood big enough to last, slide down into my nice warm puffy comforter, light a candle, and talk to my journal. I was proud…of that candle and its reflector. The flame was perfectly sheltered and bright as can be. (Sketch 6)

My state of mind at that moment was absolutely beatific. With no vast amount of effort, and in short time, and in spite of downpouring rain, I had achieved real creature comfort. I was lying on a soft, dry bed - six inches of leaf mould _is_ soft - with heat from a glorious fire reflected straight at me, and against the roof of my tent and down on me, good light to write by, and my tummy filled with satisfying food. Above me the wind made a million-stringed harp of the spruce tops, the stream chortled to itself below my feet, a thousand drops fell from the shaken trees - each making his tiny footstep sound, all around the rare and tingling smell of

Sketch Six
Candle Reflector

upland forest, and my possessions all in order and all within reach.... It was partly pride of achievement I suppose, a new and different sort of addition to my self-respect, combined with the particular exhilaration in the atmosphere. I wasn't even lonely. I was just carried out of myself with bliss. Could I have such nights, what might it not do to my daily life! Couldn't stand 'em often though. I'd burn up with white heat.

What matter if I woke up later in the night to find the fire out, a cold wind whistling round the corner, and rain beating down on the roof. I could wrap up tighter, the rain on my rag roof didn't reach me....

This morning it was so cold. A tentative arm stretched out of the blankets, let a rush of cold air in. The trees were bending and shouting under a full-mouthed wind. The sunlight was crackled into brilliant bits by the rushing shadows. Br-rr, it was cold, and colder in the creek. But the comfort of those luxuriously dried clothes made up for little troubles. Breakfast, break up camp... and march down the road. What a day! The cloud-drive again, fringy luminous white cloud against shadowy dark cloud against brilliant blue sky. Sunshine and leaping shadows. The pounding heart in tune with the charging wind and the swifter rhythm of the pack. Across another corduroy bridge, where the stream, increased in size, shoots its quicksilver water at you and dances merrily away from you. Out of the unbroken forest at last to a beautiful land of overgrown pasture, steeply sloping, patterned with areas of pointed firs. Ahead the sudden screech of a saw. A mill!... I didn't want to see one then. So I detoured up into the pasture to my left. And high on the hillside, looking back, I was a thousand-fold rewarded. Sweeping round about was the great blue ridge of the cirque

Mary's Way

down which I had come about halfway, forest clad and pat-
terned with moving shadows. Nearer were the varied
growths of the pasture itself, interrupted ferns, as tall as I,
Indian paintbrush, great red clovers, young willows (yellow-
green on their lower leaves, rich orange and delicate red on
the tops). And the shadows, the wind, the blood, the air!

I think more than any other one thing, now that it is all
over, my trip's been patterned to the rhythm of the hymn 'Oh,
worship the King, all glorious above'. Sometimes, in the city,
those words seem fulsome, stilted, affected a little. Here,
under the sky, they are the only possible words:

> *'Oh, worship the King, all glorious above*
> *And gratefully sing his power and his love,*
> *Our shield and defender, the ancient of days,*
> *Pavilioned in splendor and girded with praise.*
> *Whose robe is the light, whose canopy space,*
> *His chariots of wrath the deep thunderclouds form*
> *and dark is his path on the wings of the storm....'*

I have not tried to feel worshipful, but I could not help
it. I am sure that God made the world, and made it so beau-
tiful that our hearts ache to see it. Why do we try to destroy
that beauty, to change it, darken it, soil it, make it common
or garish or drab?... I think that always now, no matter how
common or garish or drab my surroundings may be, I shall
be conscious of the great, majestic beauties there are some-
where, and of the spot in my heart that's in tune with it all.

At the end of the journal Mary methodically listed what she
took for clothing and supplies and evaluated how she might do it
differently another time. For the most part, she decided she had
planned well, and she wrote, *"Now I am wild to go again!"*

So much of Mary comes across in her reporting of this trip.
The trek had its down sides - mosquitoes, black flies, porcupines,
slash - yet she saw it as mostly a highflying adventure. The
detailed descriptive observations she penned reflected the natural-
ist-artist in her. Her devout nature speaks from every page.
Sometime that summer of 1930 she penned the following psalm;
possibly in response to the feelings aroused during this Long Trail
odyssey.

❃ ❃ Psalm on a Vermont Hillside ❃ ❃

Praise the Lord, oh my soul!
For the wide dome of the sky, deep blue of the zenith, pale amber
    and rose all around the horizon;
For the serenity of the encircling hill;
For the kindliness of that nearest hill-shoulder, bending this farm-
    hill like a protecting arm;
For the wild sweep of valley below me;
For the worn old farmstead behind me, musical now with
    children's laughter;
For the sturdy growth of the high field near me, for potatoes
    and corn and beans;
For the wall of piled old lichened stones, creeping up over
    the edge of the pasture slope;
For the trees gracing every horizon;
For the subtle brown-green of the close-clipped hummocky pasture,
    enriching to luscious yellow-green in the trampled mucky draw,
    deepening to purple and blue and sea-green in the shadowy
    spruces;
For the rose-spired steeple-bush, in clumps far and near;
For the drying grasses, the deep-colored star-moss, the buttercups,
    the grass blue-eyed like the sky;
For the reindeer moss, grey and crisp beneath my feet;
Praise the Lord, oh, my soul;
And all that is within me; bless his holy name!

Vermont Adventuring – III

Almost exactly a year later, in June 1931, after much excited planning, Mary joined Milton and his wife Marion and several friends on a week long canoe adventure along the Otter Creek into Lake Champlain and Lake George. Mary brought a special companion, her pet crow Joe (namesake of friend Joe Back, also a student at the Art Institute). The river route they took, starting just north of Rutland, paralleled Mary's Long Trail route - just off to the west and down in a valley. Mary reported for the crew.

Joe rode our bows like a sentinel.... In a beautiful mixed forest, by a sloping water's edge we found a sick crow. Joe showed no interest. We landed and examined it. He had been shot, and his leg was all shattered and gangrened. He was too sick and miserable to try to get away. We killed him swiftly, threw him in the bushes and went on. He was much larger than Joe and much glossier of plumage, and his eyes were dark. Joe may be even so when he grows up....

Saw a great many dainty shore birds, the bases of whose primaries and secondaries showed a great streak of white as they flew. We called them willets.... An amazing number of kingbirds, many swallows (barn swallows nested in the underpinning of wooden bridges; bank swallows were often seen) one or two yellow warblers, represented most of our game along the river....

Camped about an hour before sunset in a marshy mead-

*ow.… Just north of the clearing is a steep rocky hill, heavily
wooded at the base, with considerable poison ivy. Landing
was made on a mudbank;…two canoes hauled up…and
turned over, serving as walls for the tent Milt pitched - a
standard canvas fly. For water he dug a well a few feet from
the open water of the marsh. It filled in half an hour or so
and gave us plenty of sweet water. It rained very hard that
night, but it didn't matter. We all had room to sleep com-
fortably. The great drawback to this camp ground was mosquitoes. We had to fight them with citronella and mosquito
bars all night long.…*

The days were spent enjoying the river and paddling toward
Lake Champlain. Joe's antics added to the entertainment, as he
frequently flew off into nearby trees and sometimes had to be
forcibly convinced to return, usually by Milton climbing a tree to
get him. Joe learned to catch polliwogs by himself, although he
also got wet and mad in the process. He was the usual alarm clock,
often awakening very early, standing on someone and yelling for
some food. Once he got attacked by a kingbird apparently protect-
ing his nest. Each evening they pitched tents in pastures while
someone walked to a nearby farmhouse to bargain for milk. They
replenished supplies at towns along the river, such as Middlebury,
where they arranged for a truck to portage them several miles past
a succession of rapids and gorges.

Between Middlebury and Vergennes they canoed through pasture land. When they stopped to pitch camp they found they had
an impressed audience of cows who circled them and watched with
wondering mild eyes. They insisted on remaining close by, no matter how many times the campers chased them off. As Otter Creek
reached Lake Champlain after flowing through miles of marshes,
the canoers could see the New York shore, a several mile paddle
across the water.

*Then we paddled three miles…southwest to Barn Rock
Harbor across the lake in New York State. It is far and away
the most beautiful camp yet. It's a tiny sheltered harbor, not
500 feet across, with a great rocky headland on one side, a
quiet bit of level country on the other. Steep hillside all
around heavily wooded, and not a person other than our
party in sight or hearing. To reach the place we aimed from*

the mouth of the Otter for some cliffs on the other side. They looked quite near and not particularly huge, but when we reached them after a very long paddle we found them tremendous and perfectly sheer with a wonderful echo. From them we followed the shoreline…to the harbor where there is a brook and plenty of firewood on the beach and in the woods.

Many birds calling - wood thrushes fluting, chickadees, a red-eyed vireo, an ovenbird…whose voice is a single note like the loud splash of a drop into a pail of water. The next day heavy mist over the water…which cleared rapidly away under the impetus of a northeast wind, which…didn't disturb our harbor. Clear, sunny, cool in the shadows. Before breakfast I tried climbing Barn Rock by following the shore on foot as far as possible, then straight up the cliff. Sort of hair-raising to me, but really not too bad. There were plenty of hand and footholds….

On the way I had a mighty interesting time watching an adult black and white warbler feeding a full feathered youngling. The short tailed critter was sitting on a hemlock twig while papa (?) scurried around for insects. He was brownish whereas papa was black; and creamy whereas papa was white. His feathers were soft and fluffy and his mouth dropped childishly at the corners. I tried to take a picture but before I got close enough, baby took fright and flew….

Milt discovered the chickadee's nest. I had heard them calling and scolding on the shore behind the tent, but now the whole crowd of us watched the grown-ups carry insects to an old stump and disappear through a hole in the top. With a flashlight we examined the inside of the nest. Six babies crowded it, fully feathered infants, all ready to fly apparently.

About 2:30 we took off for Crown Point, twelve miles away. When we got out of the harbor, oh boy! How the waves did hit us. Driven before a northeast wind, the rollers came so high and foamy that 'twas impossible to ride across them. There was nothing to do but ride with them, which took us leaping on the wave summits and dashing for the troughs, to finally land on a windy shore a few miles down…. The *owner of the shore…whose cottage was not far off, readily gave us permission to build a fire there. So, after hauling up a canoe for a windbreak, we had a tasty supper…. The fire was a very clever one: a shallow trough in the sand, re-enforced by a length of driftwood plank on each side, which held the pots….*

As it grew darker, the waves decreased in size and the moon began to give light. We decided to make Crown Point, twelve miles away. At 8:00 p.m. we started off on a dancing lake. I have never known a more beautiful boat trip. The air was clear and bracing, the moon bright, the lights of Chimney Point bridge challenging in the distance. Vera, my canoeing partner was in madcap spirits; everyone more or less hilarious. We held the canoes together and sang for miles to the paddles' rhythm. Only the last fifteen minutes was work. But at that 'twas only 11:30 when we landed, a head-on landing on a sandy beach at the northern tip of Crown Point….

The boaters explored the ruins from French and Indian War days at Crown Point the next day and then had a long hard pull paddling against a heavy wind before reaching the landing at Fort Ticonderoga. As the lake narrows here they headed for a pasture on a high clay bluff on the Vermont side.

The field was knee-deep in buttercups and daisies…. The brilliant redheaded woodpecker and meadowlark (welcomed us). The sunset was glorious - a golden sky with long purple clouds steaming over it - a great expanse of the lake flaming in sympathy. And right in the middle of that glory came a rat-a-tat-tat and a rub-a-dub-dub and the silvery notes of a bugle in perfect time with it; pealing out from old Fort Ti across the lake…. It was surely spectacular.

Next Day

Heading for the opposite shore, once more the wind was dead against us. It was a long wallowing struggle to the opposite side. Then up the interesting marshlands of Scum Creek to Ticonderoga Village. Red-winged blackbirds aplenty here with gulls, a kingfisher and many other birds. At Ticonderoga we were portaged to Lake George. The length of the portage is only about a mile, but the rise is about 2200 feet and there are nine dams....

Into the water about 2:00 and...a long...six-mile paddle down Lake George to camp. The scenery gets grander and grander. Roger's Slide appears on the right shore: a tremendous steep slide of rock hundreds of feet high. The cliff goes steeply off into the water, which clear to the shore is that deep, black-blue that is somewhat frightening in its significance. At the end of Roger's Mountain the shore dips into the west. Right at the corner is a little island. It is only a few rods long, a steep little rock crowned with a few oak trees, a few junipers, some cedars and grass and bluebells. A long finger of rock slants gently into the open lake. A narrow strait separates it from the mainland. A sign proclaims it state land and Juniper Island.

Here we camped.... That island was Paradise, no less. From the moment we saw it our hearts claimed it. It was home. We swam right away in the clear water around it, collected wood from the mainland, cooked and ate supper, and wrapped up to sleep all in the most complete sense of well-being....

The next day after much hard paddling they retraced their portage back to Lake Champlain, where they landed near Fort Ticonderoga. They very much wanted to explore it.

When Milt had been there before he had gone through the heavy door in the lower wall. It was the nearest entrance to us, so we tried it, but it was fastened. If we were to see the fort there were two alternatives: to go way round to the entrance or to climb the wall beside the back gate. We decided to take this side, and swarmed over the breastworks, climbing beside the great cannon and dropping down on the graded lawn inside. We started toward the barracks, but a man stopped our motley crew of battered mariners with a mere word. He said, "Say." He said further, "You can't see the fort unless you go round and buy tickets in the log house. Tickets are fifty cents." And that was that. Crestfallen, we returned the way we had come, dropping over the wall beside the cannon, embarrassed under the eyes of many visitors, but chuckling at our exploit.

The voyagers then paddled south on the narrowing lake, heading toward Whitehall, their final destination. With a stiff breeze from the north pushing them along, they hardly had to paddle. In fact, after a few experiments, Milton rigged a couple of poncho sails which he attached to the three canoes, after tying them together. For fifteen miles they sailed along in luxurious idleness until they dropped anchor off Whitehall three hours before they expected to. A sunburned, carefree crew regretfully ended their voyage, aware that such opportunities would be difficult to repeat as Mary headed back to Chicago and Milton and Marion drove northeast to their home in Bangor, Maine.

Before she ended her stay in Vermont, Mary undertook a wildlife collecting adventure in the Northfield Mountains. Did she hunt there with Milton's shotgun? While she never wrote about this trip, later that year the Academy of Sciences reported she had added to its research collections: a sharp shinned hawk and red squirrel from Roxbury, Vermont, and a ring-necked pheasant from Chicago. Perhaps another challenge conquered!

Joe

❖ ❖ ❖ ❖ ❖

In her later years, Mary recalled how her joy in life built steadily through her high school and college years, peaking in 1931 in art school. Why? She fell head over heels in love with ex-cowboy, art student Joseph Wyatt Back whom she had met in 1929. Their relationship did not start auspiciously. Mary sat in a gallery of the Field Museum sketching a bear for an animal anatomy class very intent on what she was doing. Suddenly a loud voice boomed over her shoulder, "That's a hell of a bear!" Mary turned and froze the loud stranger with an angry stare, muttering to herself about the "damn tourists". Before her stood a roughly handsome young man with sparkling blue eyes, who decided pretty quickly that Mary Cooper was someone he wanted to get to know better.

Not a run-of-the-mill art student, Joe ran away from home at fifteen (unable to abide his drunkard step-father), and enrolled early in the school of hard knocks. After a stint in the navy (during World War I) he homesteaded in Wyoming and became an itinerant cowhand, working at various ranches to make ends meet. What he lacked in schooling he made up for in his native intelligence, ingenuity, reliability and wit. He was a sought-after ranch hand. Along the way, Joe sketched wherever he went, particularly loving to draw animals. At a dude ranch near Dubois, one of the dudes, a well known painter of birds, Louis Agassiz Fuertes, saw some of Joe's drawings and encouraged him to go to art school.

When Joe expressed some interest, Mr. Fuertes helped him apply to the Art Institute of Chicago. They promptly turned him down when they learned his schooling had stopped at eighth grade. Not discouraged, the artist gathered all Joe's drawings and headed for Chicago. To Joe's disbelief, the school liked what they saw so much, they decided to admit him. He settled his affairs in Wyoming, and headed for Chicago.

Mary came to marvel at how their paths had crossed. She started a journal to record this amazing event and their developing relationship.

We have both lived for quite a long time, independently and thoughtfully. We have each beaten out a philosophy on anvils of experience. We have both laughed much and often, in respect to the things we have grown to love -mountains, campfire, real people as friends, animals, painting, the open sky. Yet we are so different that we shall always be conscious of a sort of excitement in our merging.

Separated in our growing years by thousands of miles, surrounded by entirely different sets of situations (I by the restraints and privileges of high school, college, and summer camps; he by the freedom, independence and deprivations of a life on his 'own' on the open range, in the navy, in cow-camp, sheep-camp, dude ranch, trapper's cabin). It seems remarkable to me that we should acquire and be bound by the same set of sanctity and standards and that my set should seem as odd to most of the people among whom I lived and worked as his seemed strange to the people he knew. It makes us quite sure that we must have been meant for each other from the beginning of time....

I can't get over feeling surprised at myself. My life seems to be made of pieces which fit together perfectly and almost beyond my control. What an ugly duckling I was in college! And later, what an independent highbrow up at the Academy of Sciences surrounded by those priceless people. I was beginning... to acquire a humor that twinkled and even flashed sometimes, getting a skill with my hands that gave me more sureness and confidence, and beginning to use my head for myself, instead of leaning on other folks. I was to have this job with the Forest Preserve, and a life of sturdy, humorous, old maid-hood was opening before me. I would have my animals and plants, my art and love of nature, my Sunday School class, and God to keep me company. I liked the idea. Life had always been very full and busy and rich. I had always had friends. I had never been lonely for long. Of course, there were those nights of blind and vacant loneliness on the Long Trail, when in fear and silence and self-examination I knew beyond a doubt that deep inside me was a hunger for human love. But I had buried that. I was going to live my own life.

And then I fell in love…and all the world was somehow different….

How wonderful is our psychological fitness for life. I had been independent and alone of feeling - very much alone, and lonesome, and unfulfilled. What seemed like a miracle was my stepping into the fullness of a more abundant life. I feel all aglow with a new, more splendid richness. So great, so miraculous does it seem that the hard thing to believe is that others have so loved before us. Can it be that there is anywhere else such richness and fullness and glory?

It had taken two years of Joe's quiet persistence, his steady admiration, a botched kiss, and suddenly Mary knew: this was her man. By early fall 1931, they were engaged and she could think of little else besides Joe.

Strange, above all, how long it has taken me to realize this - how long it has taken me to grow up. I wonder what the causes may be. It is partly that I've been just slow to mature. My psychological organism hadn't been set to go off at the appropriate stimuli. It is partly my family - their faith and love and squareness and unity. A man must be a real man to break into that charmed circle. Partly, I am sure, it is that I was waiting for the right man. Strange how out of all the men with whom I've had contact, out of the many men I've admired and respected, Joe steps, and commands nothing less than love. A touch of Joe's lips on mine, and I'm grown up!

I have heard people talk about the instant when they turned the corner from girlhood to womanhood. I …thought 'How strange! I recall nothing like that. I must have just grown up gradually.' How was I to know that the moment just hadn't come yet? Almost twenty-five years old - surely a girl is a woman by then. But I didn't know. I grew up in a second, when Joe threw his arms around me and gave me that funny kiss that just missed, there on our front porch a week and a half ago. I have wondered about love. I have been disgusted when I saw hand-holding in public, or kissing.... It seemed to me there was a bit of shame about love. Oh, it may be that love is sometimes shameful, but it ought to be just glorious - triumphant. I am proud to bursting of every kiss Joe has given me, even of the one he stole on Wabash Avenue, right in the Loop.

He calls me 'carita mia' and they are the sweetest words in the world, almost. They come next after 'I love you'.... How few things are important right now, except the pressure of his arms round my body, of his lips on my throat, the look in his deep, clean eyes, the words he speaks....

Often at night he comes for me at the Academy, and we walk far down the windy shore. Opposite North Avenue where the embankment is broken up some, we sit and eat lunch, then walk on down the shore, sometimes clear to the municipal pier....

We have reached a stage where we talk less and less and make love more and more. We are perfectly frank about it. 'Petting', 'necking' how terrible those words are. How disgusting I used to think were the actions they referred to. But oh, it all depends! If I thought I were doing wrong, there would be a little feeling of shame about me. But there's no shame, there is pride! Pride that such a splendid, sensitive, square, honorable, sincere man is <u>mine</u>. Pride in every kiss he gives me. Pride in his big strong hands, in his wide firm lips, in his deep eyes, even in his white eyebrows! Did ever such a man rope steers and ride broncs before?...

One of the finest things for me to remember is that Joe hardly touched me until after he had asked me to marry him. Never anything more than taking my elbow crossing a street. He never tried to hold my hand, or to put his arm around me. And by the intensity of his passion now, one can guess what a grip he is keeping on himself....

After school, another talk by the shore, some foolishness and a little teasing, with Joe getting just a bit, well, masterful. It's the first time he's been that. I must watch out for it a bit, but it's mighty good for Joe. He's been too meek, too humble, too fearful of asserting himself where he might not be welcome. He needs to feel sure of himself, and he might as well practice on me. He mustn't be too sure of me though. I'm afraid that would not be good for him. I must cultivate a few feminine wiles to make him chase along a bit.

Funny how I began to feel the need for cultivating many unfamiliar feminine attitudes. These arts of coquetry are very strange to me. Whenever I try out a new one, and it works, it makes me chuckle.... I want to make him confident, but not overconfident; to make him practice winning me, again and again, in as many different ways as I can manage.... Heavens, the man has endless grit, endless mirth upon his lips. Can I keep him in endless gaiety of heart, everlasting faith? The paradox is that I can't if he is too sure of me. It's a delicate psychological problem for a young feminist to attack....

Saturday, the concert. They played the whole of Tchaikovsky's Fifth Symphony, to most tear you in two; then, to patch you together again, a gay tarantella by Saint-Saens, and folk songs by Percy Grainger. We were lucky enough to get in the front row gallery. A great symphony concert certainly stirs you to the depths and sets all your emotions on fire. Our deepest experiences with each other have come after concerts. It was the first one we went to together that gave Joe courage to ask me to marry him. It is the concert Saturday nights when it is the hardest to let Joe go, when it is hardest for him to leave....

One of the most wonderful things about Joe is his sound trustworthiness. What years of patience and of self-control you feel must lie back of his iron will, his great judgment. At the same time, those years of patience and self-control, of repression and abstinence, lie back of the fierce power of his passion, and the rich intensity of his love. He is like a river, long dammed up, hit with the flood-gates now open. But the floodgates are there, ready to stop the terrific flow before damage is done downstream.... His proposal, when my face was horribly bleared with ivy poisoning, convinced me beyond a doubt that his love is for the real me, not the husk of me.... It makes me feel perfectly safe with him, perfectly at ease.

Midst their lovemaking, they talked seriously about their future. The wild valleys and mountains of Wyoming called Joe. Mary thrilled to the idea of heading west. They dreamed about how they could get there, find a ranch of their own and become western artists. Elmer, an acquaintance of Joe's, might help them buy that ranch.

We have all the symptoms of young folks just engaged, I think. We are absent-minded as can be, when we see each other our eyes just fly together, we get all choked up and can't talk straight. But at the same time, I think we are going into this thing sanely. People speak of this impossibly romantic 'adventure' of ours. But it's the life we have both loved always. Joe has lived it all the year round for many years. He knows what emergencies will have to be met, and how to meet them. And I am not such a greenhorn - raised in the mountains myself, brought up to love and not to fear them, to know them, to know how to live in their remote fastness-es. For many people - well, for almost everyone else we know - our plan would be worse than rash. It would be mad.... Unforeseen things will happen, requiring courage and strength and forthrightness to meet, but things can't go wrong while Joe keeps to the little refrain that is choked out of him every time his arms go round me: 'I want to make you happy - to be worthy of you - and honorable to you - and square with you - and make you happy....'

A letter comes from Elmer...stating the joyful news that he has a new young son; and the lugubrious, tough, some-what associated fact that he has no money, and can't buy a ranch this year! So the architecture of our dream world will have to be changed temporarily, I'm afraid. From a log cabin in the mountains to a steam-heated flat somewhere in Chicago is a real come-down for us. How I hate the idea of having to live in Chicago. But, on thinking it over, I can see that living in Chicago with Joe would be preferable to living *without him anywhere.*

What I am afraid of is that our dream will change - that we will see the possibility of selling our wares so much more easily in town, that we will get so used to the idea of steam heat and electric lights that we won't want to do without them; that a physical inertia will set in upon us that will be difficult to break away from; that we'll really get settled in town. We both so yearn to strike down roots, that I'm afraid we will strike them too soon, and then be always a bit sorry....

There were highs and lows in 1931 and 1932. Joe gave Mary a beautiful engagement ring: turquoise set in silver and incised with Joe's old brand ⅄ (the Rocker Y). Their love affair flamed, almost too hot to handle. On the other hand, the economy fell apart. Local banks closed. The job Mary sought as curator of a new natural history museum disappeared, as the Forest Preserve did not have the funds to start the museum. No job. No ranch. Then the doctor put Mary's mother Juliet to bed because of a heart condition and Mary became her care giver. Even when the lows seemed at their worst, Mary saw something good about the situation.

...We walked through a depressing drizzle to...where Joe and Harold (his roommate) live at 16 West Ohio Street.... It's a pretty dirty neighborhood, cobbly and unromantic in the gray drizzle. But there are possibilities.... It might be very wise to live in those same rooms when we are married. It would be a great saving in money - for the three rooms he and Harold pay only $24 a month.... And it would be much more picturesque and interesting than an ordinary flat such as <u>any</u> young couple in Chicago might have. It is sort of a hole - hovel Harold calls it - but paint, soap and water, and a little feminine arranging would do wonders to it. The chief drawback is no daylight, and I don't know about bathing facilities. I suggested the idea once to Joe, and he recoiled in horror. But I think it would be great fun.... The place is close to downtown.... It's in walking distance from the Art Institute and Academy of Sciences. And those boys don't realize that one reason their place looks so desolate is the need of maid service and a lily-white feminine hand.

Really the big trouble is 'what will people say' for it is rather an unpleasant neighborhood.

It was hard to see the bright side of Juliet's health. By early December 1932, her heart and anemia problems took a back seat to the cancer found in her stomach that had also spread to her liver. Mary wrote her brothers and sisters, now living from Nebraska to Maine, warning that those who planned to come to Chicago for Christmas might be coming for their mother's funeral.

All this is very new, I mean the news is. Of course, the cancer must have been going on for years. Only a week ago the doctor made the examination.... Yesterday he had a talk with father at his office, but I learned the seriousness of the case only tonight. I stopped at the doctor's office on my way home from work to get a physical exam. (The doctor said last night that if mother had an operation, she would have to have a blood transfusion first, and I wanted to make sure there wasn't anything wrong with my blood, in case they wanted to use it. There isn't, I guess).... I met Dad at the office...and I heard his conference with the doctors. They hold out nothing at all. They say, go to Mayo's. They are the highest authority, the last word, and we will feel better to know nothing's gone undone that could be done....

Mother asked me to write you. She sends her love. I hope she doesn't know the full purport of what I am writing, but I'm sure she does. I gather from the somewhat grim yet tender smile on her face so often this evening that she is somewhat amused at our real efforts to act as if everything were normal....

On January 5, 1933, Juliet died. Joe must have been right there with Mary to help console her. Juliet, always the cheerful letter writer, had kept the Cooper tribe in touch with each other. While Frances and Mary lived in Chicago and Dorothy and her minister husband not far away, Miriam and her husband Ernest (also a minister) lived way off in the sand hill country of Nebraska. Milton and Ed and their wives both resided in northern Maine.

As the family gathered to mourn Juliet's passing, everyone agreed the letter writing Juliet could no longer do must continue. The idea of the round-robin letter emerged. It started to circulate after the funeral, helping to tie this far-flung family together.

Married Life and the Trailside Museum

Mary wrote her first Robin letter on March 13, 1933, putting her pen to paper as she rode the L home after working at the Trailside Museum. On February 19, with the depression closing banks right and left, she and Joe got married in a very intimate ceremony at the Cooper home. Her favorite cousin Mary Ellen managed to come from Detroit, though the bank closings forced her to borrow money from her father to make the trip. She joined Mary's dad, C.P. and Mary's sisters Dorothy and Frances as witnesses to the marriage. Dorothy's husband performed the ceremony. And now Mary needed to tell the other Coopers about married life.

> It was a beautiful walk to the L tonight. A heavy wet fog has settled over the city. From the Museum I walked down through deserted streets, past comfortable houses with glowing windows, streets whose vistas ended inside a block, everything shining and gray with the wet and the fog. I imagine in the city it will be denser and more exciting, with the big signs and the lighted buildings all fuzzed and effulgent, and reflected as big glowing bubbles in the misty river. And Joe and I will walk together, on air, over that misty river, and home....

> Isn't it great to be married!... We had counted on the thrill, but we didn't know ahead of time about the great peace and comfort and contentment in just being together. It

seems as if that shabby little home of ours is like a golden cup, filled to the brim with shiningness, and we are swimming in it....

About the wedding. Mary Ellen...spent Sunday up at the Museum with me. Ostensibly it was to see how I spend my time, but really it was to see that I didn't tell anyone....

At home by 6:30 I bathed and dressed in a hurry. I was congratulating myself on my calmness, when, fishing around in my bureau drawer for something, I cut off with a razor blade...half the fingernail on the index finger, together with some considerable slice of the finger. I ask you, could I have done anything more like me?

I was so determined my hands and arms were to be at their best - so two days before, I accidentally got in a fight with Bobby Gray Squirrel (at the Museum) (*See sketch 7*) and carried off half a dozen deep scratches on my left hand. Then, the very day of the wedding, my knife slipped as I was making a muscular dissection of a deer, and cut an ugly gash

Sketch Seven
Bobby Gray Squirrel

Mary's Way

in my right wrist. And besides all that, now at the last moment I had to tie up an index finger. Thank God it wasn't the ring finger!...

At last I was ready, and about then Joe came - about 7:10 p.m. We didn't give him much time to draw his breath. We were married by 7:20. Father stood at my left hand and Joe at my right. I held both their hands…. There were yellow roses in the pewter vase on the mantel, and yellow candles in the low black candlesticks. There was no light but candlelight and the red glow from the hearth. I wore the clinging blue dress that amazed you so, and a corsage of sweet peas on my shoulder…. After the 'who giveth this woman,' Dad stepped back, and I didn't have any hand but Joe's to hold. That was pretty good holding, though. He didn't act scared, or lose the ring, or anything.

At Mary's insistence, Joe added his two cents to the Robin letter which he did in his cowboy twang with a twinkle in his eye. The Coopers came to know that Mary's husband was a real tease - watch out for that sense of humor!

"Yes, and I'm proud as punch that I've a wife (there's only one like her with my name!) This is the first time I've had a personal contact with a robin….It …seems a sure way of being plumb friendly and real home folks. I'm proud and glad of the chance to be included in the Cooper circle and my pardner is just what makes life worthwhile…I hanker for some of Milton's chop suey and when Milton makes some when we are together again, we'll use the enlarger on it so we'll have more…. Ellsworth (Dorothy's husband) has been eating too many of those good cookies Dorothy makes 'cause he looks like he spent an open winter on good feed, in his pictures. But he's alright…for he did a right good job of putting the Back brand on my Mary. If Ellsworth can splice rope like he does people, he would be a good sailor…."

Their busy lives at 16 West Ohio Street left little time for each other. Thankfully Joe no longer worked almost round the clock as he had when he was still in art school. Then he had four jobs that he called his four scholarships. For 1 1/2 hours each day he carried dishes at a cafeteria and got two meals (sixty cents each) provided. From five p.m. to midnight he wheeled a cart at the American Express Freight depot. He also fit in jobs as night watchman at the

American Radiator Company and janitor at the Art Institute where he worked from seven a.m. until the start of classes. In those days he described himself as 'the sleepiest man in Chicago,' but at least he was studying art. Now he just worked in the cafeteria.

Except Sundays, Joe is free after 9 a.m. He shops in the Loop for groceries and gets home by 9:30. Then he is scheduled to paint the rest of the day. Of course these first days a part of his painting time has to be spent on fixing-up work - building shelves, putting up electric wiring, and painting the 'hovel'.... But when he gets really started on a painting you can hardly pry him loose. He eats, dreams, sleeps and wears paint. You should see his painting trousers. The right thigh, where he wipes his brushes when he gets excited, would stand alone. More than that, you could hardly bend them if you tried.... Then he gets supper for us, and leaves it so it will stay hot while he comes down to the train and meets me.... Then I change my dress and wash while Joe sets out the supper. We hold hands while we ask the blessing, and how we eat after that!... The way we spend the evening depends more or less on whether he's at one of those painting jobs you can't pry him loose from. If he is, he paints. If he isn't, mostly, we work together on something that needs doing around the house.

True to her prediction, Mary masterminded an imaginative renovation of Joe's old quarters, using lots of ingenuity and little expense.

By late summer Joe had a job opportunity he couldn't pass up, even though it meant less time with Mary. It came with regular pay - $175 a month - and would allow them to start saving for that trip west, still uppermost in their minds.

In some ways it seemed like a godsend. The city was beginning to tell on Joe. You can imagine how three years of uninterrupted heart-of-the-city life would hurt a person who had always lived in tremendous spaces. He was noticing automobiles going by. Small sounds wore on his nerves while he was painting. His appetite wasn't good.

And one morning Mr. Sauers called from the Forest Preserve Headquarters and asked Joe if he would like to have a place as foreman of a gang of fifty men, part of a crew of a thousand of Roosevelt's Conservation Army, working to turn a great marsh north of the city into a series of lagoons and lakes. He started to work just after the fourth of July, and is much browner and heartier and full of pep already....

We find it really strenuous for us both to have jobs, and I think Joe bears the brunt of it, having to get supper after working hard all day. However, he's a hero about it. We are learning more about each other all the time and liking each other better. At least I like him better and he acts as if he doesn't mind.

The natural history museum job had finally come through for Mary, so she now rode the L most days for forty-five minutes, followed by a 1 1/2 mile walk to the new Trailside Museum in Thatcher Woods. Located in the historic home of the Thatcher family, it nestled close to the DesPlaines River in River Forest. She delighted in her role as curator, even if it only paid $100 a month. The reg-

Mary Cooper
Trailside Museum Curator

ular pay helped in meeting their goal and gave her just the kinds of experiences she so badly wanted. She continued to call herself Miss Cooper at work, while she relished being Mrs. Joe Back everywhere else.

The Museum is getting along beautifully. We have a new building, a workshop out behind the museum and near the slough. That releases quite a bit of additional space for exhibits.... We don't have many new exhibits.... There is a big woodchuck, tame as a dog, called Emmett. He is quite a pet. Then there is a new squirrel and a gray gopher and a rabbit. Pricky has grown so very big, she is hard to carry around. Also her temper is more surly. She is getting more like a regular porcupine all the time.

The Museum attracted injured animals like a magnet. The basement became a makeshift hospital for small wild animals. Those who couldn't go back to the woods ended up as caged exhibits. When an animal died, Mary became the taxidermist of her dreams. She dressed their skins and immortalized them in drawings. Under Mary's guidance the Museum became a mecca for students of biology, botany, zoology, herpetology, and kindred sciences. They crowded through its four rooms where normally shy and elusive forest creatures could be seen, heard, handled and studied at arm's length. There was rarely a dull moment, as her work diary reflects.

Our coon went on the rampage two days ago and ate a fox squirrel, a sunfish, five bullheads, two salamanders, and spilled the kerosene. Quite a night!... A woodchuck broke out at the Museum again yesterday. Some damage. Many muddy windows. We are fixing up the back entry for a good strong cage for them....

Skinned and post-mortemed a nuthatch - a very small specimen. Cage finished and woodchuck put in. Kaplan came with his timber rattlers - on loan until June....The quietest Saturday I know anything about: 55 visitors. Prairie Club junior hike - one older girl fell in the river and had to be dried out and washed in our basement. Worked on maps and chart for geology....

Quite a crowd and accidents. Falco died. When skinned, it was clear he was too fat, but I doubt that was the cause. The chipmunks and Frankie were out of their cages.

Prepared for talk at Lincoln School. Showed slides, shrew and snakes to enthusiastic kids. Worked on sketch for window shelves....

Saw whet owl reported near gas tank - went to see.
Huge snapper and a big leech brought in. Skinned towhees.

Children found the Trailside Museum irresistible. Once there, many wanted to hang around and help. Soon Mary had enlisted a corps of 'junior assistants' aged 12 to 18 who made enthusiastic tour guides and interpreters (see certificate, shared by retired Judge von der Heydt of the Alaska Supreme Court).

Trailside Museum Junior Assistant Certificate

COMMISSIONERS

EMMETT WHEALAN
President
WILLIAM BUSSE
HOMER J. BYRD
MRS. EDWARD J. FLEMING
FRANK J. KASPER
MAURICE F. KAVANAGH
PETER M. KELLY
WALTER J. LaBUY
MARY McENERNEY
GEORGE A. MILLER
MRS. GLENN E. PLUMB
DANIEL RYAN
AMELIA SEARS
CHARLES H. WEBER

FOREST PRESERVE DISTRICT
of **COOK COUNTY**
ILLINOIS

CHARLES G. SAUERS, *General Superintendent*

GENERAL HEADQUARTERS
CUMMINGS SQUARE
RIVER FOREST,
ILLINOIS
TELEPHONES
COLUMBUS 8400- FOREST 4470

REAL ESTATE AND
LEGAL DEPARTMENTS
547 COUNTY BUILDING
CHICAGO,
ILLINOIS
TELEPHONE
FRANKLIN 3000

JAMES VON DER HEYDT

The Forest Preserve District of Cook County and the Chicago Academy of Sciences are glad to recognize the value of your services to Trailside Museum. Generously and without thought of reward, because of your interest in the Museum and your enthusiasm for it, you have given much time and effort to its business over a period of many weeks, assisting in its activities and supporting its policies.

For this reason, and because of the assurance that formal acknowledgement of it will make you yet more useful to the Museum in the future, you are now recognized as a Junior Assistant on its Staff.

General Superintendent, Forest Preserve District

Director, Chicago Academy of Sciences

Curator, Trailside Museum

In one report to the Academy of Sciences Mary described the museum.

Trailside Museum's informality, coupled with its concentration on the local material that he has seen and knows a bit about, has made it a paradise for small boys…. So as it has grown, the museum has naturally tended to become organized around (them). Cases and cages, signs and pictures, have been placed near the eye-level of a twelve-year-old. The directions for operating the microscopes, and the labels describing the exhibits, have been written largely for him. That's only fair, for he has contributed many of the exhibits himself. Alone and by twos and threes he brings in chipmunks, gophers, snakes, frogs, toads, salamanders, butterflies, crickets, katydids, moths, cicadas, birds' nests and spiders. He keeps the place supplied with snake food in the form of worms and small toads. And he comes in throngs every day….

From the neighborhood around the museum came families like the Wassons who got to know Mary as an alchemist who made the ordinary, magical. Isabel and Theron, who worked as geologists, came because of their love of bird watching and nature. Their six-year-old daughter Anne joined them, skipping with delight, knowing Mary would let her help clean the animal cages and maybe even hold one of the snakes! Under Mary's gentle, patient teaching, Anne joined the flocks of youngsters who left the Trailside Museum in love with wildlife and botany.

Mary became a sought-after speaker at clubs and schools, where she often arrived accompanied by live wild companions, such as an owl or snake. She wrote several short stories about museum critters that she probably told to some of her audiences. One such tale, about Blackie, a porcupine, described his life's adventures as he matured in the forest, ending when he met some humans….

One evening down by the lake he smelled the man smell. He sat up on his tail and sniffed. He walked down the shore to where the smell came from. A pointed green thing like a queer-shaped log was stranded on the beach. It was the first canoe he had ever seen. Two whittled boards, like white branches, stuck out of it in front. Paddles, if he had known better. At the back of the beach, near the ridge of the woods, two strange creatures smelling rankly of the man smell, were putting up a flappy thing that we would call a tent. The creatures were a man and a boy about ten years old. The boy's name was Carl. The man was his father, and he was taking Carl on his very first canoe-camping trip.

Blackie waited till it was dark. He watched from down the beach, while Carl and his father built a fire, winking in the evening like a red eye, and took out supper things from various boxes. Soon the keen odor of bacon stung Blackie's waiting nostrils. Licking his lips and chattering his teeth he moved forward. There was something a bit scary about the fire, so he stopped by the canoe. There was a large boulder beside the bow. By scrambling to the boulder's top he could reach the gunwale and swing himself over to the canoe's inside. He made considerable scrambling noise, but Carl was laughing at his father's stories and neither heard the porcupine. Blackie made straight for the man smell of the paddles. He took a big bite of the wood. M - m - m! Oh, so salty! Sitting on the forward rattan seat, Blackie settled himself for a long evening's gnawing.

The talk around the fire died down. "Scrunch! Scrunch! Scrunch!" went Blackie's teeth. With a sudden exclamation the man flashed a light toward the canoe and called Carl. Blackie sighed. He stopped gnawing, put his head under the shelter of the paddle handles, erected his back quills, and lashed with his tail. That had always won before, but this was different. The man, standing by the canoe said, "A baby porcupine." Carl called excitedly, "Catch it for me, can you Dad? I want it for a pet. I want to take it back to River Forest." "Well, hold the light on him, Carl," replied his dad. "Don't touch him. And wait a minute." The man emptied out a box that had groceries in it, put it by the canoe seat, poked Blackie into it with a paddle and snapped the cover down. "There!" he said. "We've got him."

Blackie was in pitch darkness now, and couldn't get out. He whined as he had when a tiny baby, before Mother had left him. His big defense hadn't worked at all. He felt lost. But all around him was the good man smell. He took a little chew. M - m - m. The wood was <u>full</u> of salt. He chewed and chewed and chewed. Never mind if he was captive. He was

going to enjoy it. All of a sudden something funny hap-
pened. Blackie smelled the clean night air. He had chewed
through his box. Why, if he could only chew a big enough
hole, he could get out. Faster and faster he gnawed. The
world outside was getting lighter. But the hole was getting
bigger. As the sun rose over the misty water Blackie pushed
through his hole and dropped to the sand. He ambled past
the quiet tent and into the edge of the woodland. Once more
he was King of the Forest.

Perhaps as Mary penned this tale she chuckled, recollecting
her own interactions with porcupines on the Long Trail. Humans
might indeed come out second best when coming up against this
critter. And yet people thought these beasts were second-rate animals. Such a puzzle!

One of the best parts of her job took her out into the Forest
Preserve surrounding the Museum to survey the animals and
plants there. Mary found it hard to believe that someone would
pay her to commune with nature.

Spring is well along out in Thatcher's Woods.... The
hepaticas are two weeks gone by, and the bloodroot is pass-
ing. Spring beauties and pepper root are like a frost over the
ground. Dutchman's-breeches is in its glory, leaves are pop-
ping, and the hawthorns are getting ready to burst into
bloom. The wild ginger is pushing up, every day May apples
are open wider. Here are lots of birds - I have 46 species on
my bird list for this year. It was more fun last night to watch
a little screech owl conning the landscape from his high cas-
tle in a dead stub over the river. Pheasants, and hermit
thrushes, and kinglets, Myrtle warblers, starlings, woodpeck-
ers, swallows, and gulls - the woods are full of birds calling....

She didn't always take the L home at night. She loved to
adventure through the city, and wrote glowingly about what she
saw on such a winter walk.

There are two ways, I have discovered...I can get home
from work. One is to walk to the nearest L station and catch
a train.... Easy, but prosaic.... The other way means a three-
mile walk, but two of the three are by the lake shore - and on
the night of the year's first snow - who'd not take the long
way?...

     Mary's Way

At five in the evening, now, when I leave the Museum, it is dark and the lights are on. Tonight they shone upon a dream-world - the same old dream-world that has been repeated every season…for a hundred thousand years - yet still full of magic and unreality. Everything in sight was just a little veiled and blurry through the mist of the falling snow. The trees are very dark against the snow - even against the sky, so pearly-hued with the city's glow - and the upper sur-face of every branch gleams with its load.

If I go this way, I must cross three unguarded highways, at this hour crowded with home-bound cars. As I stand qui-etly at the side of the first, I am bewildered by the endless lights - much larger in appearance tonight than usual - great gleaming eyes of dragons, rushing away from me. There is a space. The next dragon is creeping along on the slippery pavement. Before he can reach me, I am across.

By the side of the second boulevard there is a man changing a tire. The snow is heavy on the back of his coat as he bends by the rear wheel of his car. His hands must be cold, as he works away in the snowy air at those many bolts. I wish I might help him, but what would he think? Besides, his wife is in the car….

Through the black and gray lace of the fretted trees, I come to the lagoon, very quiet, softly gleaming in the lights from the outer drive across the way. Ice is beginning to form. Soon we will be skating. Suddenly, gleaming like liquid metal under the lights, I see what is apparently a current, where I know no current should be. Exploring in the dimness for the source, I see two black spots moving through the water - mallard ducks! Nonchalantly, lightly, they swim along, breaking off with their breasts the needles of the forming ice. They even stop to play a little, sending up small bright show-ers of spray.

Now the mallards are gone, the lagoon narrows and ends. I cross the outer drive and at last see the open shore. Over the gleaming city to the right, a stooping sky of soft amber. Over the wide invisible water to the left, a density of purple. Over my head the mysterious blending. On the wide walk…to the water's edge, only one other foot track pre-

cedes mine. A wide heavy shoe, traveling not very rapidly, it's neat tracks now filling with snow, leading off into the dimness ahead. The waves, washing up with a splashy sound, cut dark shining scallops into the gleaming white beach. The water moans a little around the great rocks of the breakwater. The dull roar of the city is softened here.

One of the most wonderful things about snow is the amount of variation in color and value it will stand without losing its character. It may go in a short distance from yellow to deep soft purple, from very high in value to very low, and you will still know it is snow….The snow is thickly powdering my shoulders, and the top of my briefcase is white. My shoes are piled and the snow is cold on my ankles. Inside me, though, I am warm, with a tingling, dancing heat, induced by swift motion and keen pleasure in every sense….

❧ ❧ Mallard Ducks ❧ ❧

You with green gleaming head,
You with soft brown dress -
Stop playing on the dark lagoon,
Stirring the cold needles of new ice,
Raising metal ripples to gleam
with street light -
Stop playing, you.
You will tear my heart in two
From envy.
Stop playing, Mallards!
Chase each other, splash, shake
*   dripping feathers.*
My heart was torn in two long ago,
And the pain you are giving me
Is all pleasure, after all.

Mary and Joe were able to salvage some time to adventure together. In late March 1933, they took a delayed honeymoon and camped in the Waukegan dune and marsh country forty miles north of Chicago. She also reported on more local trips, like the Saturday they explored Palos Park.

We walked clear across it, through mighty wild-like

country. For practically all of that two-hour walk we weren't on a path, didn't see a path and didn't meet a person. We were on our way down a four-mile stretch of highway, bending our bodies against a stiff south wind, when we walked into a blinding thunderstorm, which soaked us to the skin in no time. About the time it was over, we had reached McGinness Slough, a big marsh and the only breeding ground for water birds left in the Chicago area. …Oh, such a wealth of bird life: hundreds of ducks - pintail, mallard, scaup, blue-winged teal and others; marsh hawks, ospreys, sandpipers, black-crowned night herons, green herons - Oh boy! I almost went crazy! And while we were there with evening coming on, the sun began to come through the clouds in yellow sunset streaks, reflected in the green and gray and purple water. It was just great!…

Other real vacations took them to camp in Devil's Lake, Wisconsin where they luxuriated in almost mountain scenery, and to the Illinois hill country near Mary's sister Dorothy. Joined by Frances and C.P. (who stayed with Dorothy), Mary and Joe camped first along the Ohio and then the Mississippi Rivers. They planned to duck hunt, but instead painted to their hearts' content. Their busy lives had made them forgo regular painting sessions and this interlude recharged their art batteries, even when they returned to Ohio Street.

In the fall of 1933 Mary actually pulled herself away from Joe and the Museum and accompanied her dad and Frank (as she called her sister Frances) on a holiday to Glacier National Park. She returned even more enthusiastic about the west, but allowed that never again would she leave Joe!

The Way West

❋ ❋ ❋ ❋ ❋

Having had a taste of the West, Mary came home even more convinced that she and Joe would get there somehow. The Wyoming dreaming became really serious. She read about the Wyoming life zones in a Biological Survey publication. Her father gave her the U.S. Geodetic Survey maps for the Dubois area. By fall 1933 Mary and Joe talked of getting underway during the summer of 1934. She bought a heavy horsehide, sheepskin-lined jacket, *"What the well-dressed curator wears in Chicago,"* Mary reported in a Robin letter. Frustrated that they weren't saving money fast enough to meet their schedule, Joe and Mary moved in with C.P. and Frances in March 1934, taking over the basement. Devoting every spare minute to getting themselves ready, they now planned, more realistically, to start off in March or April 1935. Mary enthused to the Cooper clan - *"Doesn't it fire your heart just to think of (the trip)? What matter if something should happen to keep us from it? We've got our hearts on fire now!"*

Along with the move to the Maywood house, they bought the essential ingredient for the trip - a car. They doted on that 1929 gray Buick, convinced it would make their odyssey a reality.

That car is downright swell. Motor in perfect shape, nothing wrong anywhere that we can see; finish even, unscarred. It belonged to the shop foreman at the garage, and I guess he was mighty careful of it. We catch ourselves even talking of having to buy new clothes to match the car.

Can you imagine Coopers and Backs that dudish?

Then they got to work, renovating it into a 1930s version of an R.V. Joe built cupboards to fit under the dashboard. On the running boards he installed chuck boxes (for supplies), with the doors opening over them. The boxes came off easily for packing onto horses. He revamped the front seats so they lay back, connecting with the back cushions to form a double bed. Mary sewed a tent to attach to the side of the car.

By the middle of March their nervousness became almost unbearable. It now seemed possible they could leave by late April. Mary reported on the preparations currently underway.

What we are doing right now is making sketch-boxes to hold paints, turps, brushes, canvas boards, and paint-cloths - with tripods fastened on 'em so we can use them easily anywhere. I've been having such fun carpentering.... First I made a box. It sounds simple but it was a real feat for me. I show it to everyone who comes in the house. It's of 3-ply veneer, bound with galvanized metal, and it is to hold about 40 canvas-boards, our estimated supply to take with us. There are little cleats up and down to slide the wet ones between, so they won't touch each other.

Well, when the box was done, I felt so elated I said I would make my own sketch-box with its tripod. Joe holds me to it, with a kind of wondering cynicism. Heaven knows what the result will be, but I'm learning such a lot about strains and pressures and drills and bits, and wing nuts and seamers and countersinking and soldering and threading.... I'm sure sorry no one ever taught me those things when I was young. Milton, I could weep to consider the golden opportunities I let slip when you were around....

Departure day came - April 28 - and off they drove. While exhilarated to start their dream trip, those last hugs with Dad Cooper, Frank and Chicago friends must have brought tears. Friends like Merrill (Mo) McGawn gave so much help in the last days that Joe presented him with a certificate to the "grand past, present and future potentate of the Zaw (saw) an Ammer (hammer) signed Jaw Double U Bak."

It took the Backs two weeks to get to Denver as they dawdled their way cross country: visiting relatives, enjoying state parks, and spending special days in Nebraska's Sand Hills with Mary's sister, Miriam. She and her family now included four sons and two daughters between three months and nine years of age. Mary reported that by Nebraska she had added twenty-two new birds to her life list and her year list was up to one hundred ten. She reveled in the multitudes of waterfowl in the Sand Hills and thought this fine country to live in.

Two days were spent in Denver visiting Joe's ex-roommate Harold while Mary spent the time soaking up the Natural History Museum. Then on toward Yellowstone, as Mary reported in letters to Frances, C.P. and Mo McGawn.

> *Four days in the Colorado Front Range - four days of snowfall and our first experience of high <u>altitude</u>. We are acclimated now but those first days our heads were sure light and our feet heavy. Three snowy days we camped at 9100 feet. A week in the Laramie Mountains, Wyoming, in earliest spring. Two <u>very wet</u> days at the edge of the Red Desert where wet days must be scarce indeed. Great red tilted ledges rising above blue-green sage hills.... The range ponies, so wild, free, and happy, making delicate advances toward our camp, as if to inspect it, a line of eleven sensitive, playful, excitable beasts coming up, step after cautious step, until suddenly, with a snort, they all wheeled on their hind legs and dashed off over the sagebrush.... A wet drive to Lander, over exhilaratingly dangerous roads, with our bus not steering right (...easily fixed in Lander).... Began meeting Joe's old friends and carried one of them up next day the 85 miles to Dubois. A day in Dubois, which I spent trapping mice for the Chicago Academy of Sciences, and Joe spent renewing old friendships. Two weeks camping at the ranger station, twenty miles upriver from Dubois, through lovely early spring weather.*

Camping near the Sheridan Creek Ranger Station in early June, Mary went to bed for three days with a "fluey cold." The day after she got out of bed she borrowed a tub, washboard and wringer from the ranger's wife and nearly did herself in doing two weeks washing. Even though they were camping, (or perhaps because they were) this new country enthralled Mary, and it felt like a homecoming for Joe.

We are camped in a tiny meadow of grass starred with yellow cinquefoil, wild strawberries, and a stemless, mossy phlox. It's hardly more than big enough for car, tent, and fire. On one side it's bounded by a crescent-shaped hill covered with a heavy growth of tall, slim lodgepole pines, on the other by a small mountain brook roaring over stones. The swift moving brook is very curious, just one of the many complicated channels of the big delta of Sheridan Creek, where it empties into the Wind River. This high-sloping mountain delta is a funny thing to me....

Tonight the moon is nearly full, and sheds a glorious white light over everything. While we were eating supper a great horned owl flew to the top of a slender lodgepole right beside our camp, and looked down severely at us for several minutes before he flew off. He was near enough for us to see horns, great yellow eyes, and white whiskers. We are on a slope of the mighty Wind River Range, which goes up to 14,000 and more feet.... Where we are the slope is gradual and we can't see the bare rocks of timberline.... The rounded evergreen wrapped slopes remind me of Vermont. But just across the valley are the tremendously rugged Absarokas, built on the plan of the Matterhorn. They are too steep (practically vertical violet walls, and snow-capped) for vegetation.

Mary discovered pretty quickly that there was a special culture in Wyoming; some things you just didn't talk about with new acquaintances.

I have made two very bad breaches of etiquette.... I asked one man where he came from; and I asked a woman what kind of delicious meat it was we were eating!... Joe was ashamed for me. I haven't found out yet if it is a breach to ask a man his right name - I'm not going to try. The reason the meat question was embarrassing was that it was moose, and you can't hunt moose legally without a special permit which costs $100. So all the ranchers shoot 'em now and then, but don't brag about it. Moose are very common here. Moose manure is as common as horse manure near the streams. I've yet to see my first, though.

Hoping to get to Yellowstone Park, they had to cross Togwotee

Pass, still closed by snow. They awaited the mountain road's plowing so they could head that way to explore, try to sell some of their drawings or paintings, and look for a job for Mary. On June 16 (as soon as they heard the road was open) they packed the car and headed north. It was a difficult journey with six-foot snowdrifts on each side of the road at the pass, and mud hub-deep in the road. With the pass behind them, they soon reached Al Angle's cabins, filling station and ranch, thirty miles above Jackson Hole. Al welcomed them royally, glad to see Joe who had worked as guide, horse wrangler and cook for him before going to Chicago. Al agreed to act as agent to sell some of their paintings, offered Joe a job guiding that fall and showed them a gorgeous place to camp. Life was wonderful!

> *...(We are) in a natural park among the lodgepoles three miles below (Al's) place, with a view of the unreal, fantastic Tetons across the Hole. We camped there three days undisturbed except for the twice-a-day visit of ...a high hearted young horse wrangler...as he came by to look up a new 'wrangle hawse' from Al's fifty or so head that wander round on the great forested fenceless slopes of the mountain. Flowers and elk in profusion. Saw a baby red elk calf, very close.*

Then on to Yellowstone Park. They camped their way, enjoying the spectacular scenery. Mary bird-watched with a ranger's wife and Joe fished for cutthroat trout (catching more than they could eat). As they neared Mammoth Hot Springs they got ready to make an impression:

> *In the morning an extra scrubbing, including backs of ears, fingernails, and all, and a dressing up in city clothes - for we were approaching Mammoth Hot Springs - a whole village in itself and the point of entry for dressed-up dudes from the train.... We visited Mr. Haynes, who operates all post card and photograph joints in the park. Joy of joys, he bought two of Joe's big black and white drawings, for enough to finance our park trip twice over, and ordered a whole slew of small ones and a few big ones, for Joe to place in his shops. So our summer's work is cut out - I housekeep intensively for Joe while he concentrates intensively on drawings. It seemed important enough to make us decide to curtail our projected*

trip and, in Joe's vernacular, high-tail it for Dubois, to work.

Before heading back Mary also talked with park naturalists about a possible job for her - but nothing materialized. Disappointed, she still felt very satisfied to think Joe's art work had made such a hit. She put aside her own art interests and career as a naturalist to do what needed to be done to help them make it in Wyoming. Mary probably felt such a part of Joe, that she saw his victories as hers, and never knew a resentful moment. Her role as supporting partner had started early in their relationship during their courting days and continued.

On the return trip they indulged in more bird watching and fishing and also adventured into the world of Yellowstone's geysers.

...You know, we were two people who went to Old Faithful and didn't see it erupt.... So we drove on up to the Firehole, and got a much bigger thrill out of the forty minutes or so we spent discovering another unmarked, unnamed geyser. It was in sight through trees from the road, so of course we didn't discover it, but it was in a wild stretch of road, and there was no path to it.... It was really a small geyser basin, with several fumaroles, three hot springs, and, at the top of the slope, this little geyser, about three feet across.... It obligingly erupted about every five minutes, sending up a white mass of water a few feet - about as tall as I - then settling back bubbling into deep green and blue quiescence....

Al Angle offered Joe and Mary hot baths - the first since Nebraska. What a treat! Checking at the ranger station, they found a letter from Joe's friend Elmer, offering to go halves in buying a ranch! They celebrated doubly for they had also found some temporary housing. A log cabin at an unused dude ranch (the Wind River Ranch) became available and they hustled to get inside four walls, glad to forget camping for awhile. Mary experimented with wood stove cooking and luxuriated in having a bathroom - even if it only had cold water. The car continued to serve as bedroom.

As they settled in, they came upon a companion who really made that log cabin feel like their home. Mary wrote about the new addition to the Cooper tribe.

...Lady. She is a white collie pup, three months old, almost purebred.... She has a long aristocratic nose, with the

proper aquiline droop near the end, beautiful brown eyes, a
solid little figure, and a tail that curls right over. She is all
white except for tan spots over her eyes, tan ears, and two
tiny tan spots on her back. And she certainly is a lady, sensitive, intelligent, full of fun, but slightly reserved in her
demonstrations, alert and affectionate. In the three days she
has been ours she has learned these things:

<u>She belongs to us</u>. That seems marvelous to us, since her
mother and father belong to Bill Bell (caretaker of the ranch)
and she has lived with them on this same ranch all her life.
But she comes to us for food, sleeps with us, brings us things,
sits on our porch and growls under her breath if anyone
approaches, even her father.

<u>Mustn't dirty up the house</u>.... She is very sensitive to
scolding. So she housebroke in a hurry.

<u>Knows the meaning of several commands</u>. Drop it.
Bring it to me. Outside. Lie down.

<u>Mustn't come in the house while folks are eating</u>.

<u>The only thing you can chew in the house is your own
old shoe.</u> I gave her one and she seems to know it's hers....

Lady led the procession of dog companions that kept Joe and
Mary company in their over fifty years of Wind River Valley living.
These personable, affectionate associates just soaked up all the
love the Backs could give and returned the same tenfold, just one
of the necessities of life.

With Elmer's offer in hand, they started looking at ranches in
earnest, hoping to find one for sale north of Dubois, along the Wind
River. Their dream ranch also needed to come cheap. They found
what they were looking for in the Lava Creek Ranch. It became
theirs for $1500. Mary described it to her Robin audience.

Lava Creek Ranch, elevation 7800 feet, 100 acres, situat-
ed 22 miles above Dubois on the Wind River, 75 miles from
the south gate to Yellowstone. In the Washaki National
Forest. On highway U.S. 287. About 110 miles from a railroad.... Two log cabins, one we will fix for a house, the other
a workshop; a log barn, harness house, bunkhouse. High
mountains all around: Wind River Range and Absarokas
going up to 12,000 and more feet, including Gannett and

Fremont Peaks; and the Tetons, the goal of mountain climbers. Big game country: moose, elk, deer, bear. Grand fishing.

While excited, they knew an incredible amount of work awaited them: to produce the art ordered by Mr. Haynes, and make a start at getting at least a cabin ready for winter living. By September they had made that start and welcomed C.P and Frank who came as their first visitors.

Since C.P always traveled by train, he and Frances probably arrived at one of the train depots nearest the ranch: Riverton or Lander (106 miles away), Bonneville (130 miles away) or Gardiner, Montana (170 miles away). Mary and Joe perhaps met them at Gardiner so they could drive their first visitors through Yellowstone and the Tetons, conducting art business at the same time. Then up the mountain road over Togwotee Pass, surrounded by wild valleys and towering peaks, before finally reaching the Back ranch. As they entered Mary's new world, even C.P., who pretty much kept his thoughts to himself, must have beamed as he looked around. Mary had written them enthusiastically about what to expect.

It has been said that the American frontier is dead, the old west is no more, the wild places ...invaded 'til the

Lava Creek Ranch – 1937

Mary's Way

wilderness is gone. Yet moose browse the willows in our meadow and lie down to rest among the lodgepoles a short way up our creek. There are five beaver houses and dozens of dams, big and small in our lower meadow where Lava Creek joins Wind River. To the north a tangle of precipitous mountains and untouched forests extend for a hundred and fifty miles, unbroken save for one highway and a few trails. Southward it is not so far, perhaps forty-five or fifty miles by a pretty good trail for horses, over the Continental Divide and down narrow valleys, to roads and dwellings in the Green River Valley. Westward a highway leads over the divide and down into Jackson Hole at the foot of the incredible Tetons. Eastward, down the highway is strung our own community, the scattered ranches of the upper Wind River Valley.... There is the easy optimism of a new country, too. Next year perhaps the snowplow will keep the highway open. Next year we'll have a mail route. Next year....

I wonder what C.P. and Frances thought as they drank in the wild beauty, but also saw the primitive conditions Mary and Joe had for living. They joined in to help get ready for winter. After sharing early fall days they left (already talking about a return trip in June) well aware of how challenging this first year might be.

Pioneering

❊　❊　❊　❊　❊

The scrounging ingenuity Mary had used at the Ohio Street apartment in Chicago served her well as they crafted a home out of the abandoned ranch. She saw past the crude demands of the situation: no indoor plumbing, no electric lights, no washing machine, few furnishings - to luxuriate in the wealth she and Joe had in their life together.

> We are really, truly, living under pioneer conditions. Joe spends his days cutting house logs in the timber. I do the work of our 'pioneer mothers' about the house. Let me describe our layout here. There are several buildings already on the place. As far as possible we are making use of what is here, and will not build a new house until we have watched projected sites through at least a year of snow and sunshine. There are a barn, harness house, and corrals down by Lava Creek. There is a chicken house under the pines. There's a toilet against a sage and pine hill. A spring house by the creek has water running constantly through and a trough where you set food. . . . All the buildings are of logs, and were put up between 1913 and 1915. They have been abandoned for a dozen years so none are ready to winter in. It was a problem what to do. Our solution is to camp in one room of the biggest cabin and use the other room for storage while we make the middle-sized cabin tight for winter and pleasant as a home. We will move the smallest one to a sheltered

scenic spot among pines and fix it for a guest house and finally make the biggest cabin eventually into a studio and shop.

So at present we are spread around one room. Our furniture is salvaged from hither and yon. Some of it we found here. Some was given or lent by Bill Bell at the Wind River Ranch. Some stuff Joe picked up here and there. Our heating stove, for instance, Joe found in a hunting camp out in the woods, abandoned for years. Our two most comfortable chairs are the two front seats of a 1926 Chevrolet Joe just paid ten dollars for (so he could have the motor to run his saws and the washing machine I'm going to have some day).

As I sit here, I am leaning against a nest of three pillows. One we brought with us. Two I made out of sugar sacks and filled them with elk hair, which is lying in large quantities in our yard. The outer covers are cut out of the pup tents we brought with us. We have a bookcase - three orange crates piled together. The kitchen cabinet, most efficient piece of furniture, is a table, covered with oil cloth, with three apple boxes piled on the back of it. The chest of drawers, where we keep our clothes, is made of turpentine boxes, one on top of another. The clothes closet is nails on the walls, a bar across a corner for the clothes hangers. Another corner-wise bar carries a square of canvas for a curtain to hide it all. We have a nice settee, a thing of poles, with an old automobile seat for a cushion, with a

Mary and Joe Back at Lava Creek Ranch

pup tent wrapped about the seat, to hide the poles and smooth the surface. With three pillows nicely arranged it looks neat and sure feels good. There is a wash bench in the corner by the heater. Two water pails stand on it, a wash basin, and a tin can for a dipper. Above it on the wall is a soap dish Joe made out of a can. Above it too, hang wash cloth and towel. A canvas sack of meat and one of flour hang from the roof, out of the rat's way.

Today I worked pretty hard digging the hole for the fireplace foundation. Got it finished today. Meantime, Joe was hauling down poles from back in the woods, using a horse borrowed from Bill Bell. Just now we walked out through the starlit dark to the pasture where the horse, Dick, is picketed for the night. Through the thicket of low willows, Lava Creek softly shines and murmurs in the starlight. Up over a sage covered hill and down into the pasture is a cove between pointed pines and the sprawled-out, willow-fringed beaver pond. Some ducks were talking on the pond. Pretty nice.

Even so, Mary yearned for the eleven boxes of their belongings and a cedar chest still sitting in the basement of the Maywood house. Good friend Mo McGawn saw to it that they got hauled out and sent by freight to Wyoming, paying the $85 it took to make this happen.

Now they could really settle in. Mary marveled at how much pleasure they got out of their sparse possessions.

When your belongings are limited, your purse is small, and there are no shop windows to whet your desires, each object becomes more precious, so that Thanksgiving Days are every day, and you are conscious of a keen delight in the use of everything you own.

As the fall days seemed to rush by, they found themselves in a race with time to get ready for winter. Joe constructed a better wood stove out of an old gasoline drum with legs from a scavenged cot. It held a fire going all night and generated toasty warmth that dissipated all too quickly until they chinked all the cracks between the wall logs. Taking the newspapers that came stuffed in their household belongings, Mary boiled them up to mush in a big can, making papier-mâché which she stuffed into the cracks. This would do until warmer spring days when they would add mortar as a more permanent cover. A small, abandoned, scoured-out oil barrel sat on the stove, brimful of hot water. It tickled Mary to see it steaming there: all the hot water they needed, more than any of their neighbors had. Why, she could do a wash with that amount or they could take two or three baths.

Getting the firewood to feed the stove was never-ending labor. One day, when she found two salamanders wandering about the fireplace hole, she made them a home with water, rocks and moss in a big glass jar. That night they froze into a solid block of ice. Worriedly she thawed the whole thing out slowly, and as soon as they were free from ice, she watched with amazement as the two funny little animals began to crawl around apparently none the worse for the freeze up. *"You know Joe, we'd save a lot of firewood if we could model our habits after these salamanders."* She smiled, shaking her head.

Learning how to live without easy access to a grocery store took some doing. On a late October trip to Dubois Joe tried to stock up on everything they might need until May. He knew they would still have to replenish such things as flour, lard and dried fruit. They could only afford the basics, without such delicacies as lettuce, celery, cheeses or nuts. Another rancher told them about egg powder: two pounds equaled twelve dozen eggs, enough to last most of the winter. Pleased not to grocery shop all the time, Mary felt well prepared if someone dropped in for a meal.

All you do is cut off another slice of meat and open the cookie jar. I'm really getting to be quite an expert bread baker…. Bread making presents certain difficulties at this altitude. We're too far from town to get compressed yeast, so have to depend on the yeast foam. But we can't set a sponge overnight on account of the cold. The usual method is to start a ferment of dissolved yeast in a quart of potato water after lunch one day, keep it warm if possible, and make up a straight dough from the ferment in the (next) morning. I started a ferment yesterday all right, and put it in a quart jar in the warming oven of the range for overnight. This morning it had needles of ice across the surface, and it was noon before the yeast was visibly 'working'. So now at three p.m. I am keeping a fire, so the dough will keep warm on the oven door. We should have hot rolls for supper.

        Mary's Way

They remembered almost incredulously the casual way they wasted food in Chicago: lettuce leaves tossed when not quite crisp enough; whole tops of celery discarded (good flavoring when dried), orange peels abandoned (tasty when ground), strawberries with soft spots thrown out (would make grand jam), and even dabs of butter trashed, whose only sin was a messy look!

Meat mostly came from the country around them - deer, elk, or moose. Al Angle gave them the front quarter of a bull elk that amazed Mary as she got acquainted with it.

I didn't realize a front quarter was so huge. Joe tied a rope to it, put the rope over a hook in the storeroom, and told me to pull on the rope while he lifted the meat. I thought it would be easy, but when he let up on the lifting, that hunk of meat lifted me right off the floor. It was heavier than I....

Joe added to their larder when he got a hunting license. He traded his service as guide, cook and horse wrangler to Al for a week and in the process shot his own elk.

Mary stayed behind to mind the ranch but missed him dreadfully. Having Lady for company, as well as Pedro (also called Pete), a decrepit but gentle old workhorse made a big difference. The horse got so he came to the house and nudged the kitchen window with his nose if he thought it was time for hay. With Lady in the lead Mary rode Pete around the countryside, dropping in on the far flung neighbors. Joe's absence made her realize just how much he did day to day to tend to her happiness. Hardly a day went by that he didn't say, "Mary you're getting prettier every day", or "You know you're looking awfully nice tonight". While his eyes twinkled at her as he said this, it was nice not to be taken for granted. Joy welled up in her when she finally saw the truck turn up their road, and soon had Joe safe and sound at her side, along with a truck full of elk.

Before long they had additional companions who joined them as early winter cold and snows crept in. Rastus, a gentle, willing work-pack-ride horse came for the winter. He became Pete's buddy, never straying far from his side. When Pete came down with a very bad case of indigestion from eating too much hay in a hurry, Mary worried over him for days, remarking, *"I didn't realize till then that horses are as much mortal flesh as people, and that you can feel as badly and worry as much when one is in pain, as if it were one of your family. I'm afraid my spiritual conception of a horse resembled a kind of primitive automobile!"* Two more dogs joined the growing menagerie: Susie and her pup Violet. They made a nest for the two behind the stove and soon Susie acted as if she owned the cabin.

> *[She] does her best to keep Lady outside. The two are a laughable contrast in personalities. Lady is so gentle-tempered, sensitive, highbred, and eager to conciliate. She finds it impossible to believe that anyone can be deliberately unkind, and equally impossible to hold a grudge. And Sue is so squat, sullen, and ferocious in defense of her family, quick to suspect evil. Yet she is steady, brave, and as eager to be loved as Lady is.*

Mary especially delighted in Violet, watching the puppy develop. As she worked in the cabin, Violet toddled around the floor, talking, chattering and growling all to herself. One afternoon she actually contested with her mother for a bite out of Sue's food dish. She learned to come when whistled, as had the horses. Mary had to chuckle, *"Sometimes it's a little embarrassing when you find two great big horses and three dogs suddenly on hand, when all you wanted was one small puppy."*

Their first Christmas on the ranch was a milestone. Mary cooked her first Christmas dinner, making the "turkey" out of elk steaks sewn together into the shape of a big fat bird and stuffed with apple stuffing. The black dog and the white dog scampered ahead of her in wide powdery circles in the snow when she went looking for a Christmas tree. She finally found a three-foot spruce, just built for a Christmas tree. Displayed on the very large box used as a primitive dark room for developing her films, it reached the ceiling. She decorated it simply with just a silver star on top (made from cardboard covered with film wrapper) and concocted a big wreath of pine twigs with cones and hung pine boughs and blue-berried juniper in bunches on the walls.

In January, when she put the festive decorations away, she realized as she looked around that someone with a certain frame of mind, always looking for unhappiness in others, would see their ranch very differently than she did.

Wouldn't he see right away the two broken window-

panes patched with cardboard, the tar-paper wall at the point where the fireplace-is-not-yet, the ancient, filthy toilet, placed right in the middle of the choicest view, the odd-length boards leaning up here and there against the wall, and the rotting barn?… He would say in his heart 'Poor white trash. Here is a case that needs to be investigated.' If he were feeling really soft-hearted he would say, 'Those people must be in desperate circumstances. I must send them a Christmas basket. And perhaps I have some old clothes they can use….' Wouldn't that attitude miss the serene beauty of the snow-laden pines, the lovely low lines of the little cabin sheltered below them, the soaring peaks around? Wouldn't it miss the comfortable warmth of the tiny stove; the even, clear, and lovely light to work by; the whole deep happiness of the place?…

Everyone's mind must disregard some things. It's utterly impossible for any lens to focus on more than one plane at once. Everyone has got to choose. And I choose to focus on the beauty around me, and the happiness that comes my way….

So when snow buried the upper Wind River Valley and lasted into June, she just learned to snowshoe and appreciate the strange white world that lasted and lasted.

In quantity it's quite fantastic. For long stretches the fences are covered…. Drifts around the house are in places as high as the windows…. In many places along Lava Creek and on the Wind River bottoms, the willows are completely buried. Where we walk regularly, the paths stay hard and near the top of the snow. Today…we got a good demonstration of the depth of the track. Rastus and Pedro were going to water…and somehow or other Rastus got off the track. Immediately he was in over his belly. He had a dickens of a floundering time before he got himself out.

It is an eternal marvel to me the way the moose navigate in this deep snow. Of course their legs raise their bodies, stilt-like, as much as four and a half feet off the ground, but even so…. The other day I was up on the mountain snow-shoeing, when I crossed a moose track…. There was a trough over a foot deep where his belly had dragged, and the holes *where his legs had been went down, down, into jade and turquoise darkness out of sight. But his stride seemed just about what any moose's stride is, long and even.*

Mary counted the wild animals that lived nearby, mostly unseen, as special blessings. The more time she spent close to the Wind River Valley's natural world, the more certain she was that people, animals and plants were all equal parts of God's world.

…Man is not alone, an individual species standing or falling by his own efforts. Man is so much like all the other living things around him that the differences are inconsequential. Man is not more different from them, than they are different from each other.

One night she awoke from a deep sleep, the usually quiet cabin filled with sound. She listened intently.

This morning I had a strange experience. I was wakened by sweet music. It sounded like angelic voices - a choir - singing something like the 'Gloria' chorus far away. My first sleepy thought was that the radio was on and turned way down - then the hair on the back of my neck prickled and stood on end as I woke up enough to realize that the radio wasn't hooked up. I wondered if I had died during the night and was really hearing angelic voices! The chorus kept on going, grew clearer, and at last I was awake enough to realize what it was. Believe it or not, it was coyotes.

I lay there for some time listening to them, rejoicing in the fun they were having, and in the musical effect it made. One voice alone would carry the melody for awhile, in long coloratura quavers, then another would join in, higher or lower, then a whole chorus. I could see them in my mind's eye, each coyote sitting alone on his haunches in the snow on the sagebrush flat, raising his voice to the dawn, listening with a critical joy to his own tones …listening for the pitch of the other voices, sending his in with theirs harmoniously.

All day long I've been thinking about it. I remember so clearly only four years ago that the sound of a coyote's voice in the night would frighten me. It seemed to me weird, uncanny, like a dog gone crazy. Are coyotes an acquired taste, like olives?…

It's not often you can get to hear a real songfest like this morning. When a coyote raises his voice, it's really no more likely to be in song than when you raise yours; that is, it may be, but it isn't always. And when one does feel like singing, maybe his voice isn't good, or his companions aren't musical. Coyotes bark a lot, quite like dogs. Sometimes there will be a chorus of plain yapping that will last for hours. Often they squall.

It was just my good luck, I guess, that the Glee Club gathered for rehearsal on our flat this morning.

That first winter Mary and Joe had no phone, no plowed road, and no mail delivery. Getting supplies and mail from Dubois became major adventures even when their neighbor Bill Bell gave a hand. His plan was to take both his truck and his team of horses. If necessary, the team would pull the truck out of snowdrifts. So one Sunday after lunch Mary saddled Old Pete and set off with a packet of letters and her grub order, bound for Bill Bell's cabin just down the road.

I thought Pete and I would never reach the highway through the deep unbroken snow, but when we did, the going was no better. We never went faster than a slow walk and I had to let Pete stop and rest every hundred feet... There were tracks of moose crossing the highway several times.... What with the slow going and the sitting and gossiping when I at last arrived, the slow dark had settled down over the snow long before I reached our gate.... I thought of the lonely miles of unbroken road and all the moose-tracks. I thought how bold the moose are, how even the biggest and bravest of the he-men around here are cautious about them. I wondered what on earth I would do if a moose came at me. And all of a sudden a large dark shape loomed up ahead! And it was in the road! And it stayed in the road! And it kept on coming! Even the dogs were uncertain and disturbed. Gosh, I was scared.... It was a great relief when Susie, the black shepherd, decided the approaching object was friendly, and ran toward it; and more relieved when it materialized into Joe on snowshoes. He'd been thinking about the same 'worriments' as I.

A few days later a sled pulled by two horses dropped off the supplies and mail at the end of the Back's road and the driver hailed Joe who had just started into the timber after logs. Putting down the weasel she was skinning to send to the Chicago Academy of Sciences for a few extra dollars, Mary knew she would have to do mail duty again. Bundling herself up and grabbing pack-sack, gunnysack and cord she set out again on old Pete wading laboriously through snowdrifts. Finally she reached the gate which was completely clogged by an enormous drift. Leaving the horse she went on through hip deep snow, plowing a way through with her sacks to the large pile of stuff awaiting her. She was excited to see two large packages of mail, but now had the challenge of getting the mail and all the provisions (including ten pounds of cornmeal, six of coffee, five of prunes, two of cocoa and butter) into the bags, back to the horse and tied onto the saddle horn. *"Things stuck out so far I could hardly get on, and, as Pete was anxious to get back, he wouldn't leave me long to make up my mind how to do it,"* she wrote Milton as she tried to help him understand what it meant to get mail.

Given such isolation, Frank wondered how to get word to Mary when C.P. collapsed on a hike in March, 1936 and died. She sent a telegram and Mary described how she got it.

Bill Moriarty brought us word that we had a telegram. He is a tall man, about Joe's age, with young eyes in a deeply lined face and painfully shy. Though our nearest neighbor, he has never been in our house before. It must have required a great effort of will for him to come. He came in and sat down, and he and Joe engaged in conversation, which consisted mostly of his monosyllabic replies to Joe's fluent line. After some time, Joe got on the subject of machinery, and took Bill out to look at the buzz saw. Half an hour later they came back in, and I set out lunch with apple pie all round. And about that time Bill stated his errand, that we had a telegram down at the phone office, and that he thought it was urgent.... After lunch we all put on our snowshoes and walked back a bit less than a mile to Moriarty's and the phone.

Mary could hardly believe the message. C.P had seemed so well, and so full of plans for the future. How could he be dead? She wrote Frances her thoughts.

...I can't imagine a more perfect way for Father to have

gone. Doing what he liked best, among congenial people, and with no premonition and no pain. It is very hard for me to believe that he is really gone. I have written no one but you since your telegram, thinking that I surely must have misunderstood. But a letter of sympathy came two or three days ago…so then I knew.

But most things we think of about him give us real reason for Thanksgiving. We are so glad he saw our place. It was a great thing to have had the privilege of knowing him, anyway. He was …so silent…(yet) he always seemed to know how to get happiness out of what happened to him. He filled his life full of experiences, loved his children, and saw them all happy. And life certainly hasn't been the same for him since Mother died.

Unable to return to Chicago for his funeral, Mary said her farewell to him from her mountain ranch, with his image fresh in her mind as he had walked her acres, and plunged into the ranch chores. As part of settling his estate, which would take more than a year, Mary received the elegant large wooden cuckoo clock from Germany that had always decorated the Cooper home. It became a fixture in Joe and Mary's home too. They also received some monies that came just when they didn't know how they were going to survive financially.

Mary had no time to sit around and mourn her dad. Tasks called for her attention everywhere she looked. While Joe was the tree cutter, fence and bridge builder, and constructor and repairer of cabins, Mary did whatever else needed doing. Daubing cabins with mortar to seal them for winter was "fun", while hand digging a cellar was "Hell". She planned and constructed a kitchen that first winter that included such details as a bread box lined with tin from tin cans. While the plan showed a sink, no running water came indoors, and Mary carried the grey water (slop) out and deposited it away from the cabin. Bathroom and cold food storage were outside.

The novice carpenter of Chicago days had developed into an able craftswoman. She delighted in tinkering around the house, freeing Joe for the heavier work she didn't feel up to. Needing straight backed chairs she undertook building them, whistling with the joy she felt as they took shape under her hands. Mary wore the hats of cook, scrub-board-tub laundress, and seamstress. When chores needed doing she did them; bundling up on the cold winter days to go get water, empty the slop pail of its dirty water, check and fill the kerosene lamps and get firewood. Writing about these daily tasks she described them as enjoyable adventures.

First we have to get the supply of water for the night and for breakfast.... It's not far to the water hole, not more than a hundred feet, much less than most folks round here have to go for their water. Just far enough so we can get a good look at the glorious sunset sky. The west is richly patterned with wild bannered purple storm clouds, spaced so that in the cracks between them you catch glimpses of brilliant turquoise sky. But more than brilliant are the luminous fringes of the purple clouds, white gold against the turquoise. All the rest of the sky is pearly opalescent, grading infinitesimally from the wavering tints of the zenith to the whirling snow dervishes in the yard. It's the spirit of storm, stopping just this side of being too wild to be lovely.

But what is Paint doing, standing so contentedly in the midst of the snowbanks of the back yard? He's eating the cushion off Joe's bobsled! So I set down the water pails, rush back to the house and tell Joe.... He is quite unperturbed. 'If the old cuss wants it that much, I'll make another one tomorrow,' says he with philosophy. The cushion is just hay stuffed in a gunnysack....

Now back to the water hole. In the summer the little stream which forms a pool here deep enough to dip up a whole pailful without striking bottom, is the beginning of the irrigation ditch.... Now...the shoveled path ends at a round hole about three feet across. You look down about three feet to clear water running swiftly below you. It is a sort of a well, with walls of solid blue-white ice.... There is a long iron crowbar leaning against the springhouse nearby. That is to break the ice with. After that is accomplished, squat down as low as you can on the edge of the hole, and dip up a pailful, being careful to get a good grip on the edge with your free hand, so you don't fall in. And if Violet jumps on you playfully while you are in this position, give her a swift kick if you can.... Now the other pail.... Six gallons of water do weigh quite a little…but oh, boy, it is grand to have so much of such good, soft water so close.

Even with all this to do and more, they both painted during the winter of 1936. Oh how Mary needed to catch some of the ranch scenes in paint on canvas. She liked the results, hoping they would also please next summer's customers. Once Joe got into a painting he worked passionately, forgetting all else. Those cold days immersed in art exhilarated them - just what they had hoped for back in Chicago.

As both a trained artist and naturalist Mary enthusiastically recorded her impressions both in paint and words. As spring 1937 tried to push its way into the upper Wind River landscape, she noticed.

Last night in the late dusk I stood on the snowy hillside behind the house and wondered at the feeling of tenseness and expectancy in the air. The stars were lightly sprinkled on a deep blue sky. The snow, white underfoot, went off by infinitesimal degrees into blueness, soft and indefinite. The air was very still. The dark masses of the pines all around gave me a feeling as of life just about to stir or speak. Many of them had tips of limbs still buried under snowdrifts. The portions above the snow were curved in a position of lifting strain. I thought that the moment was such that if God would just say 'Boo!' - not loud, but with swift emphasis - the tree limbs would pull out and pop up to normal, the snow would run off in trickles and rivulets, and flowers would push up suddenly from the wet brown earth.

Perhaps God did say 'Boo!' because today when we got up it was raining. Raining! For the first time since last October. Almost all day it has rained, sometimes almost snow, sometimes barely a drizzle, sometimes a smart shower. The snow is fast running off, in trickles and rivulets. There are crooked black channels in the yard. Around every bare spot there grew a widening margin, the color of pewter, where the snow was water-soaked. Small separated bare spots began to coalesce. I watched tree limbs pulling free, changing shape from a position of lifting strain to one of graceful repose - but those once-buried limbs will never again point toward the sky.

And by the springhouse I picked a few pussy willow sprays for the table - golden stems, with soft gray catkins rosy-flushed at the base. And by the house I saw, where the snow had barely disappeared, small clumps of bright green grass, and the tiny green jagged leaves of a sprouting dandelion! And the first robins called from the pines along the highway, where I heard them first last year!

While neighbors from upper valley ranches looked on skeptically, Mary undertook to create a garden as the snow deteriorated.

We are planning to attempt an experimental garden. The great risk is frost in summer. As we used to raise gardens in Vermont in spite of the risk, I think it could be done here…. We are planning to have a couple of short rows each of half a dozen quick-growing and hardy plants - lettuce, Swiss chard, carrots, radishes, beets, and peas. We will start them in window boxes in the house in early May, and set them out in early June. We will make our garden by the south wall of the big cabin, where we can lead water in by a very short ditch from Lava Creek. We will have to build it up, of course, with charcoal, ashes, bottom land loam, and manure - mixed up on top of the stony ground that is there, and held in by a low rock wall. We will have a stout pole railing around it, and it will be just the size of our biggest tarpaulin, so that when it looks like frost we can cover the whole thing.

Even the presence of snow into June did not deter the rows of peas, chard, radishes, lettuce and carrots Mary had planted. They just *"smiled serenely and kept on growing."* That year she moved lots of dirt to create lawn and gardens and transplanted wild trees, vines, and bushes around the cabins.

Irrigation fascinated her. Water diverted from Lava Creek by way of a ditch resembled *"a gay little mountain brook as it boils down in front of the cabins."* Subdividing to nourish the hay fields and yard and garden, each branch became smaller, until all the water soaked into the ground, with little draining back into the main ditch.

The idea of irrigation is to lead the water down the tops of the ridges instead of the bottoms of gullies…. When the water is on, every time you walk around to watch the ditch-

es, you are bound to find some places where the earth side of one has sprung a leak, and water is going where it shouldn't, so you have to spring to its rescue with a spade and another little gob of dirt. It is lots of fun, just like a kid playing in the mud.

So, instead of carrying watering pails and putting it where I need it, as I did last year (or attaching the hose and sprinkler, as in Maywood) now I take a spade to the yard take-out, and remove the sods that block the flow.... I do it in late afternoon, about the time you would turn on the sprinkler in town. Then the water goes streaming round to all the little ditches and ditch-lets, soaking up everything in grand shape, and making soft music as it does so. I go back in to get supper, but come out every few minutes to take a look around, repair a broken ditch-wall, shunt water from one place that is getting too soggy and is washing into another that hasn't enough, and so on. Then before I go to bed I throw the sods into the take-out again....

May days with clouds massed thickly around the mountains brought welcome rain. The rising river and creek overflowed their banks, flooding the flats between the ranch and the highway where Joe hoped to grow swamp hay. He hustled there directing the water through quickly dug trenches to nourish the hoped for crop; returning to the cabin every few hours to change his drenched clothes. The log bridge he had so carefully built to enable them to cross the Wind River stood firm, partly because the river spilled into this shallow draw that stretched below the ranch. The flooded road stymied the Buick one afternoon. After struggling to get free, they decided to leave the car on the highway side of the flood.

Their road also served another ranch where new neighbors, the Stringers, had recently settled. Ernest Stringer had a reputation as a go getter, but also as a man who struck hard bargains. He had not seemed very interested when Joe suggested they work together to breach the draw with a forty-five foot bridge. As Joe headed back to the ranch for supper he saw Ernest turn off the main road with a load of lumber for his cabins. "Watch out for the crossing, it's real bad - we got stuck", Joe hollered to him.

"Thanks", called Ernest and kept going. Later Mary described the scene.

Ernest was very cocksure. He was convinced that the truck he drove was enough higher and more powerful than the Buick so he was in no danger. He splashed across and drove on up to his place with his lumber.... Joe...drove off to make some business calls, so I was all alone when Ernest came back to make the return passage, just as it was getting really dark. He had his wife and daughter with him, and was in a hurry to get back to Dubois to close up his garage.

And he got so stuck! He struggled and struggled, and fought that draw every way he could. He borrowed a shovel and flashlight and hip boots from me. He backed and ground forward and tried different angles. He drowned the engine twice, and had to wipe off the distributor and wait for it to get dry. Once, trying a new angle, he got really bogged down in a mudhole and it seemed he would never get out....I suppose if I had been really anxious to help him out I would have made some effort to locate the horses to try to give him a pull. But they were loose somewhere, and would sure be hard to find in the dark; and besides, he had been...pooh-poohing the necessity of building a bridge to avoid that spot, so I did want to rub the lesson in. So I just stood helpfully around with his womenfolks, and threw out doleful remarks like, 'It took us an hour and a half to get out this morning, and the water's a lot higher now', and, 'Joe hoped to have both bridges done by now, but he has found it pretty slow working alone.'

Then we womenfolk came up to the Back cabin and talked...aimlessly, until the straining of the motor got unbearably on our nerves, so we wandered back again. As it got on toward midnight, I made a big pot of coffee, and took it...down to the truck, to find that Ernest had finally given up and decided to sleep at his place and try again in the morning. So I asked them up to our house for the coffee and tarts. By this time the caretaker and his wife had come over from Stringer's place, so there was quite a midnight party. Under the mellowing influence of the coffee, Ernest declared that something must be done about that bridge.

The next day after lots of work and plenty of swearing, the Stringer truck was freed. By the next week, his caretaker was busy building the bridge with Joe.

Real summer weather at the end of June found Joe and Mary building again. Mary constructed the fireplace for their cabin using lava boulders she found around the yard and a hearth from red flat stones hauled from near Dubois. She smiled proudly at the results, even if the chimney did leak where it adjoined the roof. While she worked she also paid attention to the landscape around her, happy to be outdoors near Joe who was rebuilding the big cabin. Something caught Joe's attention near the willows by the creek and they stopped to look.

… There was a strange bird in the edge of the willows. I had one good look at it, as it walked across an opening in the willows, way below me…a darkish bird about the size of a pheasant, but the shape was somehow wrong. Behind her dragged a spotted tail at least two feet long! Joe and I looked at each other incredulously. "Go on down and find out what it is; I'm eaten up with curiosity," said Joe. I went down the hill, across the flat, and into the labyrinth of the willows, following grassy openings in the general direction the bird had been going. In a short while they brought me to the edge of a grassy pond where there was motion…among the stems of grass and horsetail. Feeding with brisk motions of head and neck, and whirlings of their bodies, were a mother cinnamon teal and eight youngsters. They kept on for some moments after I saw them, but suddenly the mother saw me. I could see no flurry of warning; but the youngsters swiftly lined up behind mother, who swam to shore in the lead. She walked quite quickly into the bushes - and the orderly parade of ducklings behind her was a perfect long spotted tail!…

By late August Joe had restructured the big cabin into a fine house for co-owner Elmer Davies who arrived to spend six weeks at the ranch with his wife, two young sons and Negro cook, John. By now, Joe had a beautiful if somewhat wild riding horse, Paint, and Elmer added another riding horse, Tommy, a pregnant mare, Mollie, and her colt to the ranch livestock. On the late summer days Mary enthusiastically joined the guests on horseback explorations up into the high land behind their spread. Later Joe guided Elmer on a hunting foray while Mary tried to figure out how to live with the Davies' cook. She admitted it took some adjusting.

(The Davies) brought their …cook with them, with the idea of giving me a vacation. But, of course, since they are southerners, raised in a different cuisine entirely, we had little materials the cook was used to, and he didn't know how to cook what we had…. He was used to being able to phone the grocery in a hurry whenever he was out of anything; so nearly every day someone had to run in to Dubois, a trifling jaunt of forty-four miles after something that had been forgotten. We never did get to feel at home, having someone come up behind you and put a dish at your left side, for you to select from - much more butlerish and ritzy than in any restaurant I ever ate in.

And I found I was continually violating some sacred tradition of eating, trying to use the wrong things together. Brook trout, for instance, must never be rolled in meal and fried in lard, but always must be broiled in butter. And when you serve fish, you must never serve biscuits or light bread with them, but corn cakes…. I am very, very crude. When I am hungry, the most barbarous mixtures will please my palate….

When the hunters returned on a warm September week, Mary rushed to preserve the meat before it spoiled: devoting all her energies to the heavy work of canning, corning and jerking it.

Joe promised that in November the two of them would go off on a hunting trip together and Mary could hardly wait. Just after election day they set off with grub for four or five days, cooking utensils, tent, bedding, guns, ammunition and nearly one hundred pounds of oats and grub for the five horses and colt. Joe instructed her how to assign the horses to their loads, making sure to figure on how to carry back four quarters of meat when a single horse can't carry much more than two quarters. Pete and Rastus would each carry a heavy pack and pregnant Mollie a light pack. Mary would ride Tommy, and Joe, his favorite horse, Paint. On the way back Mollie would carry the gear and the big horses the meat. But things didn't work out the way they planned, as Mary reported to Frances.

Going up a steep sidehill covered with snow, we came to a pretty slick spot. Mollie, just ahead of me, fell down, then scrambled to her feet. I thought if Tommy got a little faster start, he could probably make it; but the result was he just fell down faster. As he slid off his feet, I jumped off and up on the sidehill above him. But there wasn't a thing to hold on to, so I slid right down onto Tommy, and we started to get up at the same time. Unluckily I was under his rear feet,... and all of a sudden I got a paralyzing sock in the chest. When I got my wind back and got over being sick - which didn't take so long - we looked me over and decided there was nothing broken and we might as well go on.

I was pretty shaky, but we had to go slowly anyhow, because the pack horses insisted they wanted to go home and had to be forever chased back to the trail. I had to laugh, watching Joe trying to herd the colt back onto the trail once. She tore out at right angles across an open park, and Joe just couldn't turn her. Finally he gave up, and rode back to the trail. The colt whirled when he did and, head up and little golden mane flying, she <u>chased</u> him back! Tag, thought she.

It was sunset when we plowed through the fairly deep snow at the pass, and darkening all the time we were descending the steep slopes on the other side - looking for a spot that was level enough for camping. By the time we found one, it was plumb dark, and my feet felt frozen. But in the course of time Joe had a fire built, a tepee up, and the horses cared for. I got supper and made the bed up, and we were pretty snug. We went to sleep with the wild chorus of coyotes and the melody of the horsebells in our ears.

The next day they hunted on foot for a bit, following a maze of fresh elk tracks, before they discovered they were close to another hunting camp. They moved their camp into thick timber at the edge of a small park at a somewhat more secluded spot and rode up the mountain where they walked quietly, expecting an elk to pop out of the woods at any minute. Mary tired rapidly and Joe went on leaving her to rest on a log. After a while Joe hurried partway back, calling, "I've found very fresh tracks spattered with blood." Cautiously they set off following the great scarlet stains in the snow. The trail tangled around into thick timber criss-crossed with deadfalls. Soon the blood stains petered out and the elk's tracks blended in with many others. Giving up, they found their horses just as it got dark, and Mary collapsed on Tommy unable to take another step. Back in camp, with supper in them and a fire going, energy returned as they made plans to get up at dawn and bag their meat right then.

You never can tell what will happen in a night. Joe must have been feeling pretty confident when he went to put hobbles and bells on the horses, and picketed Paint, so he would be on hand first thing in the morning. It was a lovely night, the horses were in fine shape, Mary was asleep, getting the good rest that she needed, we would surely get our meat tomorrow.

But I woke in the night with a frightful pain across my back and (it) hurt (to) breathe. By the time I was awake enough to figure out what was wrong, there was a crash and a thrashing out in the brush, and Joe woke up. He was afraid that it was Paint, tangled up somehow and fallen, and had to get up to see about him. It was awfully cold, somewhere below zero, I suppose, so Joe had to build up the fire and dress before he could go out into the snow.

Then I heard him curse in a despairing tone; and after awhile there were footsteps close by, and he led Paint into the firelight. The horse's face looked bewildered and bleak, and he ran his tongue constantly over his lips, the way people sometimes do at an unexpected stroke of pain. His right foreleg crumpled under him at each step. Joe said that in his eagerness to get with the other horses he had first tangled his picket-line, then pulled so hard against it that he had pulled himself over, and apparently given himself some kind of a wrench as he fell.

When Mary added to Joe's woes by telling him how she felt, he looked at her with great concern, shook his head and with alarm in his voice said, "We've got to get you out of here first thing after daybreak. Hunting will have to wait. With Paint lame, we can't even think about carrying meat back." Being fifteen miles from the road hadn't seemed so far until this emergency happened.

The sun rose on a mild, beautiful day but it was a dismal procession that wound its way slowly back up to the pass.

Paint was pretty wretched. He could bear no weight on the bad foot at all, and got along by jumping with his two hind feet and landing his full thousand pounds on the good left foot, keeping the right one curled up…. I still can't understand how Paint jumped up those precipitous slopes. Sometimes he and Joe would get very far behind, and I would have to wait, wondering hollowly if perhaps Paint had gone over backwards down some bad place.

At the top of the pass they rested briefly, not daring to linger long as Paint was dripping with sweat and the west wind at ten thousand feet was mighty cold. Old Pete took the lead, happy to be homeward bound moving carefully down the steep slippery trail, with everyone else following, trusting his judgment as to the best route to follow. About four miles from home Paint gave up and just refused to walk any further. So they left him there to get Mary back for a hot bath, good rubbing with Musterole and a sound sleep on the couch. The next day Joe went back to get Paint, packing a gun in case he couldn't rescue the horse. But he did.

It took Mary and Paint many days of recuperation before they were back to normal. Joe would have to again go on a solo hunt to get their winter meat. While she hated to admit it, Mary found herself agreeing with Joe's dogma that winter pack trips are not for women; though she said she did so with reservations.

As winter took over, Mary and Joe could feel their roots taking hold deep in their ranch soil. Their place felt like home now, especially with Christmas coming. This year it would be a time to socialize with neighbors. A real celebration.

Our Christmas Day was quite different from the traditional one, yet characteristic enough of the Dubois country.

It takes a lot of preparation to start a car in this climate

We had been invited to have Christmas with Violet Shippen and her family. (Glenn Shippen is the game warden).... All Christmas Eve it snowed and blew, piling up the drifts two- and even three-feet deep right on the road across the flats. We had planned to leave the car up by the gate ...starting after Christmas, but the weather sure caught us. When starting a car in this climate, you have to make a lot of preparations. An hour or so before you plan to leave, you put a bucket of hot coals under the oil pan. Then you get about ten gallons of water almost boiling - it takes the wife and lots of firewood to accomplish that in the least possible time. Then you pour hot water over the manifold, and finally start the car in the accepted fashion. Now, you are ready to start bucking snow. Because we drive so little, we feel we can't afford Prestone anti-freeze, so we drain the radiator each time, and have to carry water to fill it. Well, we got out to the highway, and had to shovel about a hundred yards, and weren't late for dinner, either.

The place was a good old Christmas madhouse, such as I haven't taken part in since the Evergreen Avenue days (in Rutland). Four kids, ranging in age from five to fourteen, all terrifically excited over the presents, and needing to show them off.... And there was the Christmas dinner with the first turkey I have eaten in three years, and all the trimmings. Afterwards the kids cleared out and went skating, the men assembled by the tree and - from what I overheard - talked about car engines, while the women washed the dishes, and then sat around for a good old round of gossip.

Joe and I left early.... It was still snowing and blowing at a great rate as we climbed up the valley, and as dark as a winter night can get. The road began to be badly drifted in places, for the snowplow man was celebrating Christmas in town. Of course with each mile the snow got deeper. So you can imagine our surprise when our headlights picked out of the swirl ahead three human figures plodding along toward us - yes, walking! They told us they were from Nebraska, and their car was stuck in a snowdrift five miles up the road (it proved later to be only three). They just happened to come upon us, and it was a good thing too because they would have had to walk eight miles to get to Mabel McFarland's, the first occupied ranch with a phone.

…We tucked them in where we could in our loaded car. We were carrying in the back seat a barrel of gas, three big buckets, two shovels, a coil of rope, and about a dozen Christmas packages…. At our gate we finally accomplished the job of turning the car around in the tricky drifts. We had to leave it close to the highway so as to be able to get out easily, yet far enough off it so it wouldn't be buried by the ridge thrown out by the snowplow. Then we walked in through the drifts, with the dark wind pushing us down the valley, if it could. The hundred yards of shoveling done in the morning was obliterated. You'd be surprised how hard it was in the dark and the wind and the snow to set a straight course for the invisible house! But we made it. When the fires were bright in the stove and the fireplace, and the lamp was lit, we got a chance to see our Christmas guests, and they had a chance to thaw out. They were a young man, his wife (soft and golden-blond) and their dark little seventeen-year-old niece…. All of them were dressed inappropriately for such a jaunt, and the niece didn't even have overshoes. When she got the rags that were tied around her feet and ankles off, you could see she had only thin silk stockings and flimsy high-heeled sandals. It's a wonder none were hurt by their experience, but they weren't.

Dude Ranching - Part I

❈ ❈ ❈ ❈ ❈

As 1936 drew to a close, the Back cabin hummed with ongoing conversations about moneymaking. So far they had not made a living from their art, and Mary's hope that they might survive by acting as a photo developer-supplier for the area seemed impractical. Elmer's visit got them thinking about creating a dude ranch. *"We will just have to build more cabins and take in summer and hunting season guests,"* mused Mary. *"You can guide and I'll be cook, laundress, and day trip entertainer."*

"And we'll both paint to beat the band off season," agreed Joe.

A name: they needed a name to attract folks. Why not use Joe's brand (the Rocker Y) as their invitation to the public? With that decided, they got to work. Joe steadily brought out of the woods the logs needed to build three dude cabins. As they couldn't afford to purchase lumber, he improvised a sawmill, using an old Chevrolet engine to run it and he and Mary worked as a team to create their own building materials. Mary described the operation.

The mill makes an exciting rhythm, like music in your blood. The motor is a steady roar that you can't talk over, but you forget about it after awhile. The saw rings against the wooden pegs that guide it, and screams shrilly as it goes through the logs. The carriage brings the logs through the saw, then whips them back again to starting position like magic....

And I, your machinery-ignorant sister, have been the engineer!... You may not believe it but that's about the most satisfying work I know. The main job is to stand at the throttle and give her all the power she has for the cuts, then cut it off to idling speed between cuts. Auxiliary jobs are to keep the bearings oiled, keep the engine cool - in going through the logs, that engine boils up a hundred gallons in a day. Joe took off the radiator and put a 15-gallon steel barrel in its place. The fifteen gallons boil so soon that he has to open a faucet in the bottom and let it run, then the engineer has to take a moment every now and then while the log is being pulled back for the next cut to pour in another bucket of water. If we had the pipe, we'd pipe it from the creek and just keep a stream running. Other jobs for the engineer are to keep a canny eye on oil pressure, battery charging, belt slipping, and to rush around to the other side of the mill every little while and pick up the short boards...and stack them.

When a particularly beautiful board comes off, I pick it up and pat it lovingly, then look over to exchange with Joe an understanding look of pride. We cut only dead timber, 'seasoned on the stump.' Reason is that we can get a free permit for it from the Forest Service, while green timber costs money, and you can only cut what the ranger marks. But we find there are lots of advantages to the dead timber. It doesn't shrink much, it planes beautifully, and it does come in the

Joe at the saw mill

Mary's Way

loveliest colors. Main color is ivory white when fresh-cut, yellowing on exposure. There are often narrow silver streaks, where moisture has penetrated. Sometimes there are beautiful stripes of rusty red. Resin around the knots makes them pale orange....

As they worked, they relished a new sense of community. By February 1937, Mary and Joe had a telephone - an important link to human-kind.

Our isolation has been nowhere near as great as last year. In fact, by contrast we lead almost the gay life of a city butterfly! There are four families up here at the end of the valley, in close touch however fierce the storms may roar.... The Shippens, Moriartys, Backs, and Carpenters constitute high society on (upper) Wind River. The grandest foe of isolation is the party line with its camaraderie. Everyone listens in on anyone's conversation whenever he wants to, just as a matter of course. It is even good form to break in on a conversation.... At least once a day Mrs. Shippen, Mrs. Moriarty, and I have a three-way conversation. It is hard to see now how we did without the phone last year.

Every now and then we all get together. Last Sunday we all went up to Shippens, and a rooster was sacrificed to the occasion - a most welcome change from the universal elk meat. Joe went on snowshoes, I on skis (it's about two miles) and Violet dragged her little toboggan with at least twenty pounds of books and magazines lashed on. At Moriarty's we left some of the magazines,

Mary with Violet and her pup

took on some more,… and added Mrs. Moriarty and Bill to the party, she on webs and he on skis. It snowed all day long, a very wet, clinging sort of snow, but a high wind split the clouds just at sunset as we …headed homeward. Sure grand, the flame-colored clouds, the driving snow, the cry of the pine trees, the wide stretch of a dim valley below us.

Back at the ranch the horses were good company, as were the dogs that now included Violet, who 'sang' when Joe played the harmonica, and Stubby. Both dogs had puppies, although Stubby's disappeared when they were only a few days old. Mary and Joe had long talks worrying about how they could afford to feed Violet's six pups. With the pups weaned Mary finally forced herself to drown the three bitches. She just wiped away the tears, knowing she had to do it; living so close to the edge of their resources was hard!

Finding dudes became a difficult and ongoing concern that provoked Mary into creating a brochure. (*See sketch 8*) They asked everyone they knew to help them find people who wanted to visit a dude ranch. Mary wrote invitingly in the brochure:

You'll glory in the winds, the dizzy space, the brilliant flowers of timberline. You'll chuckle in the firelight at tall tales of the West. You'll ride through the moonlit sage, and sleep in a cozy log cabin or under the stars that look so near in Wyoming skies.

All this for the price of $35 per person for a week with meals or $15 per person without. Co-investor Elmer helped locate guests, and his horses helped make the

Dude ranching means spending more time on horseback

promised riding possible. When a family friend, Warren, came to visit and help out on the ranch a few weeks, even Mary took time to enjoy the horses.

We have been doing quite a little riding…. Tommy has tamed down amazingly, so now just about anyone who knows anything about riding can manage him. But he is still

Sketch Eight
Cover of Rocker Y brochure

plenty peppy. Today…I rode… for a couple of hours around on top of the aspen ridge above the ranch, trying to get a look at some elk; but all we saw was a lot of fresh sign. Some of it was so very fresh that it looked as if the critters were hanging about at their ease, and just lit out when they heard us coming…. As we passed the pond on Lava Creek, we got a good look at a big beaver. He was swimming with an aspen to

IF YOU LIKE THE MOUNTAINS •
We're on top of the continent, right in the heart of the Rockies• North — the Absarokas and Yellowstone Park• West—Jackson Hole and the Tetons• South — the Gros Ventres and the Wind River Range• East—the Wind River Badlands•

IF YOU LIKE WIDE-OPEN SPACES •
We're at the edge of the timber, where the sage hills of the cattle range rise to the forested shoulders of the Rockies, haunt of elk, deer, moose, bear, mountain sheep •
Some figures: North—150 miles to settled country• South—30 miles, across the Continental Divide, to the nearest ranch• East—14 miles to Dubois, nearest village; 100 to Lander; Riverton, the nearest railroad• West—18 miles to the Continental Divide, 60 to the Tetons, 80 to Yellowstone Park•

IF YOU LIKE ANIMALS — the whitefaced cattle of the grassy hills; the big and small wild game of the forest; the colts, broncs, and saddle stock of our horse herd •
We've the right horse for you, whether you're a green hand or an old timer that's known horses from away back•

(AND THERE'S NO EXTRA CHARGE FOR YOUR HORSE!)

IF YOU LIKE TO GET AWAY FROM CROWDS•
Our four guest cabins, one to three rooms in each, are scattered for privacy among the pines and aspen at the foot of the Home Ridge • We are full up when there are fourteen guests •

Sketch Eight
Rocker Y brochure

Mary's Way

put on the big raft - winter supplies - I suppose that floated in front of his house.

Lately we have had beautiful moonlight, which has tempted us successfully to ride out after dark. It is surely thrilling to ride across the sage hills and through the pine woods under the blue-white moon....

Tommy threw Warren twice - doing no more damage

Sketch Eight
Rocker Y brochure

than stiffening muscles and slightly wounding the self-respect. The self-respect was quite restored this afternoon though when he had the privilege of seeing Tommy dump me off <u>twice</u> in the course of one ride. He was all tamed down, and sweet as anything you ever saw, until the last three days, when he has sure been spooky....

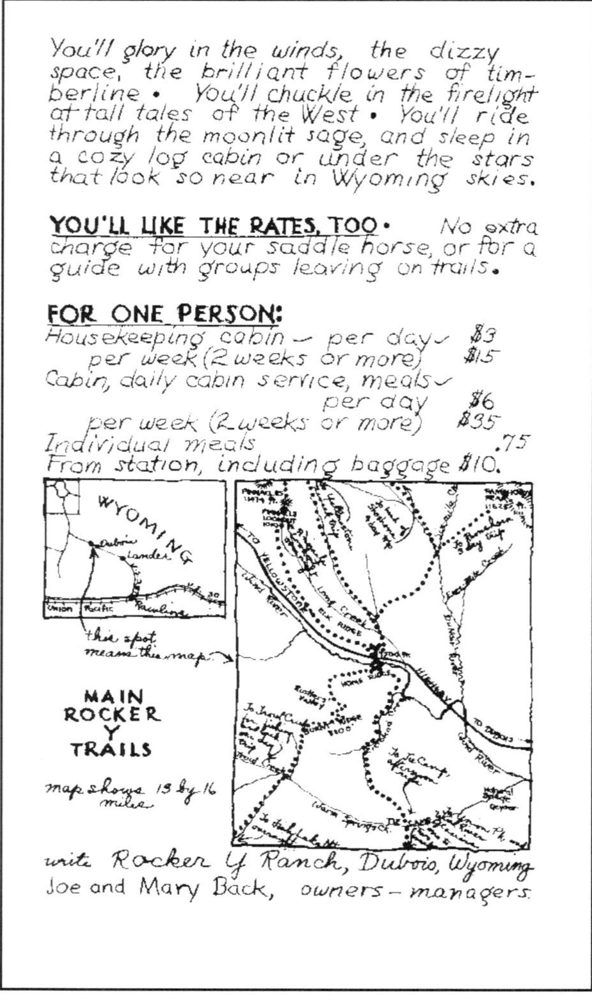

Sketch Eight

Back of Rocker Y brochure

June 1937 brought Mary's sister Frances' wedding to Mo McGawn in Maywood. Mary would have given anything to go but with their first dude season almost upon them, she couldn't get away. Cabin building preoccupied them with the first one not quite ready for the planned July guests. They obligingly camped for a few days enjoying the Back's scenery. By fall Mary reported they had hosted enough guests to "just about make our winter's grub-stake" and pay off the mortgage.

In September, Mary surprised Frank with some mighty important news which she slipped into a letter.

I am a pretty lonesome girl tonight....Joe is away - gone for the whole (hunting) season, probably until early December. He is guiding hunting parties for Al Angle, going after elk, deer, bear, and moose. We can certainly use the money ...and I am sure it is good for both of us to be apart for awhile. It's the first time we've been separated for as long as overnight since his hunting trip two years ago, and that was only for a few days. This getting far away from domesticity and having more than two months right out in the open, among the mountains of the Continental Divide, is going to pep him up a lot for painting. He is sure to have a lot of interesting encounters with animals, and some funny ones with hunters. For my part, I do have a lot more time free for doing all the other things that housework usually crowds out.... But just the same - how I do miss Joe!

As for the reason why we especially need the money that Joe is after. We have recently discovered that a new little Back is due to greet the big world sometime in February!... You may wonder at my saying that it is a recent discovery when here the time is already halfway gone. But I have just been so ridiculously healthy, and more active this summer than ever before in my life, that I never gave my state of health a thought until my overall buttons got too tight! So a couple of weeks ago I went down to Lander, saw the doctor, who confirmed my suspicions and at the same time gave me a clean bill of health, a few simple directions, ...and publications that are most enlightening. I made tentative arrangements at the hospital and at a boarding house; and came home all excited.

You know full well how completely I'm <u>not</u> qualified by past experience to have anything at all to do with babies. My ignorance is quite abysmal, though, to be sure, not as complete as it was a couple of weeks back.... Mae Shippen gave up a whole morning to me, going over the Wards catalog baby section item by item, telling me what was essential, what was advisable, and what was pure frill.... To make room for the extra occupant in my little house I have to construct a new series of cupboards and drawers. So it's lucky I feel so very well. I intend to get the carpentry out of the way as soon as possible, and then do my sewing when it's not so easy to get around, bend, and so on.

The doctor puts the approximate date for the newcomer's arrival at about February 17; but myself, I don't really expect him - or her - until about March 1. But in any case, I plan to go down to Lander about February 1, that being as late as it would really be safe to stay in the snow country. So there seems no way out of staying at a boarding house and just waiting until the time comes to go to the hospital....

After Joe returned from hunting camp, they pondered baby names and by Christmas had decided on Charles Wyatt (for both their fathers) or Martha Anne. While Joe rode up into the timber every day to cut house logs, Mary giggled at the scene left behind. She plugged around the house in a dignified elephantine fashion accompanied by the two dogs who were also about to become mothers. *"We all have an amusing similarity of contour,"* she noted to Joe on his return. A letter from her sister Miriam came full of worry about their isolation and urging Mary to come stay with her in Nebraska and have the baby there. Mary reassured her that she had the best of doctors and that help wasn't that far away if needed; she and Joe were educating themselves to know how to handle an early delivery. She really couldn't afford to come and she couldn't imagine being that far away from Joe.

In case of a real emergency, I should ...call...Mrs. Moriarty.... She has brought more than one baby successfully into the world for other women. She is a swell person, a live wire with a good sense of humor. (She) came to this valley in 1889, at the age of ten. Her family were the very first settlers in the upper valley. Her own four children were born right over there where they live now,…quite without benefit of doctors….

Prenatal care was no easy matter when the closest doctor was in Lander, over 100 miles away. Just the same Joe drove Mary there in January for a check-up.

Monday morning we got ready to go out to Lander…. It took all morning. Joe waded the drifts - often knee-deep - bent against the terrific snow-laden wind sweeping down the valley, to get the car lined up. We are keeping it over by the mailbox, right on the edge of the pavement. (While he was getting the car ready) I got clothes ready. There was Joe's suit to press (he wears it about twice a year), all the underwear, socks, and so on to be checked over, my own dress to have a few stitches taken and a new collar to finish, the overnight bag to pack, a whole wash-boiler of water to heat (six gallons for the car, the rest for our baths), besides the routine housework and lunch to get.

Joe warned me it was cold and that the snow was drifting very fast. So while he was bathing and dressing, I supplemented my downtown outfit considerably: an extra wool scarf under my coat, pair of long wool stockings and another pair of heavy knee-length socks pulled on over my dress shoes, and my overshoes…pulled on and fastened over all, and heavy wool mittens pulled on over gloves. I sure felt overstuffed….

So we left about noon, Joe carrying the two covered pails of hot water, I with the overnight bag in one hand and the electric lantern in the other. Joe broke trail, turning around solicitously every little way, asking 'Getting along all right - both of you?'

After so laborious a start, it certainly was cozy to sit in a nice warm car and watch the scene change. Seven miles down the valley the snow was gone, though the clouds pressed low and dark and the grass and sage showed the wind was still wild. At Dubois clouds of dust were flying high. Ten miles further down the sun shone out from the tattered edges of clouds and soon all the storm was behind us, though the peaks and upper canyons of the Wind River range were hidden in a wild white smother of plumed and tossing snow clouds. But in the fields by the river horses walked contentedly through golden stubble, or came down to drink from the tumbling green water. It looked like early May or late October. It got warmer and warmer. Item after item I discarded: my wraps, overshoes, socks, stockings, mittens, and scarf....

Joe thought I was going too far when I took my coat off; but you would think that as you continued down the valley it would keep right on getting warmer. It sure was a surprise to me when we topped the hill this side of Fort Washakie, and looked down into winter again. From the Fort to Lander... the process reversed itself, until at Lander we were back in fairly deep snow and a whistling wind.

Friends treated us to supper and overnight. We had to smile to think of the way we kept waking up on account of the too-comfortable inner-spring mattress. But the change in diet was welcome - no one offered us elk meat, and we found lettuce on every hand!

The doctor pronounced me in fine shape, and we arranged for me to come down about February 5. We did our annual shopping and came home yesterday. Found that the high wind had drifted the road pretty badly above the ranger station. But we had no trouble until we were clear to our mailbox, when we went in above the running boards, and were stuck. So we walked on to the house, called up the snowplow man to let him know about the drifts, and went to bed. This morning Joe shoveled almost four hours, to get enough of the road clear so he could turn the car and get it off the pavement onto the top of our drive.

In early February Joe drove Mary to Lander to board with friends until the baby's birth and for a few weeks of recovery. He had to return to the ranch, so they hoped they wouldn't have long to wait. Unfortunately, days - then weeks - passed and still Mary waited.

The waiting (was) ghastly long. Every night I...hoped ...I'd be sick, and go to the hospital by morning - a curious reversal of normal desires. So many people were good to me. I was taken out to dinner, and the movies, and for many *drives, and I had many things to do besides. I cut the wood-block for the letterheads, typed a bunch of rate sheets, wrote a lot of letters, painted two small watercolor portraits and eight landscapes, took many walks, read lots of library books, and helped with the …housework….*

The main part of course was missing Joe. He got down only once; early in March. We talked on the phone a few times, but it was too expensive to indulge in often. Worst of all was the fact that it didn't storm. Here I came down two weeks early, and had to wait five weeks and all that time the weather stayed fine and the road …open clear to the ranch gate. It was maddening to think of that long open road and Joe at the end of it, and no chance of getting together.

Finally in the early hours of March 9, her labor started and off she went to the small hospital, where *"there was a regular shower of babies that morning."* Mary tolerated the severe pains certain that this was all just part of having a normal birth. Toward the end they put her under with chloroform.

Next thing I knew I was conscious of being in a private room, which surprised me as I had asked for the ward, and the doctor was coming in. Before I could get the whirling stopped enough to ask for my baby, he said 'Girlie, we lost,' and told me about it. And I had been so <u>sure</u>, that my first feeling was just plain amazement. I thought he must be talking about someone else. But he wasn't….

He explained that the baby had come all tangled in the cord and all bunched up, with the cord tightened around her neck. The circulation had been cut off just too long. There was a faint heartbeat at birth, but he couldn't get her to breathe. I was quite badly torn…and had to be sewed up. A visitor last night…said the doctor told her that I had the hardest time of any patient he had had in years, so I have the cold comfort of that distinction. He said he could have saved the baby by a Cesarean operation, had he known ahead of time; but the x-ray, of course, doesn't show the soft parts, so there wasn't any way to know until too late. He said he had called Joe and told him, and he was coming down right away. It was just 12:30 p.m. then.

Through the fog of her lingering anesthesia Mary tried to

make sense of what had happened. Was something she had done responsible? After the head nurse reassured her, she brought the baby girl for Mary to see. Marveling at the perfectly formed little body topped with a mop of yellow hair, Mary bonded sadly with the baby, wondering how she and Joe ever produced anyone so beautiful. The rest of the afternoon she spent looking for Joe.

From the window I could see way below the hospital hill, half a mile of the road he would have to travel.... I kept my eyes on the cars for several hours, though I didn't expect him much before five. And I tried to make all the adjustments to living...though I suppose I will go right on making these for a long time to come. There will be no new routine to get used to, no baby cries in the night. Something will have to be done with all those baby clothes. And there will always be a little grave on the hill across the creek (from the ranch).

Joe finally came at quarter-to-four, much earlier than I had thought possible. And when I saw his face, all drawn up and sunken in with worry and fear, I felt so <u>sorry</u> for him that I cried and cried. He didn't know how I was, you know, and was scared for me. He came down the eighty-six miles from Dubois in an hour and three-quarters, hitting seventy much of the time.

They decided to bury Martha Anne on the terrace across the creek, and the sad task fell to Joe. Their good neighbor Gordon Shippen volunteered to accompany Joe and help out. Joe wrote Frank the sorrowful news, reflecting, "Mother Nature, I guess works in queer ways at times." Mary had many days of recuperating at the hospital ahead of her.

She absorbed the new situation with her usual spunk, commenting to Frank, *"It's an experience in living, one that I certainly wouldn't have asked for; but it isn't going to hurt me permanently."* She commented on how much it helped to write her sister. *"I like to use you as a confidant. Often I have found that I could exorcise pain, or anger, or chagrin or grief by writing it all out."* Then she looked on the bright side of her hospitalization.

This is a pleasant place to be. It is on a high hill overlooking the town and overlooked by the main (mountain) range. From the window I can see miles beyond the town to where the road to Dubois goes over a far-off brown hill. At

Mary's Way

night when the headlights of the cars swing down those curves, I can pretend one pair belongs to the old Buick, bringing Joe down to see me. The nurses are just a dandy group…. They know everyone and everyone knows them, they are companionable and cheerful and not at all aloof or impersonal.

Around March 21 Joe came back for her and they attempted to pick up the pieces of their lives. In later years Mary would remember this as the lowest point in her life; she felt deserted by the God of love she had always had such faith in. The deaths of her parents had been hard, but she understood them. How could God let this baby die before she even had a chance at life? She still tried to look at the bright side, but it was a struggle to do so.

The poverty they faced intensified the psychological burden of Martha's death. Mary's hospitalization costs had wiped out their financial cushion, and it became imperative to spend as little as possible and make do as best they could. The pressure to work hard was overwhelming. Some days Joe came home so bitterly tired from working in the timber, he hadn't the strength to do the chores. With the dogs at her heels, Mary got the wood and water and later carried out the slops, worried about how he was overdoing. They bought very little - if they could make it or improvise they did so.

Tickled me to (hear about) buying metal shelves…saying they were cheaper than wood ones. I am now wrestling with the problem of storage (mouse-proof) of paintings and drawings. When I settle upon the construction of the cabinet, Joe goes and cuts the logs, wrestles them onto a wagon… and hauls them to his mill. Then the saw must be adjusted, perhaps filed and set, the motor tuned up, gas on hand, logs cut to board length and finally sawed. Then I select the boards I want. If Joe is around he hauls them down - if not, I carry them one at a time - to the big cabin I am working in (and on). I have to plane each board on all four sides. THEN - I'm ready to begin building my cabinet.

It was more important than ever to sell paintings and good frames made a big difference.. The hours spent constructing frames exhausted them both.

Today we have been framing pictures. Joe has…a new

workbench in the shop with a new window over it, all for framing.... So he has been making frames, and I have been cutting glass and fitting drawings and glass into the frames. And of all the nerve-wracking work , cutting glass is the worst that I have ever done. I am so terribly tensed up for fear of breaking some of those big pieces, that I just about break down when the strain is over. I was more tired at suppertime than I've been in ever so long - maybe since we left Chicago (for there I would get nervously tired the same way). So Joe and I got to roaring at each other, and we had a real time; ending, in the usual fashion, with me sitting on his lap and crying on his shoulder. Now the storm is all over, and I am ready to cut more glass tomorrow.

They had great hopes for the 1938 dude season. Mary had graduated to attempting heavy carpentry work, as she sought to turn their big cabin into a kitchen-dining room. She proudly built and hung two doors and created the frame of a wall to separate the kitchen from a storeroom. Joe cut the boards for the wall and she did the planing. *"Gee it is grand to feel good and to be able to do such things,"* she enthused. All their efforts to get ready led to a busy July, but no guests in August. Poverty loomed closer than ever.

Anxious to bring in a little cash, Mary began baking bread for sale. Paintings were sent to Denver where Joe's former roommate hoped to find buyers. Joe decided to open a lumbering business on the side and started selling posts, poles and house logs. He guided during hunting season and regretfully began to harvest beaver for their pelts.

Joe will soon have to begin harvesting his beaver crop. They are trying to take our lower meadow. Just in the last few weeks they have raised all their dams, backing the water right over the hay land. Joe has a permit to take them, and thinks he can get quite a few without dangerously reducing the population. We hate to kill them, for they are such interesting little engineers; but after all, if you encourage them too much they are pests like mice. Last night we saw several swimming around down there, and you should see the palace they are building. More of our land is in beaver ponds, I am afraid, than hay....

Joe (skinned a beaver) yesterday, so I volunteered to do

this one, thinking maybe I could do it better. It's <u>some</u> job! I admire Bridger, Bonneville, and all the others much more than I did before; that they made their living at it. Joe shot these two. It seemed easier than trapping. I think it's easier on the beaver, too. He hopes to get four or five more this fall. The dogs like beaver meat. We both hate to kill them; they are such peaceable, busy, smart animals, but we must have our hay land. Joe was telling how two frisky little pups were having a picnic building a play dam out beside their home one.

Making do took on new meanings as they struggled to survive until the next dude season.

We are mustering all our resources right now for food alone, and at that we won't eat fancy. When the winter food problem is settled, we'll try to figure out what to do about such things as taxes, phone bill, our license and Christmas.

I had thought I knew a little about economy, but I have learned a lot I never dreamed of before, about how to make food go a long way. For the first time I am making my own soap, from lye and elk tallow. I found that you can save the tea ball from one meal and make quite acceptable tea for the next. By putting in more baking powder, you can make quite good flapjacks entirely without eggs. The same goes for cake and gingerbread - eggs are entirely beyond our reach any more. I am sure glad when Joe gets beaver, for the meat saves the dogs' cornmeal mush. Mrs. Moriarty says they are not bad eating either. They smell willowy, though, like moose, so I think I'll feed (them to) the dogs and eat their mush instead! Well, it's all in a lifetime, and it's an interesting experience. It is too bad, though, to get so parsimonious that I begrudge the suet I have fed in past years to chickadees!...

I've been doing quite a little sewing.... I am astonished at how long good stuff will wear if it's cared for. Joe is still wearing the woolen underwear, wool shirts, breeches, and, believe it or not, socks, that he got in Chicago. Much patched, of course.... His Chicago pajamas are only just giving up the ghost; got so they won't hold patches any more. I was in despair for materials to make new ones, (but) finally used some cheap unbleached muslin (5 1/2 cents a yard at Ward's) that I had bought for making mattress pads. They turned out just fine, wash and press well, and look not bad at all. So I made myself a pair, too, trimmed with plaid gingham! (Out of the old overcoat of Dad's) I made myself a short sport coat for hunting…. Joe wanted a short slicker, easy to use in the timber, but not cumbersome to work in. I made a canvas jacket (from pup tent material) using his overall jacket for a pattern, then painted it with waterproofing (the same stuff we used on the tent before we left Maywood). He says it's just fine, sheds rain, is light and manageable….

(Joe) traded several hundred posts to Rosbrook for winter oats for the horses. They are beautiful oats. I can see myself cooking some for the family if times get really hard before spring.

Mary adored her darkroom and the experimenting she did there, printing the films she took with her camera. In their state of financial disrepair, she worried how she could afford to carry on with this hobby which also provided them with good advertising photos. When Frank and her husband Mo sent her a large box full of photo supplies for her birthday she confessed,

I've not had any film since last year. I <u>had</u> to have some for Christmas pictures. So I gathered together my refund checks from Wards (there is nearly always a little one comes back when I order: something wasn't in stock, or they reduced the price of something, or I sent too much postage). They usually amount to four or five cents. Altogether the ones I found totaled sixty-five cents, so with them I ordered a roll of film and half a dozen developer tubes. That, with some paper left over from last year, was the total of my photographic supplies when your gift arrived.

Mary could count on her brothers and sisters to come to her aid as best they could. Miriam was herself struggling as the wife of a Nebraska Sand Hills preacher, and could offer little more than comforting words in frequent letters. Dorothy, also married to a minister and living near Chicago, offered to try to help find dude prospects for the ranch. Ed, a schoolteacher in Massachusetts with a young family, worried about Mary but had neither the time nor money to help out much. Frank and Mo were frequent contributors of photos and equipment. Living as they did in Maywood, they kept Joe and Mary posted about Art Institute happenings. While Mary enjoyed looking over the catalogs of exhibitions they sent, Joe just poured over them, reliving Art Institute days, reminiscing happily about acquaintances and relaxing as he seldom did any more.

She had always depended a great deal on my father - Milton - and he continued to be her strong supporter. Extra money for Christmas, a loan when they were desperate, his offer to try to sell some of their paintings...or find dude customers - he did what he could. He had sent Mary a diagram for making a kitchen cupboard with an extendible leaf. It pulled out for use and pushed back to save space. Mary proudly built it according to his plan. When Milton and our family managed to get to the Rocker Y, he always found a project he could engineer, and usually shed some pounds carrying it out. The weir (small dam) he made one year proved invaluable.

Do you remember the weir you built?... Its remains are still across the creek, and were we ever grateful a couple of weeks ago! We'd had some hot weather...melting the snow up in the mountains at a great rate. The creeks got higher and higher. Finally the old wooden dam a mile up the creek went out, and we had a flood for awhile. Well, the weir caught all the boards and trees and other refuse that came down, making a new shaggy-looking dam ten feet high and extending about thirty feet upstream. Somewhat more than the normal creek flow came through and under the loose dam. The rest was diverted by it to the other side of the valley, making a new channel and scouring away the approaches at the farther end of the bridge.... If the weir hadn't caught the flotsam, I'm afraid the bridge would have, and sent the surplus water straight down to the house, where it might have done some damage....

While Mary and Joe's Wyoming neighbors lived some distance away, Wind River upper valley folks looked out for each other. Their caring and concern certainly helped brighten the days as the Backs worked their way toward 1939. They particularly enjoyed a Thanksgiving expedition to Lu and Grace Long's ranch, way up near Ramshorn peak, towering high above the valley. Joe and Mary drove to within three miles, where the Longs promised to meet them with a team of horses and sled.

...We started out bright and early. Had to get up at five to get all the preparations done so we could leave at eight. The plants were put in a big cardboard carton and set on the kitchen table near the stove. So were the cabbages and onions. I wrapped quilts around the four hundred pounds of potatoes in the cellar. Joe shaved and got all dressed up - white shirt and of all things, a tie, under a woolen army shirt. He had on his best chokebores (which is what they all call breeches in this country), the red plaid jacket, ...rubber-footed leather boots, Scotch cap, and mittens. This was to be one of the rare occasions when I step out in a dress, but my choice of dresses was strictly limited, not only by my small wardrobe, but even more by the thought of the three-mile ride in an open sled. Over the woolen dress with red buttons, and the silk stockings, I wore a red sweater, blue ski pants, sheepskin pack, buckle overshoes, wool socks, heavy short coat, and plaid wool muffler. Then there was a wool crocheted cap, wool gloves, and leather mittens. ...Can you reconstruct the picture of the well-dressed Wind River pair setting out from their estate in the upper valley, bound for a social gathering in winter weather?

It was tough going to get to where Lu met us with the sled. Even with chains on there were places where the powerful old Buick couldn't buck the drifted and hard-packed snow. One place Joe had to shovel not only tracks, but the whole width of the road. But we made it...up...in a narrow valley between bare high ridges, where Lu had built a little fire in the bottom of a thicket of spruce. The team of white horses was drawn up close to the trees. It was sure enough a cold ride. The wind came so sharply against my face that I tied my muffler right over it. We stopped once to warm up in the cabin of a trapper, a huge man with shining blue eyes, then went on while the valley narrowed, and the forest came closer. Once we watched a good sized buck...as he stood on a hillside among quaking aspen above the road, and he watched us in turn. We topped a ridge, and there, spread out below us were the cabins of the Long ranch, on a little flat at the head of a valley, with wooded ridges and the naked gray spine of the Ramshorn above and behind it. Soon the two *little boys came dodging out of the willows, and we were at the end of the road.*

The Longs are just delightful people. Luther has been in this part of the country about as long as Joe. He comes from Missouri, has an imagination and picturesque way of phrasing things.... He's a fine logger , a good carpenter, a hard worker, and lots of fun, with a solemn-faced, dry wit. Grace is a few years older than I, with a smooth oval face and love-ly almond-shaped eyes that crinkle into a lovely smile. She was a student at the Kansas City Art Institute when she was married. In our interests, experiences, and activities, she and I seem just about alike. When we get together, we just talk ourselves hoarse. We plan kitchens, exchange recipes, discuss dude ranch problems, and are constantly surprised that our problems are so nearly identical, and that we solve them in so much the same way.

And the boys are such fine youngsters. You know how youngsters are apt to be when they are raised in a log cabin at the head of the hollow - wild as rabbits, shy, untrained. But these boys, aged six and seven, are as friendly and un-self-conscious as any you could find. The older one draws all the time - astonishing productions of a curious, wide-rang-ing imagination. The younger one's talent is friendliness. So we all had fun. The Longs never get out, or even less than we do. So an occasion like that marks a high spot in all our lives.

Christmas brought an avalanche of mail, as friends and fami-ly remembered the Wyoming Backs. Joe and Mary invited the Shippens to dinner and the weather cooperated by giving plenty of snow for skiing. For Mary, preparing the meal was a major under-taking.

Main dish was roast chicken. Joe tried to win us a turkey at the American Legion shoot, but wasn't quite good enough.... A neighbor gave us a chicken, alive. Neither of us had killed, defeathered, singed, dressed, cleaned, stuffed, trussed, or roasted any poultry before, so we had to rely heavily on the Boston Cook Book.... The Merc (Mercantile) gave away Christmas presents of half pound packages of... bacon, much better quality than I ever can buy, so it was just right to drape a couple of slices over the chickie's bosom dur-

ing the roasting. To piece out we had elk …croquettes with brown gravy. There were mashed potatoes, salad of chopped apples, cabbage, dates, and nuts and pumpkin pie (adapted) out of the squash that Warren gave us last fall. The vegetable was carrot out of my garden. You can see it was quite grand.

By April 1939 Mary felt increasingly optimistic about the approaching summer. She thrived on early spring days when she spent as many hours outside as she could; usually busy solving some problem or other…

(As I worked in the rock garden yesterday) I felt like Archimedes. There was a (big prong of a rock) right by the kitchen door, so I decided to eliminate it. I dug all round it down to the bottom, and gee whiz it was big! About the dimensions of a heavily upholstered two seated bench, (made of) very fine lava, no big holes to make it lighter. Joe wasn't there and I was mad at it by then, so I got a crowbar, and, by taking all afternoon to it, got it pried triumphantly out. I'd raise it on one side a couple of inches, put a rock under it, then go round to the other side and do likewise. So when it was out the hole was all filled with rocks, and I was hardly tired at all. I was sure impressed by the power of a lever. With a little brick-sized stone for a pivot, I could lift that enormous thing by the pressure of one hand, hold it with my knee while adjusting the stones under it. Yes, sir, I was sure that if there were only something for a pivot, I could move the world!…

This afternoon I worked on the 'water system.' Mrs. Moriarty suggested it to me. I had been wishing so hard for running water in the house, that the simple substitute never occurred to me. A tiny irrigation ditch (for watering the lawn) runs right by the kitchen door. All I need is to deepen it to carry a larger stream, build a trough and a waterbox to (use) to dip up pails from, and bank it all with sods, and there is convenience and beauty as well.

Water at the front door! The cuckoo clock up on the wall after months in storage! Some drawings, watercolors and beaver skins sold! Above all, reservations and down payments for the summer kept arriving, while Joe worked to finish a new big cabin, complete with a built in icebox. The work load seemed so much lighter when life looked so encouraging. Heavy duty cleaning of cabins involved chloroxing walls, oiling floors and painting ceiling boards from Mary's perch on enormous sawhorses (four and a half feet high). Curtains awaited ironing. Before she could transplant cabbage seedlings she had to break the sod for a new garden patch. A lot to do!

Dude business overwhelmed them in summer 1939. Their cabins could sleep fifteen guests, but for three days one extra person had to sleep under the stars. There was never a dull moment as they took folks on pack trips, fishing and horseback riding. Mary relished the arrival of her cousins Mary Ellen and Aline who joined the Smith family (of cough drop fame) on horseback excursions. One bright, cold, windy day Mary led the way to Pinnacle Point where they traversed land so steep they often dismounted and walked the horses. They laughed over lunch by a protected spring, for their sandwiches had nearly disintegrated from the jolting ride. Life could hardly be better than this.

While Mary took a casual approach to housekeeping and cooking, she still found herself busy almost every minute. She sought to keep the linen clean with her hand wash method which was exhausting and time consuming. She delighted in greeting one guest who had been one of her campers at Camp Teela-wooket in Vermont. Then Bob Allen, a former junior assistant of Mary's at the Trailside Museum showed up. He came to take pictures and stayed at the ranch all summer, working for his board. Sleeping in the woods, he tried his hand at many new occupations, including digging ditches, building roads, shoeing horses, cutting firewood, and even washing dishes. Joe marveled that a raw city kid with absolutely no experience with farm or ranch life could adapt himself so readily and be so all round useful. He became a trusted hand who even felled trees just about where he aimed them.

By early September with the guests gone Mary breathed a sigh of relief. Now she could think about painting, although she had a long list of projects calling for attention. For one she had a sink and cupboards under construction. This meant the end of having to haul out slop buckets!

She looked forward to such new experiences as digging a cesspool complete with a deep trench to the house, and installing the sink plumbing. She could hardly wait to get in the thick of the work. She also wanted to make copies of her rustic chairs for dudes who had ordered them. She sure could use the extra money, besides she really enjoyed fitting the pine poles together and covering them with laced raw cowhide. Canning called for Mary's attention: spinach and chard plucked from the garden before the first frost and bottled, buffalo berries made into jam, and a bushel of peaches in the larder preserved before they went bad. She had sewing projects galore including making a wool shirt for Joe, pajamas, underwear, sheet-blankets, quilts and sleeping bags. She hoped to knit socks, gloves and caps for winter. Then, of course, she needed to keep up with the dirty clothes. When Joe complained he had no undershirts, Mary realized she had neglected doing the laundry for two weeks. Besides, she remembered, she had worn his shirts herself!

To Mary's great joy, they could now afford a washing machine! Ordered from Montgomery Wards, the source of many of their durable supplies, it cost $60, including an engine to run it.

The tub is steel, heavily enameled in dark green stipple-work. It has a Lovell pressure wringer, with an automatic safety release. (The engine is hardly) larger than an electric washing machine motor, yet it runs like a car motor. It has one little cylinder, air cooled. The oil pan holds less than a cup, and I add it by the teaspoonful, and when I drain it - only once so far, - drain it into a sauce dish. The gas tank holds a quart, and lasts for about five ordinary washings. There is a long snaky exhaust tube, that you coil up when not using the motor and stick (it) under the machine. When in use, you have to stick the end out the door (to drain out the water). I can see it may be a decided inconvenience in mid-winter; but don't believe I'll keep the door shut just the same! It's hard to see now how I managed to do without it all this time. Less than an hour's operation is usually enough to get a big bunch of really dirty clothes all clean.

Before Joe left for hunting camp, he began the urgent task of building a pickup out of a 1927 Buick sedan to replace their truck that had finally died. Mary was immensely proud of his tinkering skills. He could take an abandoned engine, hand make new parts for it, and end up with a first class buzz saw motor. The sedan, pur-

   Mary's Way

chased for $25 had only 40,000 miles on it. It cried out to be used somehow.

> *So after several weeks consideration, while it sat in front of the house as a decoration, he cut the body in two (back of the seat), removed the back part, and the old roof, and built a very neat back and roof out of metal from the worn-out old truck. (This in the meantime he made into a wagon that is his delight to use.) The back has a regulation car seat back built into it, and a large plate glass window. He built a regular-sized pickup box of heavy planed planks, put together with iron saved from old cot frames rescued from a road camp junk pile! After it was done, I painted it black outside. I have just lately been finishing the inside, using plywood paneling above the seat back and inside the roof, and strips of it to finish around the doors. Where there was a space between the outside and inside, I stuffed it full of old mattress stuffing. I am painting it tile red, trimmed with black…. Then I made pockets of leatherette…and screwed them to the back panel to hold mail, packages, purse and so on. Joe put in the heater from the big Buick, and now it's sure comfortable.*

With the retrofitted truck available, Joe and Mary set out for Idaho in October on a trip to stock up on supplies. As they climbed in and settled themselves, proud of their handiwork, they also worried how this untried hodgepodge of a vehicle would handle the trip.

> *The trip is quite something, taking us 250 miles from home, over three mountain ranges at a time of year when any kind of blizzard might happen on short notice. Before we reached Togwotee Pass the car stopped, with that sudden out-of-gas way. The vacuum tank was empty…. We were to find out that with long use of second gear, either climbing or going down, the tank empties. Joe hasn't found out why. It never happens on our side of the range, so he hasn't had occasion to monkey with it. But the tank had to be refilled twice going up Teton Pass, and once going down the other side, and once again going over the Big Hole range in Idaho, and the same on the return trip….*

> *We had lovely, fine, clear, crisp weather all three days….*

The leaves were still gorgeous, and every turn of the road gave us exciting new views. I enjoyed the trip, even though we were rather under a tension all the way home, because we were much overloaded. (We carried about 1400 pounds, which was much too much for the passenger car springs Joe hadn't yet replaced or strengthened. The load sank right down on the axles, and he had to raise it with wooden blocks wired to the axles. It rode like a lumber wagon). You should have seen us preparing for Teton Pass, as one would prepare for a trip to Little America. We stopped at the foot of the steep grade where a Forest Service campground opened a space in the thick black spruce and golden quakers (aspen). Joe tightened all the brakes, filled the vacuum tank, filled the radiator, checked the tires; I stowed my purse, magazines, and so on, in the back, so nothing would be in my way if I had to leap. I hunted up a big wedge-shaped rock to stuff under a wheel if necessary. Joe put extra gas for the vacuum tank in a pail. I held it between my knees, and the rock on my lap, and we started. Two miles from the top is a sign at a stream crossing: 'Waterhole Canyon - last water'. We stopped there by prearrangement; no difficulty so far. The radiator was boiling, so we waited around awhile, filled it with cold water, filled the vacuum tank, and pulled slowly on to the top. I could feel every pound of that load dragging us back....

Getting home finally, safe and sound, Mary marveled at the good deal they had made on potatoes. They paid fifty cents a sack for three 100-pound (plus) bags that they filled from the farmer's potato cellar. She had never seen bigger ones: all at least a pound, some over two and all spotlessly clean. They were culls - somewhat imperfect - but would make mighty good eating in the months ahead. She supposed the farmer was probably bragging about how he hung it on that Wyoming outfit - getting fifty cents a sack for culls!

Now Joe and Mary could really concentrate on painting. As usual Joe got so carried away with his oils that he forgot to eat. Mary enjoyed working with watercolors, but also made trinkets out of elk horn to sell. She got caught up in sewing projects, too. Intent on replacing Joe's threadbare red plaid hunting jacket she used the

     Mary's Way

old one as a pattern. Blankets Milton had given her provided a perfect fabric and canvas made a good lining. *"I put a zipper on it, like the old coat. I'm sinfully proud of it. It looks tailored, fits beautifully and I know it's as strongly made as I could manage."*

She improvised outfits for herself too, overhauling dresses that looked worn, and creating a new one. Using bright assorted leftover curtain material *"that would make your hair stand on end"* she sewed an exaggerated dirndl style dress. Its silver buttons came from three old dresses. While she thought it really cute and fit her well, she worried that everyone would think, *'Hello dress, where's Mary?'* (*See sketch 9*)

She suddenly needed more 'going to town' duds as Dubois attractions drew her to town frequently. She gave a 4-H talk, and sometimes chaired meetings of the American Legion Auxiliary of which she was now president. Some days she helped out at the library, "2200 books in an ancient log shack". In 1940 she became the official librarian, driving to Dubois to hold fort in the tiny building two afternoons a week (for which she received $16 a month). The donated cabin and its trove of donated books and magazines hardly resembled the Berea College library, but Mary enjoyed being part of the community effort to encourage reading in the valley. She also delighted in bringing home the extra money. She expected the unexpected, so the day a Holstein bull walked through the door didn't faze her. She just marched him back outside - all in an afternoon's library duty.

Sketch Nine
Mary's Dress

Dude Ranching - Part II

Joe and Mary discovered big changes afoot on their trip to Idaho. On the way they waved to highway crews setting snow height poles along the road over Teton and Togwotee Passes, indicating that for the first time they intended to plow the road and keep the passes open all winter. Since the Northwestern Railroad promised to help open Jackson Hole to winter sports, possibly some skiers might make it to the Wind River Valley - could mean some winter business. Amazingly, the post office planned a winter mail route on their road with twice-a-week delivery expected all winter.

The most significant changes, however, happened much closer to home. Co-owning the ranch with Elmer just had not worked out well. They needed to run their own place. After months of frustrating protracted negotiations with him, he finally agreed to buy out their share of the Rocker Y. Right up to the last minute it seemed the sale might fall through. Then suddenly they closed the deal, sighed with relief, and began looking for a new home. The Moriarity place was not for sale; and the Rosbrook ranch, while attractive, cost too much.

They finally settled on the Gordon Shippen place, seven miles closer to town, with the Ramshorn practically right in the front yard and the Wind River running through it. Finding it both available and affordable they agreed, "Let's do it!"

By the end of January 1940, they had moved in, thankful to have their own ranch. Leaving Martha in the grave on the hill was hard and they must have wondered about all the work they said goodbye to: the gardens, buildings and many improvements. What better way to welcome the new year though, than to celebrate at the new Rocker Y.

It's much larger than the upper place, with more than twice the hay land.... The growing season is all of six weeks longer, and the ground is not stony.... As we sold only the land and permanent improvements we have complete equipment to go right ahead. A week ago Sunday we took down our last load, and since then we have been more than busy building.... The ranch house of the new Rocker Y was, we thought, entirely hopeless, just a sort of lair we could crawl into until we could get something else organized. But to my delight, as we work with it we can see it has lots of possibilities. It's a tight, sound cabin, with no leaks in the roof. Mostly what it needs is cleaning and plenty of cupboards. As fast as I can get to it I am giving it both.

It's thirteen by fifteen feet inside, or rather smaller than...the smallest on our upper place. It was built some twenty years ago, and has been inhabited almost entirely by bachelors, including a Swedish tie hack locally famous for his avoidance of soap and water, and a gang of moonshiners during prohibition days. An illustration of the conditions we faced is the first remark made by our nearest neighbor, Mrs. Weeks, on the occasion of our first dinner party....'Why,' she said, 'you've laid a new floor! This cabin always had a dirt floor!' The joke was that we had only scrubbed the floor....

The tiny cabin challenged Mary's ingenuity. How would they ever cram everything they needed to keep house into it? Finally she sacrificed two and a half feet, the whole length of one wall, and built a series of closets. Then she enumerated with amazement their holdings *"all our clothes, three hundred pounds of potatoes, thirty of onions, the winter supply of carrots, rutabagas, and parsnips, the sewing machine, the washing machine, clothes basket, boiler, ...bed linens, towels....mending and fancy work, carpenter's tools, water barrels, woodbox, and quantities of canned goods."*

Having become a confident carpenter, she next attacked the worst of the cabin's problems only to discover she didn't need much skill to fix things, at least temporarily. The door was so black and

Mary's Way

greasy, she puzzled over what to do with it. With scrubbing, it astonished her with its white pretty raw wood. Looking into why it sagged badly, she discovered all she needed to do was substitute screws for nails. The windows appalled her. Crookedly cut, carelessly made casings, and sashes just tacked on the outside of the house made them nearly useless. Cleaning helped a bit, and she planned to recut the window holes and put in new windows in the spring.

Mary delighted in the setting of the new Rocker Y and explored it when the tasks at hand became overwhelming.

Joe has been spending much of his time in the timber, getting out house logs and saw logs for our new construction. I went up the logging road back of the place the other day to see what it was like. It's quite a ways to really good timber, about three miles, though you are going through woods all the way. But when you do get into it, the timber is so beautiful you could eat it, so straight and trim and clean of limb....

The timbered ridge back of our place is fascinating. It's more fun for short horseback rides than anything around the upper place, because there are so many interlacing ridges in an intricate chain, and there are such grand views. Too much timber where we were before; but here the pine, fir and aspen alternates delightfully with bare sagebrush look-offs.... (For example, you should have seen) the pinnacles yesterday morning. At sunrise these grim and craggy rocks were most delicately and inappropriately wrapped in a sheer cloud of baby-pink. Joe said it looked like a thug in a pretty nightgown!...

It's an odd thing that though we are lower and hence more nearly out of the timber, yet the house is right among the trees, much closer than before. Chickadees, Clark's nutcrackers, woodpeckers, and squirrels are almost constantly on the feeding ledges about the door and windows.

By April renovations and building had taken over their lives. Bob Allen arrived to help out and then the progress really accelerated.

Bob is already planning what he is going to do next winter to improve the ranch! He and Joe are quite in cahoots as junk collectors. They think they have spotted a pretty good electric light plant they can trade poles for. Yesterday and today Bob cleared willows from a place for a vegetable garden for me, and this afternoon he and Joe plowed it.... (They) have built a fine solid cabin for a bunkhouse, a dandy two-span bridge across Wind River and gravelled the road, dug a well, and sawed up a lot of lumber. The place is sure changing fast. Next on the program is a dude cabin, a fine three-room one with cellar and a terrace. The cellar is already dug and the first row of logs laid....

Cabin building is quite an industry around here. There are almost no other types of buildings. The Episcopal church is of logs, so is the new high school. So a great many of the men are keenly interested in new developments in log cabin building.... Aristocrat of methods is the old Swedish coped style, with each log hollowed on its undersurface to conform perfectly to the upper surface of the log below it. In placing the logs, each has a line of oakum spread on its upper surface to seal the joint.... It's warm and satisfactory if done right, but very expensive. Commonest construction (that we use) is the saddle-and-notched corners, leaving narrow cracks between the logs. These are most commonly chinked with splits or quarter rounds of poles inside, and daubed with mortar outside.... It is a common and popular practice to have the logs slabbed on three sides, and put up with the round side out. The inside is then walled with plywood or... plastered.

Mary was anxious to tackle some building of her own, and looked forward to adding a wing for a bedroom. Before the summer of 1940 hit them, she had it completed, *"pushed and pulled and prodded into shape around us like a robin building her nest."* The particularly welcome rush of guests included Frank, her husband Mo, daughter Janet and their Scottie dog as well as Mary's cousins Mary Ellen and Aline and friends (all of whom came as paying dudes). The homestead cabin became a dining hall and Joe and Mary moved into the new three-room cabin which felt like a palace.

Although somewhat disappointed by the dude business that first summer after the move, they reckoned they did as well as they could with only three cabins and no advertising. Progress in paving the last few miles of the main road put the Rocker Y on a detour, which made it hard for casual tourists to find them. The march of troops in Europe alarmed many Americans, and one family had canceled, afraid to leave home.

Nevertheless time just sped by, and suddenly fall approached before they had time to think about winterizing their palatial cabin. The cracks between the logs needed sealing, and it was now too cold to use mortar and apply it outside. Mary made up a mix of ashes, salt and water and daubed all the cracks on the inside, including those high up under the roof line where the bitter west wind pushed itself inside. The little stove roared at full throttle below scorching her feet, while her hands nearly froze. Mary's niece, Eleanor, who had come for an unexpected visit got called on to help.

Miriam's seventeen-year-old daughter had materialized out of the thin blue mountain air one Saturday evening as Mary fumbled with the key to open the door to the Dubois library.

It developed that some neighbors were driving out this way, and took her along. They were visiting with some of their friends and relatives and would leave her with us for three days. Five of them had come from Nebraska in a pick-up - two men in the cab, Eleanor and a boy and girl about her age wrapped in blankets in the back. The youngsters at least were having a perfect picnic.

As we got acquainted, it seemed that three days was a terribly short time to have her here. She was very enthusiastic about staying, and it did sound as if she could be spared awhile. So we let the neighbors go home without her, and we don't yet know what Miriam will have to say. I guess it's something in the nature of a kidnapping. It sure seems odd to have such a grown-up young person addressing me as Aunt Mary!...

So Eleanor oiled the walls while Mary tackled the floor, using a mix of turpentine, boiled linseed oil and paraffin *"put on as hot as you can stand it"* to produce easy-care surfaces. Eleanor fit right in, helping with chores, giving Mary some precious moments to herself. After admiring Mary's rag wagon wheel rug, Eleanor asked timidly if she could learn how to create such a rug as a gift for her mother.

So I got at my semi-annual clothes-sorting, and we had a sort of carpet-rag spree. She took the pile of discards from the still-wearables, sorted them into colors, studied them for half an hour or so with complete concentration. (She had already asked me about the principle of weaving on the wagon tire as a frame and I had made her a sketch or two of different types of patterns.) Then she got out a pencil and paper, and in another half-hour or so had a most interesting design worked out. When it was done, she efficiently packed in a flour sack for me to store all the colors she wouldn't use, and started making rolls of carpet rags from the others. Now she is putting her design together, and I must say it is ever so much better than mine, both in basic pattern and in workmanship. There are eight spokes about three inches wide, closely woven of dark reddish brown. The pie-shaped spaces between are filled with a pattern of arrowheads fitting into each other, in turquoise, tangerine, orchid, and ecru. It's going to be really stunning....

Eleanor had quite an education in 'make-do living,' which came naturally to her as she had faced much economizing at home in the Sand Hills of Nebraska. Those days with Mary and Joe were decisive. She arrived just a kid, and became so much more as she became engrossed in the Backs' lives. They treated her as an adult and involved her in working out the steady procession of problems and chores that occurred on a dude ranch. Watching Mary's artistic energy inspired Eleanor to try some efforts of her own, with Mary's enthusiastic encouragement. She went home a much more confident young woman.

Then Joe and Mary settled back into their busy-every-minute lifestyle. They even invited the Dubois High School - a grand total of thirty students - for a post-Christmas snow party. The school was new to Dubois, as the first class of three graduated the prior June. It snowed all day, really a blizzard part of the time, but the *"powerfully lively gang of kids tumbled around as gay as you please. Skiing was pretty good, and skating all up and down the Wind River was wonderful. We sure enjoyed those kids, and they acted as if they had fun."*

But mostly hard work prevailed.

We're getting along the same as usual, grubbing along, doing everything ourselves to save money, planning twice what's possible, using extra efforts and doing about three-fourths of the plan, then feeling mad because we didn't get the rest done.... I sure laughed at Joe this evening. He came in all tired out and swearing reminiscently. 'I made a resolve,' he said, 'not to work so hard today, and then when I got in the timber I forgot all about it!' You might say he forgets his res-olutions the hard way.

Even so, this year brought a new attitude. They took time off for a March vacation. Heading for the big city of Casper with their nearest neighbors, the Weeks, the Backs decided to look for a car.

It was quite a time for hillbillies like us. Casper is about the size of Rutland, and a real metropolis, as the only 'large city' in a radius of several hundred miles... We've been dri-ving the 1927 Buick sedan-pickup renovation, and lately begun to have various motor troubles.... A Buick's motor is the last thing to go wrong, so we decided it was about the end.... We decided not to...trade in the Buick. Cars its age are quoted at about $15, and we could probably, if we wait, get a much better trade for a horse and saddle, or stock feed, or something else that Joe could use.

So I dry-cleaned Joe's wide hat, washed and pressed and stitched up the rents in our humble best, packed a full set of old warm clothes...just in case. We bathed and cleaned up fit to kill - you would love to have seen Old Bruin and his wife getting ready for TOWN. I was sinfully proud of Joe's masterful look in his suit and overcoat - about the fourth time he's had them on these last six years. The Weeks were equally impressive....

So we went to Casper. We stayed in a HOTEL, went to a MOVIE, ate three meals in RESTAURANTS, and BOUGHT A CAR.... We discovered several things that made home more desirable. It may have been an illusion, but both of us thought the lower altitude was depressing. Window shop-ping was by no means as much fun as catalog shopping. And when you see Casperites en masse, it's amazing how many of them have the pale, bland, large-faced, thick-bodied, smug look that we of the mountains have come to think typical of

Casperites (from the trickle that we know)!

Anyhow, we brought home a car,… a six-year-old Chevrolet, two-door sedan, dark blue. To our untutored eyes, it looks positively scrumptious. It had been turned in only the day before and nothing had been done to it.… We tested it pretty thoroughly, even (met) and talked with the former owner, a fragile tiny blond who said she didn't have any trouble with it, just wanted a new car. We proved to our-selves that there wasn't a knock in the engine, even in high on a steep hill; that there wasn't blue smoke in the exhaust; and that the frame had never been sprung.

The trip back home really tested the car as they had to tra-verse mostly unplowed roads in dense fog. They averaged twenty miles to the gallon and felt very proud of their new possession.

They came to regret this foray into crowds as they both came down with miserable colds (flu?) that really laid them up. All the energy they could muster they used to *"feed the horses and chickens and us and wash the dishes."* To make matters worse Mary went out in the snow without dark glasses and got her first taste of snow blindness. The curtains had to be drawn while she covered her eyes with dark glasses and a wide black woolen mask with tiny eye-holes. *"I look like a highwayman,"* she reported to Frank. Even as she suffered from this ailment, she still paid close attention to the life of the ranch, particularly enjoying watching the horses on a stormy day after Joe called them through a howling wind to come get feed.

Soon through the murk of the storm I saw heads and ears peeking over the edge of the steep hill above the barn, and then they were plunging down through the snow. It was a lovely sight. The broncs are so graceful anyway, and the wind lifted their manes and tails, and the snow swirled around them as they lifted their feet, and they were all so eager!

Thankfully by late March they both had recovered enough to start their summer preparations even though school affairs took over their lives that spring. As the town librarian, Mary found her-self at the center of an effort to secede from the Lander High School District. Angry Dubois voices accused the Lander School Board of treating the four-year-old Dubois High School very poorly. Dubois folks thought they could do a better job of running the school and scheduled a vote to decide the matter.

In order to pass, law required the yes votes had to equal more than fifty-one percent of the vote in the district in the preceding general election. The numbers voting in the presidential election the previous fall had been much larger than usual; swollen by lumberjacks, hunters and a large highway crew. Meeting the challenge of getting enough voters out in the spring took dedication.

Mary helped organize efforts to roundup possible voters and then get them across the muddy roads to reach the polls.

By working hard, sending out circulars, talking to every single potential voter, and promising cars to pick up folks (who sometimes had to walk or ride horseback as far as five miles each way to get to where a car could meet them), sixty-seven voters voted yes - just a hair above the sixty-one needed. Afterwards Mary breathed a sigh of relief and agreed that every vote sure counted that day.

Mary Ellen and four friends returned for three weeks in 1941, another busy dude season which also brought my father Milton, my mother and my sister and I. Ten guests at a time filled the ranch now; enough to keep Joe and Mary busy without having to hire help (although a high school girl did help with meals and dishes

*"That summer (of 1941) was very special," noted Mary Ellen
on this picture. Mary is seated on the ground
next to her cousin, Mary Ellen Lindley.*

this year). These family guests brought Mary great joy, making up for the disappointment she and Joe felt when a much hoped for art school camp at the Rocker Y planned by an artist friend did not materialize.

We've done quite a bit of exploring, finding new trails up into the mountains. More and more we realize what fascinating country is opened up by trails from here. (Mary Ellen and friends) took a three-day pack trip into the high Absaroka country beyond the Pinnacles. I couldn't go, for there were several guests left at the ranch. You should have seen the excitement when they came riding back. There were twelve horses in the train, and seven riders. They came in along Elk Ridge at a good clean trot, and when they came near the gate pandemonium broke out. The horses left at the place went tearing across the meadow, manes and tails flying, and shouting 'howdy';…the ones coming in answered them just as loud and excitedly. And everyone was waving and shouting and apparently in highest spirits. We had a party for the whole crowd that evening, starting with an enormous supper, which disappeared…in just no time at all….

The most exciting single happening for me, I think, was the breaking of the brown filly, Clown. She is a tall, slim brown thing, with a white diamond on her nose, and white hind feet…. Joe had let me get her familiar with all the equipment - halter first, then the pad and saddle, then the bit and bridle, then with me mounting and dismounting time and time again. But he wouldn't let me stir her out of a stand. He said there was no telling what she would do if she suddenly found herself walking with the new strange weight on her back. It was very exciting to see her ridden for the first time. She never even ventured to buck! The funny thing was that she wouldn't even move at first. I began to think she might be a naturally slow and balky horse. But it appeared that she was just figuring on doing what was expected of her, and I had convinced her previously that she was supposed to stand stock-still when a human climbed on her! Joe had to ride her with spurs at first. But even that didn't scare her. She acted as if she were only bewildered because she didn't understand what the big idea was. After two rides spurs weren't needed, and now she is obedient as an old broke horse to a little tap with your heel. At the same time she is plumb full of pep and life. And when you get off her she turns and sticks her slim soft muzzle under your arm.

Summer rains broke all records. Haying became difficult, roads washed out and "the red badlands are rimmed with green grass which looks very odd and unnatural; makes you think of mold on Roquefort cheese." Joe was apt to tell the dudes, "We've had enough rain to drown Hitler, Muscle-enie, and Stall-ine and all the armies" and then he grinned.

The other animals on the ranch that year included the dogs - Violet, Stubby and Bozo - and a newcomer cat. The dogs were in a peck of trouble for they had taken to chasing the cows that roamed the nearby hills in the summer.

And that, in this country, is one of the seven deadly sins for a dog. I should say ranked third. Dogs get shot pronto for getting rabies, or killing sheep, or running cattle. And because we think that we caught them before the habit was too well estab-lished, we are try-ing to break them by keeping them tied most of the time, and letting them off only one at a time. I will sure be thankful when Cross (the cattle owner)... cleans the cattle out from these hills.

The cat attached herself to Violet like an unwanted burr. It tickled Mary to watch their interactions.

The demon-strations of cat

Joe with a stack of freshly milled boards

psychology are interesting. Ours is intent only on her own comfort, which she arrogantly takes as her right.... Apparently a part of her comfort depends on a placid and friendly atmosphere, so her actions are tempered by the discretion called for to maintain that atmosphere. Friendliness with Violet has been her worst problem, which she has set herself steadfastly to solve. For some time now she has been at the stage where Violet will permit her to sleep against her side, or even under her chin. Funniest time was the other day when an east wind blew and the floor was cold. Violet was on a rug, but even that didn't suffice for kitty. We saw her calmly sleeping across Violet's middle, like a wide orange belt!

But Violet has, while accepting her attentions, been steadfastly refusing to reciprocate. Her reactions at the start varied from anger at the cat to shocked horror at us that we could do that to her. She has very slowly progressed through the stages of armed neutrality to sullen resignation to calm acceptance. But yesterday I shouted with glee when the cat made noises at the door and Violet very plainly asked me to let the cat in! When I did the two marched over side by side to the stove and lay down together. So I guess Kitty won.

The arrival of fall always meant hunting season: time to get their winter supply of meat. While Joe guided dudes in hunting camp for pay, he and Mary also needed time to go off into the mountains to search for their own elk, deer, or moose. In 1939 Mary wrote:

We've had several hunting trips, in which I learned a whole lot of new country and had a whale of a time. From which we brought back our winter meat - one bull elk, one yearling elk, and one buck deer. I could grow quite lyrical about the exquisite taste of the meat. We hadn't had one piece of real meat since the last dudes left the first of September.... You can't imagine how hungry you get for it; how the thought of a thick juicy steak makes your mouth water. When we got our first, we just gorged on meat, had two or three slices of steak a piece, three times a day. (A few days later I began to wonder at a sudden and unprecedented eruption of pimples!) Now we are almost back to normal....

The trips were most exciting, too, in themselves. I had two bad scares - one from men I foolishly imagined were bandits, and one from a bull moose, too independent and at too close quarters. I learned the difficult art of achieving privacy when there were two men and me, together with a stove, firewood, water, and food boxes, all in a seven by nine foot tent - in a snowstorm! And I surely did enjoy being in a great expanse of absolutely virgin timber.... And really stupendous piled-up mountains all around.

Weather made all the difference. When clear skies and mild weather continued right into December, the game animals disappeared high in the mountains away from the hunters. Finding their game and getting a successful shot took a lot of patience. Both Joe and Mary really admired the game they pursued. They needed the meat but thrilled to the wild lives and beauty. Mary counted the days in fall 1941 until she could join Joe adventuring into the mountains.

First we tried Long Creek.... The first and second days of the season we got up at 3 a.m., had breakfast by lamplight, saddled up in the frosty darkness, and were over in the parks up the East Fork...in the early dawn light. It was all very exasperating. Only a few days before we had seen 27 (elk) in one bunch on that same hill... spotted 'em while we were eating breakfast. But that hill is closed territory, and the elk knew it. Over in the legal country we saw, the first day, many fresh tracks and sign, and six elk at different times, all wilder by far than rabbits - wild like foxes. We never saw one long enough to take a shot, and we were in mortal fear that one of the other hunters

Mary hunting

should take a shot at us. I nearly passed out from fright one time when a gun went off nearby, at the same instant that I saw my shadow and realized that the ends of the bandanna I had on my head had come untucked and stood up for all the world like a pair of ears! At the end of the day, when the sun had set and the shooting light was over, we disgustedly turned our horses homeward. Just outside the open territory I saw the first fresh deer sign of the whole day.

'Joe,' I called, 'these tracks and sign are so fresh the deer must be right ahead of us.' I looked up, and there they were! Four does and a buck, jumping along lightly, turning to watch us, safe on the hill closed for hunting, and not scared at all. They knew same as we did, I guess, that a warden was camped at Cross' cow camp for the season, in easy hearing of gunshot on the hill. Just then Joe spied a big bull elk against the darkening sky, and looking closer we counted seven cows with him. He raised his head and I swear he thumbed his nose at us....

We decided it was dumb to hunt where there was access from the highway, when we had loads of country available that would be more exclusive. We hired a couple to stay on the ranch, and arranged for a substitute at the library. We laid out grub for five days, routed out the tent and made sure the sleeping bags and mattresses were sound, saddled the horses and loaded the camp stuff and the oats on the four pack horses, and set off for the wild country to the south. Joe rode Tony and I rode Clown.... Several times Clown acted as if she had bronky ideas. Once she really tried to buck.... It was a good thing for us both, that trip. Clown learned a lot about being a horse, and I a lot about riding.

We camped back of Fish Lake Mountain on the Pacific slope, about twenty miles from home and about as far from any ranches on that side. All five days we saw nobody else. The second day we each got our elk; then it took three days to get all the meat and camp in. They were enormous creatures.... Must have been lazy lummoxes, though, for the meat seems very tender. Joe's was a nice 6-point bull and mine a spike, but mine was a lot heavier.

I broke camp while Joe packed the meat. We took the

four front quarters and part of the camp stuff across the Divide to the nearest park fit to camp in on the other side - toward home. Then Joe dropped the packs, left me to care for the meat and make camp, and went back to get the hind quarters and the rest of the camp supplies. It was very exciting for me. I had to pick the campsite, pitch the tent, and everything. Joe got in with the pack string about dark. I felt very smart to have a fire lighting up the tent, a big pile of firewood ready, and liver and bacon with onions cooking in the Dutch oven for him!

With dude season over and the meat supply stashed, Joe and Mary's art interests could again claim them. Mary mulled how to create Mother Goose Rhyme illustrations for Dorothy and Frank's children.

It was just lots of fun…. I suppose because of all that time spent thinking about them, they went just like clockwork, as if they had to be the way they are, as if there were no choice of color, composition, or anything else. Monday I drew them all and inked in some of them. Yesterday I finished with the ink and colored all but one, which I finished this morning….

I hope my interpretation of the rhymes will suit. Mistress Mary is of course a mocking rhyme…. So it occurred to me that the 'pretty maids all in a row' could very well be a bunch of brats who were singing the song and pulling Mary's flowers. The pigtails will indicate that Mary is a somewhat prettified version of Aunt Mary herself. Perhaps it's a misleading interpretation to give an innocent child…. (See Sketch 10)

By late November 1941 Joe had discovered small-scale sculpting.

Stormy days, evenings when he's not too tired, and now and then whole days when he can't bear to stop it, he has been modeling small animals, heads or the whole critters. I have been learning to cast them in plaster and put on different finishes: bronze, silver, enamel, and so on. We are anxious to try casting some in plastic. We hope to have a bunch to sell next summer…. You should see them standing around on the tables and windowsills: grizzly mother with cubs, grizzly breaking open a tin can, cute little bears sitting… heads of elk.

My art work is somewhat different. For summer sale I
am working up some small carvings in elk and moose horn.
But my biggest interest right now is a mural-sized painting of
elk by a mountain lake for one of the hotels in town -
Stringers…. It's a funny deal. Last winter Joe bought his oats
from Albert Stringer. But Albert, known as the stingiest man
in town, has three times refused hard cash for those oats. He
wanted one or both of us to finish…an old painting he'd
been hanging onto for years - one that had been started by a
'buckeye' painter who dumped it out with his junk, and
Albert rescued off his trash heap. The first two times we

Sketch Ten   *Mistress Mary*

argued with him how impossible the idea was, but the third time we brought the dang thing home, tied to the roof of the car, sticking off in all directions. The only thing to do seemed to be to paint out all the original monstrosity and start over with the same general composition. The drawing was rotten, the color peculiar... but the thing that made it impossible was that he had the sun visible in his sky. I think that was why he threw it away, struggling to work around that sun.

Well, I got to work on the problem.... I began with a small black-and-white drawing, using the same composition but what I thought was a better balance of masses, with the sunlight coming from off at one side. By then it got to be fun, so I made a big watercolor study. It was more fun all the time, getting those elk with the early morning sunshine brilliant on them, the big lake behind them, the shores, the great mountains in the background. In a way it's a sort of sentimental and calendar subject, but heck, I've seen elk just about that way, and it's a real experience to put them down on paper. Now I'm at the stage where the old mural is covered up, the drawing done, and the painting started in oil. I can hardly keep from working at it by lamplight. When it is done it will perhaps be a greater monstrosity than the old one, but at least I will have had a lot of fun. If it's any good, it should be worth a lot more than the oats, except for the fun I get from it.

As Mary and Joe worked in the quiet cabin that November they had no inkling that in just a few days happenings in the Pacific Ocean would send their dude ranch plans and art dreams up in the smoke of falling bombs.

Mary's Way

The War Effort

❖　❖　❖　❖　❖

Even back country Wyoming felt the impact of the Japanese attack on Pearl Harbor on December 7, 1941. War! Mary and Joe huddled by the radio; the news crackling across the room. As the new year got underway, plans for another successful dude summer looked impossible. Day after day reports of gearing up for war reached them. What could they do? Would Joe get drafted? If not, maybe he could do something to help the war effort.

While they puzzled over their world turned topsy-turvy, Mary came down with a cold so severe she went to bed. She might not be on the front lines, but her body definitely felt under attack. With the closest doctor over a hundred miles away, Joe gave him a call when her temperature reached 102. The doctor suggested perhaps she better come to the hospital in Lander. Mary didn't really feel so badly and rather enjoyed Joe's wrapping her up in blankets, and stuffing pillows in all the chinks along the car doors.

We had a grand ride down. I loved it: the first fifty miles down the canyons in the sunset, the late sunset, and the twilight; the last fifty over the high sage plains in the moonlight, with the aloof snowy Wind River range stretching endlessly along on the right (And Palm Sunday music on the radio!).

They put me to bed and temperatured and stethoscoped me and asked me 200 questions, more or less. Then they said it wasn't pneumonia, just a chest cold, but they had better go after it with sulfa thiozol.... But Mary was contrary....

Seems I'm not one of the happy souls sulfa works miracles on. My temperature started up and up, clear out of sight, I got a splitting, blinding headache, so they had to give me hypos to get me to sleep. They took an x-ray and the doctor looked at it and said 'Well!' It was pneumonia.

Still I wasn't a proper pneumonia patient. I didn't have chills…and I didn't fight for breath…and even when I was sickest my food tasted good. After a while my temperature seemed to reach the stratospheric height it was aiming for (103.6) and dropped down. The doc said…I should have been limp and practically out of my head, not reading Charlie Chan and exchanging pleasantries with doctors and nurses. Doggone!

During her days of high fever when she may have been delirious, Mary later recalled a vivid dream, nightmare, vision or hallucination that she reported with awe, wondering what it suggested about her subconscious.

I was a part of the Aztec hierarchy, and my job was Inspector of Sacrifice. I was standing on top of one of those big steep pyramids looking toward the sunset, and in front of me, right on the edge, was a huge feathered serpent of stone with a big wide open mouth I could see the sunset through. Between me and the serpent were two priests in gorgeous robes and each had a heavy stone sledgehammer…in his hand. In the mouth of the serpent was some kind of pulley, and over it went an endless belt whose other pulley was down at the bottom of the pyramid in the dungeons of the prisoners of war. Assistants down there were busily tying prisoners, one behind the other, to the endless belt…. I gave a hand signal for the sacrifice to start. The belt moved, bringing a captive headfirst through the mouth of the serpent. One priest stepped forward, moving stiffly and rhythmically as in a ritualistic dance, raised his sledge…and whanged the captive on the head. Blood poured forth, the priest retired, the belt moved on, another head appeared in the serpent's mouth, the other priest moved forward and whanged it, more blood, and the belt moved on. I watched it critically, checking chiefly the ritual of the priests, until suddenly I noticed that the head coming through the serpents mouth had already been whanged. The belt had gone full circle. I stepped forward, gestured for the priests to stop, gave them a kind word -'O.K. That's all, boys. Good job.'

The medical arsenal available to combat pneumonia hardly existed in 1942, which often made it a life-threatening disease. Those who lived, experienced this kind of crisis and recovered, but not usually with Mary's remarkable enthusiasm and imagination.

As she recuperated, Joe spent his days at the ranch worrying about her and their precarious finances. This hospitalization was digging deep into their savings, and he doubted they could count on much coming in from the coming dude season. The more he thought about it, the more certain he became that after Mary recovered he must go where he could make money working for the war effort. The doctor warned Joe that Mary had anemia and had lost weight while sick. She needed to eat well to rebuild herself. Since they usually scrimped on their food bill, Joe just didn't know how they could manage unless he sought war work.

Once home at the Rocker Y, Mary took awhile to bounce back. Folding clean clothes a few days after she came home gave her so much pain she could hardly move her arms. Weeks later when she first tried sweeping the floor she had to stop, it hurt so to breathe. Scared, she felt her back muscles and could feel the pain there, not inside. Hungry all the time, she felt guilty, thinking about the people suffering on Corregidor for lack of food. Joe worked harder than ever, helping her and tying up loose ends around the ranch. To Mary's delight he cut out a four- by five-foot window hole in the west wall of their cabin, doubling the light in the room and letting **"the whole of the upper valley come right into the living room."**

They talked a lot about Joe's idea of working in a war-related industry to put bread on their table. While she couldn't argue with him, she felt so empty when she thought about living without him around. It just made her ache inside. Then he learned he could sign up for a course in welding at a government defense school in Casper. Since he had welded much of the ranch machinery, this sounded like just the thing for him. By June Mary felt well enough and strong enough to think she could take over running the ranch with a hired man to give a hand.

Joe took the course and returned full of news. In Oakland, California he could get a job working at Kaiser's, building Liberty ships. There were tears, and they hugged, regretting this necessary separation. Then they got him ready to go.

She wanted to join him, but they had no idea what they would do about the ranch - the horses, the dogs, cats and chickens.

Mary certainly kept busy. She grubbed a lot of sagebrush off the prospective hay meadow, tore down some unused fence and built new sections. She built a coal bin, enclosed the back porch with glass, improved the chicken house, tightened up a guest cabin and finished daubing the west wall of their house. She proudly created the window to fill Joe's window opening. Chores seemed endless: chickens and horses to attend to; coal to knock into small pieces and strong-arm into the house; wood collected and hauled up with a horse, then sawed, split and carried in; and water to haul up in barrels with horse and sled. Not very sure of herself around the workhorses, she became confident in how to handle them and manage their harnesses. Her hired help was Lester Shippen.

(He) is quite a kid, and a lot of company. He is fifteen, and undersized. I think he is just now beginning to really grow. But he has the imagination of half a dozen kids. There are projects constantly underway. He likes to paint and draw, fish and shoot, ride and swim, and Lord knows what besides. This is his first job, and he's doing quite well at it. I think I am lucky to have him. Right now I am appreciating him; for he has a week at home…and I am just finding out how much time he has been saving me by doing the chores.

A little dude business cropped up after all: three weekend fishing parties in July and the Wasson family, Mary's good friends from Trailside Museum days, for the month of August. This reunion with these professional geologists taught Mary indispensable lessons about the ancient past of the world around her.

Joe had given her such good lessons in horse packing, that she took the Wassons on a six-day pack trip into wild remote country where she learned firsthand from them about the rocky terrain while she rejoiced in her ability to guide them successfully. Later, when Joe heard about her mountain adventuring, he called her his "Mountain Gal (an awfully nice one) who must be related to both Jim Bridger or Fremont the explorer." While Joe made good money working deep in the bellies of new war ships, he sure did miss Wyoming and his Mountain Mary.

With the tourist trade way down in the Wind River Valley, an even more serious problem became the absence of men; the few remaining stayed because of responsibilities they couldn't leave. This made doing most any kind of business difficult. Mary reported to her Robin audience how all of this affected the valley.

One day I was invited to dinner at the Diamond G, which is…the largest resort in the valley, with accommodations for about one hundred…. I was appalled by the vast open spaces in the dining room. There were only eleven eating there, and six of us were at the owner's table! The feeling of emptiness was almost uncanny there….

There is a ranch near us…which has always been a fairly pretentious place. There are nearly a thousand acres of good hay land in the bottoms and they run several hundred head of cattle - controlling all the drainage of West DuNoir for their summer range…. But this summer all they could get for help was (a) 'dissolute old sot' and two (young teenagers)…. Bill Pickett and the three 'hands' ran the ranch (chores, milking, fencing, irrigating, and putting up the thousand acres of hay). Bill got his mother to come cook for them and look after the two little girls. And (his wife) Esther, who is a slender girlish person several years younger than I, went up to the cow camp in the mountains, and all alone managed the herd. We met her on the job when I took the pack outfit down West DuNoir…. She described …how she had the herd broken up into little bunches of about thirty head, cows and calves with one bull…. Each bunch was ranging up a separate draw. She had to ride all the draws… to check on each bunch, be sure they were well fixed for grass, water, and salt, and that nothing was amiss with any of them…. Believe me, she knew her watersheds and the arrangement of her herd!…

Albert Stringer was in the library the other day, going on a bit about the problems of running a hotel these days…. I was quite shocked to find out that the Stringers had been unable to get a cook or housekeeper for some time, and that Albert and his brother Oscar (both bachelors of about sixty-odd years) were now doing all the cooking and cleaning! This afternoon I stopped in to get some milk. Oscar, looking fraz-

zled but still triumphant, was wiping dishes alone in the big kitchen. He said with quiet pride, 'They was five of them stopped in at two-thirty for dinner. Five of 'em. And y' know, by three-thirty I was about ready to clean up.'

By fall, Mary luxuriated in the beautiful colors even more than usual as she had made plans to join Joe in California. She wasn't sure exactly when she might return. When she could, she lingered outside to enjoy the landscape, or stared appreciatively out the new window.

Here and there a whole willow bush has ripened into gold, and a few quaker leaves are brilliant. The fields and pastures are bright tawny, the leaves of the cinquefoil are rich red, and the skies are blue as blue. Every morning there is ice on the priming pump by the pail.... Except for being with Joe again (which is the most important thing, anyway) I do hate to go away.

Almost miraculously she had found a good man, a veteran of the Spanish American War, known simply as Honolulu, who would caretake the Rocker Y for the winter. As soon as he finished his job checking out hunters he would arrive and she would head for Oakland. *"He seems to be well educated, is very clean, and doesn't drink, which is noteworthy for Dubois"* so she could leave comfortable that the ranch would be in good hands.

She climbed aboard the bus with a lump in her throat, after stashing her bulging suitcase. She hated to leave, and yet...and yet...she could hardly wait to see Joe! Days later in San Francisco they launched their California adventure - together again.

They set up housekeeping in an apartment on Chattanooga Street in San Francisco with opposing views of the bay and high green hills. It didn't take her long to find a job as an entry level mechanic (called a mechanic's helper) at United Airlines. Both Joe and Mary traveled by long bus rides to their respective jobs, and they didn't see very much of each other. With Mary working the day shift (with Sunday off) and Joe on the swing shift (with Tuesday off), they only saw each other at breakfast which they shared at two-thirty in the morning. They also savored their Sunday mornings together and Tuesday evenings. While not ideal, it beat living in two separate states!

San Francisco captivated Mary and she delighted in the

exploring she did, especially on Sunday afternoons after Joe had gone off to work. With the mountains and the open space, she could almost imagine she was in Wyoming.

...It's wonderful for my soul that I can get out afoot from the house to high and deserted points where I can look off for miles. This is surely an Alice-in-Wonderland city. For all that it's truly cosmopolitan, it's oddly countrified. Cows and horses and goats graze here and there on the wild oats and grass that grow enthusiastically on the steep hills above the houses. Ships in gray war paint, big full-rigged sailing vessels, and speedy PT boats move about the bay. You see sailors from many nations on the streets, and soldiers with wide bands of service ribbons.... This afternoon I climbed through shifting veils of fog down a steep hill...only a mile or so from way downtown. The wind whipped my hair, gulls flew about, my shoes filled with sand, and I was mostly pre-occupied with avoiding the poison ivy and the long canes of wild blackberry, now in bloom. And not another soul was anywhere on the slope!...

The architecture continually astonishes me - the thou-sand devices used to fit houses to the peculiar slopes they occupy. On a walk last Sunday I passed a house on a corner lot, coming from the back.... I was high above the back yard, and going steeply downhill. I could look about eight feet down into a delightful back yard, where narrow terraces held roses and carrots, irises and cabbages, very companion-ably. By the time I reached the corner I'd dropped so I was outside a high retaining wall and could see nothing of the place. I turned the corner and went a few steps to where there was a grilled front gate in the wall. Inside it, steps went steeply up a full flight to the front door! (At) another place a neat flight of brick steps with a brick railing twisted and turned to get up a rock cliff at least forty feet high. On top was a cute little house with an enormous front window. I thought 'Oh, oh, I'm getting into the high-class arty section.' But there was a sign in the big window, and when I came closer I could read 'LADIES DRESS-MAKING'!

Perhaps it's the terrain that has something to do with San Franciscans being so unconventional. Perhaps the war...

or the turbulent history of the city…has something to do with it. Anyway, it's interesting and most unexpected.…

It's sharp and clear for a change, and the blue pattern of the bay, the white-speckled towns on the further shores, the slender webs of the bridges, the ranges of the Berkeley Hills in soft and intricate violet folds, with Mt. Diablo poked up in back - all made quite a picture. I can't get used to the oddi-ties of this climate. Judging from the flowers, it's not tropical at all, in spite of a few stumpy palms. The flowers are famil-iar, really almost the same as the ones we knew in Vermont. But they mix the seasons up so. I saw growing almost within arms' reach…wild iris, buttercups, roses and goldenrod! On the ledgy stretches were dwarf wild blackberries in full bloom. All that richly waving grass over the hills above the crowded houses makes you think what a wonderful stock country it must have been in the days of the Spaniards.

One thing I had been dreading…was the bright lights. So many years of living where the night was velvet black if the moon and stars were hidden, without even one neigh-bor's light in view - had made me selfish. (I dreaded) to have the sky hidden by the city glow. But the 'dim-out' changed all that. The streets are lighted only enough to guide your steps. When I leave for work in the blackness before the dawn, I tell you it really is dark. From the street car I can't read the street names at the corners.… They have heavily painted the top half of each street light - no, the top two-thirds. No shop or theater signs are allowed.… So everything is quite pleasant-ly obscured, the stars shine peacefully visible, the strings of lights on the hills are picturesque without being in any way obnoxious.…

Supremely happy with her job, Mary knew the only thing that could make life better would be more time with Joe. But the job was wonderful!

I feel it's really doing essential war work, helping to repair the big planes. It enables me to use much of the expe-rience I gained on the ranch, and is constantly teaching me more that I can use when I go back. It's active work, keeping my muscles busy and…gives me a legitimate excuse to wear Levis and shirts and…get my hands dirty.… I can't under-

*stand why I never got greatly interested in mechanics before.
I think it's fascinating. I spend all my time around engines
and parts of engines, learning more every day, and soaking it
up as if I were parched for it....*

After two months on the job she got a raise, and began studying a correspondence course in aircraft engines. Dreaming of getting her aircraft mechanic's rating, she could hardly wait to start
physics and then the electricity home-study courses. *"With all the
family interest in such subjects, why on earth didn't I get started
before,"* she wondered.

> *Let me make it clear that I'm not working in a factory....
> I work at an overhaul base...for the Air Transport
> Command.... It's always much more interesting to handle
> used rather than new parts - parts that already have a histo-
> ry, that have had things happen to them, and carry the
> marks.... Our planes come back again and again. We get to
> know them. We know their pilots and flight mechanics. We
> hear about the performances of the big craft. Our own work
> comes back to our hands, and we learn if it was done well or
> ill.... The responsibility is rather frightening at times, as it
> may well involve men's lives, but it is certainly exhilarating
> too.*

The fast pace of this new San Francisco life pushed Mary to
think about a new look. Handling those braids that needed to be
done freshly each day and firmly attached circling her head, took
too much time. Besides, Joe encouraged her to think about getting
a permanent. Finally, off she went to a beauty parlor's *"chamber of
horrors,"* and came back with a head full of curls. When she looked
in the mirror she kept thinking she saw her sister Frank. All that
hair at the back of her neck worried her, but since Joe liked the
fluffy style, Mary guessed she could adapt to it.

Even with the tyranny of their long work hours, they both
found some precious time to paint and sculpt. Working up some
Wyoming landscape sketches into full paintings provided Mary a
great release from city life. Joe relaxed modeling horses and bear.
Working the clay until an animal emerged, brought a whistle to his
lips and a sparkle to his eyes. All in all, they were content.

In April 1943, someone had to return to the ranch to make new
arrangements, as Honolulu had to go on to other work. Mary set

off flying half-fare to Salt Lake but on the return trip got bumped by priority mail and had to take the thirty-hour bus ride back. That first flight in an airplane filled her with excitement, while at the same time gave her pause as she wondered who had checked its mechanical parts! Back home she found that while the Wind River Valley had suffered from a very hard winter, spring with its greening grass and horses returning to pasture was at hand. She just couldn't find anyone to take Honolulu's place. Finally in desperation she asked Frankie Moriarty if she could serve as caretaker for awhile. After Frankie agreed Mary hurried back to San Francisco.

Unfortunately, the arrangement just didn't work out, and finally Frankie wrote that some horses appeared to be missing and the grass didn't look good - someone better come. So in September, Joe quit his job and went to check things out. While the horses and grass looked all right, nobody wanted to caretake. After staying a month - in which he busied himself shoring up the bridge, and building a barn - he found a winter home for the horses and arranged for someone to keep an eye on the ranch. As he pondered the problem, he decided they would just have to find work closer to home so they could keep track of the ranch situation.

Whatever were they going to do? After asking around they discovered that they both could get jobs in Cheyenne, Wyoming, 350 miles from Dubois at United Airlines facilities there. Joe found work in the sheet metal shop and Mary, while hoping for a job just like she had in California, settled for working in the engine overhaul shop. This allowed her to get the experience she needed to qualify to take the tests to become a licensed airplane mechanic.

She could hardly contain her excitement about her good fortune in having access to the United courses. *"Meteorology, trigonometry, celestial navigation, radio communication"* - the words tumbled from her lips as she described all the possibilities she could take. She was currently eagerly studying basic math, beginning physics, and airplane engines. As she completed each topic, off it would go to the Chicago office for correction and comment; back would come new lessons. Mary just couldn't understand why she had always avoided such technical subjects - and now getting that mechanic's license looked very possible.

After an unsettled summer, they made the move, thankful to

be at least in the same state as the Rocker Y. Cheyenne was a big letdown after San Francisco. While Mary enjoyed her job and they could even walk to work, they disliked the housing. FHA apartments at Frontier Park offered tiny living spaces for over a thousand war workers attracted there. Long low buildings with eight apartments in a unit, spread out across the former Indian village of Cheyenne's famous rodeo grounds. While adequate and warm, their apartment had no room for the nine- by twelve-foot rug they had brought from San Francisco. They cut it into two pieces in order to use it. A windowless L off the living room served as the kitchen, and the windowless bathroom even lacked a wash basin!

Mary and Joe in Cheyenne during World War II

While Joe just put in his time at work, Mary came home each day pleased as punch with what she had done, and what she had learned.

They set me at tearing down engines to begin with - about the dirtiest job I ever got into, but certainly the best way to get the hand of the way they are built.... (The engines) weigh 1500 pounds apiece without any accessories. It's wonderful how you can get to handle them....

(There are) tracks all over the ceiling and chain hoists hanging from them.. Nobody lifts any very heavy parts. You set the switches right, drag a chain hoist along its track to where you want it, fasten a lifting eye to your crankshaft (or whatever) put the hook of the hoist through that eye, and pull it right up by the lifting chain. That way I can do as much as anyone else....

After a few weeks of pulling engines apart, and arranging the parts in orderly fashion (and that is no joke, for you must never mix any two engines up in any of their parts...), the foreman moved me to final assembly.... That's very interesting and quite responsible, putting all the cases together, installing the cylinders, timing the engine, getting it so it will run; then installing it in the test stand and seeing if it runs; and finally servicing it for storage....

One of the real benefits of Cheyenne was the time they had for ART. Their drawings and paintings attracted a lot of attention and they even made some sales. For Joe, whose job did not particularly excite or interest him, painting became his life. Mary thought his painting better than ever when she peeked over his shoulder in their crowded quarters.

Joe's body had suffered in the California shipyard job and now, to her relief, his eye, ear, and throat problems began clearing up. Even the rheumatism which had bothered him in California improved.

The hours spent with paint and brushes also made them homesick. They had just about had all they wanted of crowds and city living, and decided to head for the Wind River Valley and home. They hoped to spend the spring and summer of 1944 there fixing the place up, living on their savings and look for war work again in the fall.

But before they left Cheyenne that April, Mary wrote she had gotten her airplane mechanic's license.

It was no cinch to get. The technical knowledge will serve me in very good stead on the ranch, I am sure. The six exams were good and stiff. I took them all the same day, and it took all day and left me all done up. They were on carburetion, lubrication, engine theory, ignition, propellers, and CAA rules and regulations. All but the last two can be well applied to a whole lot of ranch machinery, from washing machine to buzz saw to winch to lathe to truck. I've not previously been much use where engines were concerned. Maybe I'll be worth more now.

Pleased to put Cheyenne behind them, they drove back through the increasingly familiar landscape, visiting with friends along the way. Excitement built until finally they crossed Joe's sturdy bridge and then stretched their legs exploring THEIR PLACE. So good to be home - so much to catch up on! They had great hopes Milton, Frank, or Mary Ellen would get to the ranch that summer, but wartime restrictions on travel made such trips impossible.

Summer plans evaporated when Joe began having severe trouble with his back in July. For three weeks he couldn't even do the chores. Unable to stand straight, his back was curved sidewise in a sort of bow, and hurt excruciatingly all the time. In order to try to stand, he had to crawl up a wall from an all fours position. Terribly worried about him, Mary drove him the many miles to Riverton (near Lander) to a doctor. After looking Joe over, the doctor said his spine looked fine; the problem came from spasms and cramps in the muscles around the spine.

"Perhaps they lack calcium," he pondered.

Not enough milk? Joe and Mary were astounded and gaped at each other. Well, they could do something about that! Within days, two cows joined the horses and Joe began drinking two quarts a day and seemed to recover completely. By the end of August he felt so energetic, he hired onto a ten-day pack trip adventuring into the southeast corner of Yellowstone National Park.

Wouldn't Mary have liked to go, but someone had to stay home to milk the cows.

Boy what a chore! I learned how only the last day before

Joe left. The first three days I didn't do anything else! It took me two hours each time and between times I just went to bed, all tuckered out.... Besides the milking, there's always the problem of discipline. If you stick to their schedule - and you had better - you'll find them waiting near the gates.... When they are corralled, with the help of a willow switch, Annie must be tied up by a rope round her horns, but Judy stands pretty quiet - though either one will kick the pail over given half a chance.

Then you brush them off thoroughly around the bag and get down to business. Until you've practiced quite a lot, it's hard to aim. A lot of the milk will go into your shoes or up your sleeves, or even in your face!

Sometime after the cows arrived Charles Larsen (Miriam's eldest son) showed up. They extended a warm welcome to this experienced ranch hand, thankful that while he waited to go into the service, he satisfied his curiosity about the Wind River Valley and came to stay with them a few weeks. He arrived on the mail stage (truck) and slept in the bunkhouse.

He seems a family member of long standing,... He's a fine boy. Yesterday he rode the home ridge looking for our horses...and brought them in. He is helping Joe put a hip roof on the new log barn. He's increased our milk supply almost one-third by proving that Judy, the black Jersey holds up her milk (so nothing comes out of her teats when milked) until she reaches her calf!

The plan to look for war jobs evaporated as they relished their ranch life and the freedom to really work on the new animal model business. Instead, Mary found a job, practically right under her nose; one that would keep her even busier than usual through the end of the war.

I'm a schoolma'm now. It's something I have never tried before, and is quite an experience. I am sure trying to do a good job. It's our nearest district school, a little log building ten miles down the road. I have eleven pupils in the first, fourth, fifth and eighth grades. Most of them are bright and all of them are lively. I'm so new at teaching, that making out lesson plans for the next day sometimes keeps me up until after midnight....

> *One of my pupils, little Mimi Pickett, aged ten, is boarding with me for a couple of weeks. It's a very special occasion for both of us. Mimi has a brand new baby brother. So Mother is in the Lander hospital, Daddy is batching at the ranch (nine miles north...), baby sister Margy is with other neighbors, and I rate Mimi. She's a joy to have around, a slow-spoken, humorous, easy-going little girl, whose hobbies are horses, cattle, dogs, the forest and reading....*

Mimi remembers learning more in that one year of school than any year before or since. They went on Mary-improvised field trips to see extinct geysers and warm springs and to the railroad tie camp. The kids talked to old-timers and recorded some of their stories. They read about local history that Mary had written and typed. Mimi and Mary snowshoed the half mile to the school bus, dodging moose along the way. Some days they counted twelve on the way to the gate, and passed twenty or so on the way to school.

Mary of course learned at least as much as her pupils. She grappled with history, geography, arithmetic, how to test, devised games and stunts to put over various ideas, and even conquered the coal stove. She felt constantly stretched by the rewarding but exhausting work. She even oversaw a Christmas play that filled the tiny school with forty-four proud family observers who watched the students perform on a make-shift stage, with a blanket as stage curtain.

I wonder if Mary ever took a minute to catch her breath and consider the way her life had evolved. She had tackled successfully an amazing variety of occupations: naturalist, painter, dude rancher, librarian, airplane mechanic, schoolteacher, and lately helping technician to Joe's model business. This lady of many talents probably just wouldn't understand how unusual she was. She just did what needed doing.

Wintering the horses became a problem as they couldn't find anyone to oversee caring for them in a more sheltered valley. Finally, most of them were turned loose to graze on the windswept slopes of Whisky Mountain (below Dubois), joining others from another ranch. The three they kept at the ranch seemed to enjoy each other and the two cows. Joe had a knack for finding bargain animals who had deformities that didn't interfere with their usefulness. Babe, the mare, had a buck knee that made her throw her front foot sidewise when she ran. This didn't keep her from skidding logs all day in the timber, returning home in the evening pulling the bobsled at a smart trot. Her partner was Nig, a gelding that Mary described as *"a prince among horses."* The two grew up together and seemed devoted to each other.

The cows amazed the Backs with their productivity. Their cream went by daily mail truck from Dubois to a dairy in Riverton. In the winter the market for all their milk dried up, and even with the Backs drinking a gallon a day, and using all they could in cooking they still had an excess couple of gallons. This they usually just threw out. This bothered Mary terribly but they couldn't afford to purchase bottles to supply customers, and she didn't have time to bother with making such products as cottage cheese. Winter snows made it difficult to even give the milk away to neighbors.

Joe and Mary, so caught up in ranch affairs and art business, hardly acknowledged the end of the war in August 1945. It did mean the Valley could now try to return to more normal living. For some months they had found they could just barely get by on their sales of drawings, paintings, and sculptures (with Joe's animal models the heart of the business). While this encouraged them, they acknowledged they lived poorly and worked very hard for what they earned. Their hopes were high though, that with time the market for their artistic creations would expand, and in the meantime they just put their all into their art.

Moving On

By spring 1946 the animal model business had taken over their lives. Mary loved the menagerie of animals - bears, deer, bighorn sheep, elk, moose, coyotes, rabbits and horses - that their home factory produced. With her help they moved from Joe's clay original to plaster mold, to kiln, to finish work, to distribution. After hiring a housekeeper so Mary could work full time in the assembly line, she paused one day and looked at her plaster covered hands. How were they ever going to add the dude business to what they were doing? Joe had become a big worry too, ever since that day he'd come inside, complaining of pains in his chest.

Finally she convinced him to go to the doctor in Riverton. The doctor (who knew Joe well) shook his head after checking Joe over. "Joe, your heart is complaining! You just put your body through too much stress. Something has to give, if you want to have a future!" Mary thought about all Joe did, year after year: logger, builder, rancher, problem solver as well as artist. They stared at each other, knowing they had to make some changes. I imagine the truck was quiet on that long drive home until Mary saw the bright side. They would just say goodbye to dude ranching and really become the artists they had always wanted to be. Somehow they would manage. Joe knew she was right.

This meant moving to a smaller ranch. They found just the right five acres in milder country two and one-half miles southeast of Dubois, still along the Wind River. At the same moment a buyer for the Rocker Y showed up, so they grabbed the opportunity and moved out. There was no house on the new property and no easy access to their land on the other side of the river. Setting up four tents to serve as house, workshop, storehouse and bunkhouse along the road facing their home site, Joe got to work building a bridge while Mary continued to process sculpture orders, but now in a tent.

Joe had some help on the big bridge project as Ed Lyon, 15-year-old son of Mary's sister Dorothy, came for the summer and became Joe's right-hand man. Since Joe was supposed to take life easy, they hired some Swedes to build their log cabin. Joe hoped to build the bridge before the Swedes would be ready to do the house. However, with the bridge about half-built the cabin builders drove up, all set to start. Life got very complicated! The foundation still had to be poured, and animal models delivered on a two-day trip to Yellowstone and Teton National Parks.

There _were_ other unreliable ways to reach the Back property. One could travel along a rough dirt road through neighbor Bill Leseberg's hayfield but, during the summer, irrigating made it boggy. Luckily, the water to the fields had been turned off the week before, so a load of house logs and foundation supplies got through to the house that way. When Mary, Joe and Ed left to deliver the sculptures, they expected the foundation would get started while the Swedes peeled the logs. Returning two days later they found Bill had turned on the irrigation water and the road was impass-able again!

Joe grumbled as he faced the problem, and then sighed. They would have to use the old nearby river crossing that for so many years (before the present highway) allowed passage through the river. Too deep for a truck, a wagon and horses could barely make it. They owned a wagon built from an old truck chassis, but had sold their team of workhorses. They made do by borrowing an old work mare from one neighbor and an enormous aged white gelding from another. With this mismatched couple, supplies and workers were hauled through, although the lumber very nearly floated away. Finally cabin work got under way.

Young Ed Lyon learned a lot that summer - about bridge build-ing, about tackling insurmountably difficult projects, and about being willing to try new things. While Mary kept the animal model orders moving, Joe taught Ed how to create big trusses on the river bank and use the winch and cable to move them down into place in the river. He spent many hours with cart and horse gathering thousands of pounds of rocks in the badlands behind the Back's ranch, and bringing them back to dump around the bridge supports.

With the bridge finally finished and the cabin well underway, they moved all their gear proudly, traveling <u>over</u> the river on Joe's masterpiece of a bridge. As they settled in as best they could in the unfinished house, Joe and Mary took a good look at the new country surrounding them. Across the river, beyond the main road, rose Whiskey Mountain and the towering Wind River range. The badlands behind their spread were something very different. The ruddy striped cliffs made an undulating wall they could watch from their kitchen window; changing with the sun and cloud cover as the severely eroded turrets and castle-like formations caught the light or disappeared into shadow. Also from the kitchen they could look up the valley clear to Lava Mountain and pinpoint the location of their old ranch. They watched it snowing there as they luxuriated in a Christmas Day drive across snowless terrain up into the badlands, exploring *"among the fantastic monuments on the rich brown grass that carpets the slopes."*

Mary and Joe looked forward to their completed cabin which would have electricity and indoor plumbing! In the meantime, that first winter was pretty rough living, as they camped in one bedroom and worked on finishing the interior and sculpture reproductions. Taking stock at the end of 1946 Joe did so with regret.

"Looking back, on our building up the little ranch at Lava Creek and then putting in a lot of work on the place we sold this spring, makes me realize that about ten years were thrown away (as far as art aspirations go). But that is swift water under the bridge. After modeling a few animals in miniature and finding a sale for them reminded me very forcibly that down deep, after all, I was just a long-haired guy at heart.... So we are now just about to get our 'studio' into operation.... I just want to mention that Mary has still the art complex just as much as I and lucky for me she is ALL FOR IT! All for ART and ART for ALL!"

Practically speaking, since the sales of art provided only a modest income, Joe took on other jobs when they came along while

Mary kept the production line going. Sometimes he became game warden, or hired onto construction projects. In 1947 he welded pipeline, creating a flume to carry irrigation water through a narrow canyon west of Dubois. Mary observed,

Unlike most of the manual labor he's had to do from time to time, it neither toughens his fingers nor stiffens his muscles. Far from making it harder to turn back to drawing and modeling, it increases the precision and delicacy of his touch.

Every fall, hunting season demanded their attention, both as a way for Joe to make money guiding, and as their source of meat. Joe reported in his inimitable style on a successful trip he and Mary took in 1946.

"Mary and I took a truck we have, put our 2 horses, saddles, tent, grub, beds, stove, oats, hopes, fears, gas, oil, sacks, chains, ropes, wire, axe, shovel, tools, clothes and selves in same, journeyed over Togwotee Pass in a snowstorm, camped below Angle's ...Lodge 2 miles...and we walked, rode, cussed, looked, listened, stopped, rested, ate, slept, got cold, got warm, got mad, laughed, frowned, argued, went up, went down, slipped, slid, fell, tripped and finally in eight days we came home with two elk (not alive).... And when we get back home we have scars, less weight, less clothes, less soles, and a GREAT HANKERING FOR A HOUSE where the roof don't flap at night, a bed not on the ground, no pine needles in the coffee, no mice in your bed, no wind to blow the stove over, and to sleep without a bear breathing down your neck!"

The two of them also joined a hunting camp, Joe as guide and Mary as cook (her first experience as camp cook). She reveled in the beautiful wild country of Caldwell Creek Canyon *"two days by pack train from the nearest outlying ranch, which itself was twelve miles off the highway."* This country - of vertical violet volcanic rock walls, steep slopes covered heavily by virgin timber, and natural open parks in the valley bottoms - caught her artist's eye. Mary sketched this ideal big game country and later created an oil portrait of the dramatic landscape and the pack train. Unfortunately Joe had two accidents. *"One horse knocked him over with her picket log, while another kicked him on the thigh - raised him right off the ground and heaved him fifteen feet into a bunch of spruce trees."*

While he could hardly make the ride out, and was mighty sore for many days, fortunately nothing broke.

Keeping to a regular schedule of art work constantly challenged them because hunting, carpentry, welding, gardening, cooking, plumbing and a wild variety of other jobs threatened to intervene. The animal reproductions (see Mary's price list) called for attention seven hours a day, with all other responsibilities fit in around the edges. The popular horse models came as pack trains or saddle horses, complete with gear and custom brands. In that first summer of freelancing in the animal model game, the Burlington Railroad thrilled them by buying reproductions for dis-

Joe and Mary Back

Animal Models.
Retail Price list   March 21 1951

Pack Horse, with booklet "How to Tie the Diamond Hitch" $14.00
    and complete pack gear, 10 separate pieces.
Saddle Horse, with bitless bridle, wool pad, better saddle   14.00
Horse, same model as above, no gear   10.00
    All horses are colored and branded to order.
Moose   12.00
Elk   14.00
Antelope   7.00
Mule deer fawn   2.00
Mountain sheep, Rocky Mountain Bighorn   5.00
Mountain sheep head   3.00
Horse Head, color to order   2.00
Standing bear   1.00 .75
Boxing cub   .75
Seated cub   .75
Laughing rabbit   3.00
Bear family book ends, pair   3.00
Bear and honey book ends, pair   3.00
Cubs and log and rabbits, each piece   8.00
    Story telling set of three   5.00
Cowboy and paddle   4.00
Singing cowboy   2.00
Coyote, barking or howling   1.00
Cub ashtray   1.50
Cub and log ash tray
Bird pins — bluebird, killdeer, magpie, Stellar Jay, Mountain
    chickadee, red winged blackbird — each 1.00

plays in Chicago. Producing stock to sell, touring area shops, dude ranches and camps to sell items and take orders, made for a frantic life. One big order came from a boy's camp where twenty-eight boys ordered horses to duplicate the ones ridden at camp.

Howard Harris, a new summer resident from the east coast, delighted in the small sculptures. He told Joe and Mary about his Woodstown, New Jersey livestock auction house called Cow Town that could sure use one of Joe's sculptures. What Harris had in mind though was large scale. He wanted a cow one and one half times life size that he could use as an advertisement. Joe was intrigued. He sent a small scale replica of a proposed cow to Harris and soon heard back. Could they come to New Jersey to build it? What excitement! What an opportunity! They'd get in family visits cross country, and at Cow Town they'd be just a few minutes from my father Milton and our family! Other business would have to wait.

Setting off in their 1935 Chevrolet in November 1947, it

Howard Harris, owner of the Cow Town Livestock Auction in Woodstown, N.J., commissioned Joe to build this thirteen by eight foot advertisement

seemed their happy spirits would float them all the way east. The car, however, had other ideas. It acted up right away. A layover in Casper fixed the brakes and the gearshift, but the generator burned out as they neared the Nebraska Sand Hills where they hoped to visit Mary's sister Miriam and her family. As it was the day before Thanksgiving and the Backs were behind schedule, they had to cut the visit short and drive on to find a good hearted mechanic who worked late putting in a new generator. That got them into Iowa, as Mary remembered later.

There were two main signs to show when you passed from the West into the East. One is the disappearance of sagebrush and its replacement by sumac. The other is the disappearance of jack rabbits killed on the pavement, and the appearance of possums, likewise killed on the pavement....

Pretty country, long grades, considerable timber, hardly any traffic. But all of a sudden, in the middle of the state, the engine quit functioning. It didn't break to pieces with alarming noises; there was no racket as of universals going bad. Just first it was going along smoothly and then it wasn't going at all. Joe coasted down the hill...and nearly to the top of the next one. He went through the motions of looking under the hood, but that didn't do any good. We weren't very far from a farmhouse, so, Joe headed for it, while I tried vainly to think what it might be.

Calling the garage in the nearby town, a wrecker came and hauled them in. Expecting they might be there some time, they registered at the local hotel, where Mary used the time to finish a pair of nylon pajamas she had cut from a parachute back in Dubois. Back at the garage, the engine was pulled apart and by the next night, $42 worth of repairs and a new set of spark plugs sent them on their way again.

Nearing Naperville, Illinois where they planned a stop with Mary's sister Dorothy, they ran into deep snow and ice. Worst of all, the car began to whistle, a high-pitched shriek. This was the car's last complaint, before it settled down to allow them to complete the journey without incident. After memorable visits first with Dorothy and family, and later with Frank, Mo and kids in Chicago, they ventured on. After crossing seemingly endless Pennsylvania and then the five-mile-wide Delaware River on a ferry, they finally nosed the car into Cow Town. Mary breathed a sigh of joyful relief. Now to create a cow and soon visit my family, just twenty-seven miles away.

Harris and his wife made Joe and Mary welcome, settling them into a small house close by. Joe got busy welding a skeleton from rods of an old silo. Cow Town was quite a place to spend six weeks. Harris' business centered around the livestock auction barn with 1400 head sold every Tuesday. He also rented spaces to vendors in a vast open-sided structure: an enormous flea market. In this lively setting, Joe masterminded building a body onto the skeleton, with Mary helping as an apprentice. When a fierce cold snap froze their water pipes, Mary's chores included wiggling through a small hole in the cement block foundation to thaw the pipes using hot water and rags. Joe would never have fit and she noted *"were I a trifle more bosomy I couldn't make it either."* By the end of January 1948, the cow sculpture sat ready for waterproofing and permanent installation: thirteen feet from tip of tail to nose; standing eight feet from horns to toes. Harris' staff would take over now.

On the east coast the Backs emerged as social butterflies. Weekends they soaked up family, went sightseeing, enjoyed plays, concerts and even the Ice Follies. With the cow completed, they spent a few weeks in the Harris cottage working on paintings and drawings they hoped to sell in New York City. Then, with the car freshly overhauled in Harris' garage, they set off hopefully for the big city. They encountered enough traffic to last them a lifetime.

A visit in Glen Ridge, New Jersey, with brother Ed and his family gave them a close look at upscale suburban living that astonished Mary. Then dude friends, Bill and Grace Smith, guided them to New York City. The Smiths had spent August with Joe and Mary in Dubois, and now reciprocated in grand style. What an adventure: fancy hotel entertaining, French restaurant dining, Broadway theater, mansion living in Poughkeepsie, tour of the Smith cough drop plant, and visit to Vassar College! Their heads whirled. Even so, Joe came prepared to tickle the Smiths' funny bones. He brought along a trick spoon that melted when used in hot water. When Bill Smith stirred his tea with it, those at the table also melted into shrieks of laughter.

Along with the visiting and touring, Mary and Joe put on their best apparel and knocked on publishers' doors. Joe had brought his wildly exuberant <u>Side Hill Wampus</u> story and illustrations, hoping to find an interested publisher. In office after office, folks listened, nodded and smiled as they heard about this imaginary beast. Longer on one side than the other, it had evolved into one peculiar beastie, perfectly adapted to mountain-side living. *"Time was all they gave us," mused Mary. "We can say we have been diplomatically brushed off by some mighty fine people."*

Much more rewarding was the pilgrimage they undertook searching for information to help them with their art and animal miniatures. Needing a way to make the plaster models sturdier, they sought advice at Ed's employer, the big Plastic Research Lab of the Dupont Company and at a little hole-in-the-wall workshop on 37th Street where several industrial designers had developed amazing techniques using plastics in crafts.

They relished the Museum of Natural History and the New York Public Library and asked questions at a rubber company laboratory high up in Rockefeller Center and a copper company in a Wall Street tower. Glad to say goodbye to the city's congestion, they headed for Mt. Vernon to talk to taxidermist and sculptor, John Jonas, followed by visits to other sculptors in New Hope, Pennsylvania.

Apparently the Back's return trip to Wyoming went smoothly. They paused along the way to visit friends and family and explore northern Ohio where Joe had lived as a child. Finally in late March 1948 they drove across the bridge and up to their cabin. Home! Within a few days Mary found herself impelled to go mountain climbing.

>*...to make sure the peaks and valleys were still properly arranged I climbed as fast as I could straight south from the house, up the foothills of Windy Peak until the snow got too deep. Sure enough, there were all the miles and miles of Absarokas...and all the jagged canyons between.... When I got home, I found I wasn't properly toughened for such a jaunt...because I was stiff and sore for days.*

So good to be back, but every minute burst with projects! There were the animal model back orders, a fireplace-chimney to build for the house, Mary's Dubois library work, and Joe's "How to Tie a Diamond Hitch" project. This booklet, designed to accompany the horse pack train models, captured every free moment he could give to it. He puzzled over how to give clear, straightforward directions detailing how to properly pack a horse, yet include smidgens of Joe Back humor and artistic illustrations.

With the arrival in early summer of my sister Ellen and me (young teenagers from the east coast) and Joe's young nephew Bob from Omaha, the place really bustled. Having youngsters in the house brought unaccustomed joys but also worries, especially when I came down with a mysterious feverish illness. I no sooner recovered, when we three kids got caught in the badlands during a rain storm; experiencing the flash flooding that can happen there. While we emerged safely, Mary and Joe breathed more easily when their weeks of foster parenting ended.

A call from Charlie Moore of the CM dude ranch brought an invitation they couldn't pass up. Would Joe guide and Mary cook for a five-week summer pack trip into the high country around the head of the Yellowstone? They dropped everything and went. Mary didn't really look forward to the cooking, but she didn't want to miss out on the chance to adventure in the back country and even get paid for it. In all their dude years they never had both been able to go off together on such summer trips, so they agreed now was the time to go. They tried not to think about the models crying for attention, and instead thought about all the ideas they'd get for paintings and sculptures.

The plan was to start from Brooks Lake with one family of five for two weeks, take them back, pick up another party of four and adventure for three more weeks. The twenty-two horses needed to carry riders and supplies made finding good camping spots tricky.

You have to have a meadow with water; a meadow of more than twenty or thirty acres. And your camping spot must be at a narrow point on the homeward side of the meadow. There aren't any fences…. You can't keep the horses tied up. They have to feed. And the rule among horses is, when you get full-fed, you try to go home.

One night the horses did just that, getting past the sleepers in the tents before their pounding hoofs and wild jangle of bells awoke everyone. Grabbing clothes they rushed off after the disappearing ponies, managing to grab them before all that horseflesh disappeared up a steep mountain trail. Mary found herself making

184   *Mary's Way*

breakfast at four a.m. for the exhausted crew.

She enjoyed observing the two dude families and described them in word pictures. The first party, a fox-hunting family from Virginia, consisted of Mr. and Mrs. H. and their three teenaged kids.

Mr. H. had served through the war…and was very much an army-style man, bluff and hearty and full of orders. In his family he was something of a martinet. However, his children…were of no temper to be cowed, so there were some lively family set-tos…. One would gather that the army way was the only right way to do anything; and if you didn't happen to know the army way, he'd be glad to teach you….

They wondered at first about how well the youngest child would do. Albert, a big fat kid with exotic tastes, also had a unique sense of humor. The cheerful butt of jokes, he gave better than he got and kept the whole party laughing.

The whole H. family worked together to get Albert set-tled in his saddle. All are riders, but him. The first day was his worst. Along the way we stopped once for a bit of a rest, and some of the party got off. Albert started to. At once the family formed a hollow square, facing in. 'Albert: Don't you dare get off that horse.' Albert bit his lips, looked comical, and sank back into the saddle. Family relaxed.

The second family, Mr. E. (a recent widower) and his three children, came from a monied New York family.

Mr. E. is a tall, dry, cadaverous mortal, looking rather like the white knight and talking like an Englishman. He was brought up and educated in England and at the fashionable places on the Continent…. He's of the fraternity of big-game hunters - tigers in India…,Tien Shan sheep in China, gaur in Burma…. He's used to being waited on, glad to do his part whenever he is told what that is, quite absent-minded.

The oldest boy, Duncan, is a pre-medical student at Harvard; a round-eyed, big fat boy with no sense of humor and an inexhaustible store of the kind of innocent questions that make him ready prey for a storyteller like Joe.

The wild country captured Mary's attention and she absorbed the scenery knowing she would paint it another day.

Most beautiful sight of the whole trip…was the first

view of the South Fork of the Buffalo from high on the cliffs
above Cub Creek. The fact that it was close to sunset, that I'd
been up since five-thirty, riding since eight, and that camp
would be made down there, no doubt added to the magical
quality. We were facing into the late-afternoon sun. Enough
clouds were on hand to shade our eyes, but not enough to
keep the sun from shining on the valley. It was level floored,
lying between steep rocky cliffs and a thousand feet below
us. The stream was wide and swift, sending silver flashes
back to our eyes. The valley floor was patterned with the
bright windings of the river, with tweedy gravel bars, with
the bright yellow-green splash of an enormous meadow,
with patches and masses of dark timber, with the blue shad-
ow of a gaunt granite crag that closed the valley several miles
to the west. The cliffs were vari-colored, cream and purple
and ochre and rust, with ragged timber along the ledges and
brilliant accents of light and blue shadow. And far away,
framed in the narrow V where you could see out past the
granite crag, swimming up out of a blue haze were the fan-
tastic outlines of Mt. Moran of the Tetons.

As the days sped past, they discovered that Joe's horse Clown
liked garbage at least as much as Bobby, the husky-shepherd pup
that tagged along with the train.

Fishing was so good, and there was so much fish show-
ing up in the scrap pan, that Bobbie got bored with it and
wouldn't eat it all. Clown would amble casually over to the
cook tent in the evening to see what was what. And if there
was some fish left in Bobbie's dish, darned if she wouldn't eat
it. Bob would try to get his nose in then - but Clown's was too
big. One night Joe and I heard dishes rattling in the cook tent,
and he got up prepared to chase a bear. But that was Clown,
too.

When Mary picketed her nine-year-old horse, Susie, one
evening and looked around at the mountains she thought life just
couldn't be better. The next morning, though, brought an unpleasant surprise. As she hurried to get Susie, she discovered the horse
lying down, stretched out on her side, stiff - as if dead.

I started to run toward her. She heard me, and lifted up
a bloody, shapeless mass where a head should be, and out of

     Mary's Way

*that mess of beaten flesh came a choked nicker!... We decid-
ed she had been scratching mosquito bites under her chin
with a hind foot. The halter rope had caught under the back
of her shoe. Finding herself caught, she'd become panic-
stricken and had fought like a demon until she was exhausted. But she didn't get exhausted until she had fought the halter clear off over her head, and pulled the shoe clear off her
foot. In the process, she very nearly hanged herself, nearly
put out both eyes, cut the insides of both front legs..., done
some damage to her kidneys and tied her large muscles into
knots with cramps. She was bleeding at her legs, and from
her eyes, nose, mouth, and kidneys. Her tongue was swollen
until it was too big for her mouth, and forced her jaws apart
until we could see it - a horrible lump of yellow and green.*

If there had been a gun in camp, Joe would probably have shot
her. Instead, Mary undertook some unusual nursing. With everyone helping, they managed to get Susie on her feet. With absorbine
for her muscles, merthiolate for the cuts, and water and Epsom
salts to drink, Susie finally managed to drink a pail of Wheatena
gruel. Since a prostrate horse can develop pneumonia, someone
had to be with Susie all the time encouraging her to stand and
move about. Joe rode off to the nearest ranch, ten miles away, and
brought back lysol for the cuts and rolled oats. Once the swelling
in her mouth went down, Susie relished the oats. To everyone's
amazement, the horse was able to make the return trip to Brooks
Lake under her own power.

Much as they enjoyed the back country, home looked mighty
good - and not just for Susie's sake. Their eastern trip had given
them many ideas for improving the animal reproductions and they
needed time to experiment. Mary also enjoyed living closer to
Dubois. One Sunday after they returned, she decided to go to
church. For all the years they had lived in Wyoming, her strong
sense of religion had brewed quietly on a back burner. She had
watched nature and mulled how everything she saw related to
everything else. While her religious understanding deepened, she
missed church. The only protestant church in Dubois was St.
Thomas Episcopal Church, so there she went.

*It seemed to me that the Lord's Supper, as celebrated in
the Episcopal ritual, is essentially a magic ritual, an invoca-*

tion aimed at a divine blessing, and not greatly different in its feeling and purpose from the Sun Dance, performed in all reverence every summer at Fort Washakie (on the Indian reservation).

Reading the very simple story of the Last Supper, I wondered suddenly what it would do to my thinking if I were to take it literally, try to see it from the point of Jesus, not from that of a disciple or of Leonard da Vinci, or of the 2000 years of formalism of the church.

He took bread, and broke it, and gave it to his disciples, saying, 'This is my body broken for you.... Take, eat.... As oft as ye do it, this do in remembrance of me.'

The more Mary thought about this, the more she marveled and the more she got herself to church on Sunday. It seemed clear to her that Jesus was talking about all life. If she took his words very literally, his words took on amazing meaning.

'This is my body, broken for you (I am the wheat, the yeast, the fat, the bees, that made the honey. I am part of life. And life is being given up for your sake, in order for you to live)...Take, eat.... As oft as ye do it (three times a day, or oftener) do this in remembrance of me'.... Why don't we eat the Lord's Supper, according to his own words, every time we eat, every time we drink?...

Thinking of all life as coequal with equal right upon the earth,...it is sad and humbling to consider the carnage necessary...to keep us alive. Much as I enjoy elk meat, I am often impressed strongly with that point of view when on a hunting trip. I do not so often think about it when forcibly pulling a carrot out of the ground.

She thought about hunting season and how to deal with killing another life to continue her own. She wrote in the family Robin, struggling to explain her thoughts.

There are always mixed emotions during a hunt, and a now familiar pattern of thinking.... There is the excitement of being up in the thin crisp air of the high mountains, the stiff climbs bringing the blood singing in the ears, the breathtaking spread of country underfoot. There is the frustration of a long day's hunt for nothing, the exciting sudden chance at a shot, the sharp agony of actually taking life, the hard, bloody work of dressing and dragging out, the period of remorseful appreciation when the doe lies by the jeep, her slender legs and delicate feet describing precise shapes, her insides gone, her gentle bunny-like face composed and quiet. There is the uncanny shock of realizing she might well be saying, 'This is my body which is given for you. Take it and eat it. Do this in remembrance of me.'

There is no way out of this trespass against life. No way but Jesus' 'Give us this day our daily bread - and forgive us…our trespasses as we forgive those who trespass against us.' It's a sin to eat if you have a grudge against anyone. Every possible effort of kindness is necessary just to earn the right to eat.

So, as always, in the end I just give up, accepting my position in life, and thankful that I am close enough to elemental facts to see vividly and sensitively this all-pervading unity of life, hidden from so many by the multiplied complexities of modern life.

Mary became a regular at St. Thomas as she worked to develop a working theology while immersed in the business of art.

The Art Business

Experimenting with the plastic resin they had bought in the East kept them both busy with the animal models. By adding the resin to the plaster process they hoped to produce less fragile sculptures. Days spent dipping and baking finally produced results they liked. Mary did find the resin fumes unpleasant to work with but the results were superior: brown sculptures that were both beautiful (after a little polishing) and sturdy.

Teaching herself to use an air brush to paint some of them took great concentration. She frowned intently as she practiced this new technology, then called delightedly, *"Joe, come see. **This is wonderful!**"*

"Boy, I guess you're right," allowed Joe, keeping his delight under wraps as he eyed the smooth bright finish. Mary, his art partner and engineer, who constantly solved the small animal models' technical problems, was some gal! She even put aside her own painting to ride herd on these little critters, knowing they paid the bills.

Each of his clay figures sculpted over a wire framework began the process. For each new piece, she created a rubber mold that could be reused many times. Mary painted liquid rubber over the clay sculpture and while still wet, laid nylon strips (made from worn-out panty hose) over it for reinforcement. After applying multiple layers, she had a rubber mold that she dried before making a two piece plaster mold based on it. Then placing the rubber mold into the completed plaster mold pieces (held together by rubber bands made from inner tubes) she poured a plaster mix into the mold opening. First, though, tails and legs had heavy pieces of wire inserted to strengthen them. The filled molds were then jiggled to eliminate air bubbles and allowed to set overnight to harden.

Ellen Butner, one of several neighbors who joined the assembly line Joe and Mary eventually set up, remembers carefully separating the casts from the molds. Then she trimmed the fragile molds to remove seams caused by the rubber. She also recalls how Mary developed procedures that used whatever she had on hand. "Mary had an old-time icebox …she figured out how to use for her oven. It was heated with various wattages of light bulbs throughout. She had experimented and found what she needed to reach the required temperature. There was also a cooling down period before the reproductions came out - so they wouldn't crack."

After donning rubber gloves and face mask, Mary dipped the pieces very carefully into the brown plastic resin. Another period of baking followed with the stench of the plastic infiltrating everywhere. Antlers made from lucite followed a similar mold making process. Ellen remembers how hard the plaster was on hands. "No amount of lotion kept them 'the skin you love to touch'." She was often joined by her two pre-schoolers, who took part in any interesting side activities, like Mary's bread baking.

Mary did love to make bread and cherished the time she took to knead the dough. As she struggled to work out her new theology, she saw the bread making process in a new light.

> *I have always enjoyed making bread, largely because of the feeling of the living force under my hands; a force which it was up to me to guide and control. People have laughed at me because I have stoutly maintained that as an activity making bread was rather like breaking a horse. I'm sure it's true. The thing, though, that always seems unfair, is that after coddling the yeast, keeping it warm, feeding it properly, watching it proudly grow, cutting it down to size, shaping it, watching it grow again to its proper final shape — THEN – we put it in a hot oven and kill it! ('This is my body, broken for you'.)*

Even when busy overseeing the model production, her

thoughts swirled in other directions that she shared with her brothers and sisters through the Robin letters.

Up the long history of the saints and sages, I don't recall any other (besides Jesus) who so strongly identified himself with all life, except St. Francis of Assisi. And we still think him quaint...for referring to the birds and flowers as his brothers and sisters.... I wonder with what right humans think they are better than other creatures? Because they have brains, why are they therefore better than wheat, which is just as much alive?

How can a person, who has learned to identify himself with all life, ever be lonely? Life is all around us, our brothers and sisters. Taking a walk this evening, just before dark, for a mile or two along the river, I was filled with a greater sense than ever before, of 'belonging.' My great family was all around me - the grass underfoot, the rattling seedpods of the iris, the slender red withes of the willows, a group of 15 mallards ruffling their feathers and paddling in an eddy, our slim and greatly enthusiastic dog Monkey, splashing madly across the river, shaking the drops off his fur into the cold west wind, a horned owl waiting for us in a cottonwood near the house, lowering his head and circling it, to watch us with those enormous yellow eyes. My brothers and sisters.

Monkey taught Mary much about nature. She observed his interactions with wild animals with wonder. There was the day he chased a rabbit. As Mary watched, the rabbit stopped and turned around. Both dog and rabbit approached each other with little short steps. The rabbit stood up straight and smelled Monkey's nose and Monkey smelled his. Then the rabbit hopped off with Monkey after him. Mary decided they were just playing a game between friends.

Monkey was a very resourceful dog. He amazed everyone who came to visit. A lighted match or glowing ember on the fireplace hearth caught his immediate attention. With a rush he scuffed out the flame with his paws. While Mary always had tales to tell about her four-pawed friends, perhaps her favorite had to do with this black and tan mongrel who lived with them in their first house east of Dubois and died on the highway. Mary relished one tale in particular.

Some years ago Monkey took to wandering and staying away. After various futile measures, we had him castrated, and thereafter he stayed home. Then a year and a half ago we got Moses, as a tiny puppy. Monkey resented him, but, inhibited any demonstration, acting the patient martyr. Evidently the inhibitions induced a regular neurosis. Anyway, Monkey began acting erratic and peculiar. Among other things, he began going away from home again. He knows our schedule, and would try to arrange to catch a ride home…. His favorite time to leave could be Friday or Saturday afternoon. Then he'd meet me Sunday morning at church.

We discovered he was spending his nights with Queenie Jacobsen, evidently the personality girl of Dubois dog society. With Monkey it's evidently completely platonic - the more so because Queenie's been spayed! Queenie is a big rangy orange-colored short-haired hound, not at all the gentle feminine type. Yet she certainly attracts admirers, who evidently love her for her personality alone. When Monkey started his visits,…she already had a steady. He was a stray who stayed. Jacobsens called him 'Butch' but never fed him or owned him. He rustled for himself, and spent his nights in Queenie's doghouse. Well, when Monkey showed up, apparently Butch just moved over, and they all three shared the doghouse.

Moses was our pride and joy for a home-staying dog. He just never left home. But about a month ago he did leave one day with Monkey; and has never come back…. Monkey took him to Dubois and introduced him to Queenie!

Then Monkey caught the car at church and came home, and has never left since. His neurosis is apparently completely cured; he no longer gets a wild and haunted look in his eye; he behaves like a normal, well-adjusted pet dog, secure in his position in the family. When you ask him where Moses is, he just grins and looks sly, as if to say 'Aha! We sure got rid of him!'

Much too busy overseeing the model production and working in the Dubois library three days a week, Mary didn't pay too much attention when Al Conger, field man for the University of

Wyoming, questioned her about teaching painting in an extension class. When he kept asking, she agreed reluctantly (certain no one would sign up), *"Well, yes, I guess I could do that."* When he called back to say ten women had registered for a Dubois class in Creative Oil Painting, she could hardly believe it. As the class got under-way, she relished the time with the enthusiastic women who had never even seen an oil painting brush before. Teaching was won-derful! The additional income was also a real blessing.

When the extension department put out feelers in Riverton and Lander, more hopeful artists materialized. By the end of 1949, she was on the road with the old truck stuffed with art supplies for sixty-five students. This exhausting life certainly did have its rewards: not only the extra money but also the joy of watching ranch wives, mothers, cowboys, storekeepers, youngsters and lum-berjacks catch the painting bug. While she taught in Dubois mid-week, every other weekend she squeezed two classes into Sunday: the Lander class in the afternoon, and Riverton at night. Some-times she made the 200 mile round trip that day while other weeks she stayed overnight in Riverton, and bumped out to the nearby coal mine to restock the Back's coal supply before heading to Dubois.

Summertime gave a respite, and in 1951 they forsook the sculptures again and went on a 42-day pack trip along the Buffalo River, northwest of Dubois. As they explored this wild, mountain-ous land, Mary worked out her own religious creed. When they returned home, she sat right down to put her thoughts on paper. Central to her beliefs was the idea of love.

> ...I BELIEVE that God is love. I believe that in every prayer the word Love may be perfectly substituted for the word God. I believe that <u>every</u> manifestation of love is a manifestation of God.
>
> I BELIEVE that the great creation of Love is Life. I believe that Life is a material creation - a thing of length, breadth and thickness, but without limit in time. Life, con-stantly changing in form, is in time everlasting and eternal. Life is a wonderful tapestry spread over the surface of the earth - here thick and matted, there fine and tenuous; hold-ing to and part of the earth itself, yet constantly moving, flowing, growing, reaching out from the earth. Life is com-

posed of almost countless forms, the various creatures: dogs, mosquitoes, men, pine trees, horses, gentians, coneys, fungi, bacteria of decay, pondweed, elk, rainbow trout, and millions of other forms.

Each individual creature has three functions:

(1) To play his momentary part in the great picture or tapestry, enriching it according to his ability;

(2) To spend his time, in part, in transforming other forms of life into his particular form (hunger is the urge to effect these transformations);

(3) To finally sacrifice his own body thus to be transformed into other living creatures (that is to say, as other shapes in the same great pattern of Life).

I BELIEVE that, as life is one unit created by Love, so all living creatures are equal before Love....

I BELIEVE that salvation is orientation - the individual finding his place in the scheme of things. I believe that the individual's place in the great whole of Life depends less on his relationship with his own species than on his relationship with the many, many other forms of life....

I BELIEVE in Jesus, as the greatest interpreter of this way of thinking. I believe it was the oneness of all Life to which he referred at the Last Supper, and not to his own personal sacrifice.... I believe that Jesus is divine, as the child of Love..., just as all living creatures are... divine in so far as they manifest love.

I BELIEVE in the resurrection of the body as a continuing fact in changing forms, and in everlasting Life.

I BELIEVE in the Church as the organization best equipped to help humanity become oriented into the whole of life.

I BELIEVE in the service of communion. It continually recalls the words of Jesus which are the key to personal orientation into Life through Love.

She sent off her creed in the Robin letter and awaited responses from her family. Miriam's reply remembered how hard it had been for Mary at age twelve to accept killing pet chickens for family meals. Was that still an issue for her? Mary smiled and wrote her right back.

You are quite right, too, in thinking that ever since, that has remained a central problem with me. The reasoning is simple and obvious. If God made me, he is my Father. If he made everything else, he is their Father, too. If he is Father to the elk and the cottonwoods, the mosquitoes and the dogs, and the ducks and the snakes and me, they are my brothers and sisters-in-love. And by what right do I eat my brothers and sisters?...

To make sense of what at first seemed senseless killing of brothers and sisters, Mary returned again and again to the flash of insight that came to her about the meaning of Jesus, communion, and his sacrifice at the crucifixion.

There are not two conflicting forces, Love and Greed, with Greed often the victor. Love is the master creator and guide, of a great single body whose name we call Life. Individual lives are constantly sacrificed to feed other parts of the body of an eternal Life. Each individual, during his lifetime, accepts the sacrifice of many more lives than he can possibly repay by the sacrifice of his own. The only repayment can be with constant determination to make life better for all the forms of Life with whom we come in contact.

There was my answer - a great illumination of the present, the past, and the future, with the conviction that I am no single, frail individual, but a living part of the body of an eternal Life. It solves the problem of the sacrifice of life, to the point where it actually makes my meals taste better!...

Letter writing had to be put aside, for Mary's life got even busier as the painting classes continued to expand. Crowheart, on the Indian reservation brought together thirteen folks for a Friday night gathering, to paint, exhibit and talk painting. By 1954, more sites were added and Mary acknowledged, *"It looks like I'll be running around all winter."* She became a familiar sight on Wyoming roads, a miniature arty wagon, with Mary at the wheel. While it was a chore for her to get to the several hundred students she had reached by then, it was no easier for some of the fledgling artists who rode horseback or drove jeeps or station wagons for many miles to get to the classes. Art was definitely flourishing in the Wyoming back country, and Mary was right in the middle of it.

Starting at the end of the very first semester, Mary included an exhibit of class efforts attracting both her students and proud families and friends. As the classes and students grew, the exhibits mushroomed, finally becoming centralized in Dubois - a summertime event known as the Wind River Valley Art Exhibit. When its success skyrocketed, Mary and some of her students formed the Wind River Valley Artists Guild in 1954. By 1957, three hundred forty pieces were hung and prizes were awarded. Exhibitors were not only local people; paintings came from California, Kentucky and even Afghanistan! Its original purpose of running the exhibit, rapidly expanded until today, years after Mary's death, the Guild is a major facilitator of artistic efforts and events and still organizes the annual national exhibit.

As Mary's itinerant art teaching grew, something had to give. She found she hardly had time to paint anything herself, to say nothing about getting out for an occasional mountain walk. Her letter writing to family suffered so much that an inquiring letter soon came from Mo and Frank asking what had happened to the Backs. This egged Joe into one of his typical fun-filled responses.

"Mary still does the cooking, sleeps in same bed (at least she must - I hear the snores). She could find a better husband, no doubt about it, but she still has the same ball and chain.... Mary still bears me and hasn't thrown anything at me except - BIG WORDS - which floor me worse than guided missiles...."

How could they make their lives a bit less hectic and boost their art business at the same time? An inspiration hit them, and they thought long and hard about it. Why not build a studio-shop right on the highway under tourists' noses? They could live there and sell their paintings and the animal sculptures directly to the public. Renting their house would give some more income, too. When they found they could buy land cheap at the entrance to their road, it seemed destined to happen. In January 1954, Mary wrote Miriam, who was mending from breast cancer surgery, about the preparations.

> *Joe is doing all the building himself, and, with the interruptions of winter weather, it's exasperatingly slow going. It's built of round logs - and thereby hangs a tale. We weren't getting any action, last October, from the man we'd dealt with to get out the logs. So at last Joe had a talk with the forest ranger, and arranged for Joe himself to get the logs from a*

…small ridge by Brook Lake Falls, some thirty miles up the valley. For about a week we went up every day in the pickup; it turned out to be the week of the first winter storm!

Snow piled up about eighteen inches deep. Every day my first job was to locate and sweep off the logs Joe had already cut, so they wouldn't get lost…. Joe worked all day long with power saw and axe, felling trees and trimming them. My job was to spot more dead trees, measuring them and tallying them, since our permit called for 1500 running feet. The snow was deep enough so Joe had to carry a shovel to get down to the less than ten-inch stump required by the Forest Service. It was a strenuous time, but beautiful there in the pine forest, filled with the smell of snow and resin, with the murmur and cry of the wind and of the falls, with the snap of the cold and the light-headedness of high altitude.

The sequel was that the man with whom we'd arranged for logs,…got worried about Joe's operations, put on extra steam, and got out all the ones ordered…. So we had twice as many as we needed…. Now we think maybe we'll build another house to rent.

We got the foundations dug, forms built, and concrete poured in October, the logs peeled in November, and since then Joe has been sculpturing logs. He's doing a perfectly beautiful job, setting each log down solidly and firmly over the one below, hollowed out on its bottom so it covers and grips the log below, and matched so you couldn't get a tooth-pick between.

It's a big building, twenty by fifty feet, so it's slow. Plans

On July 6, 1954, the Backs' store opened for business.

call for four rooms: a big salesroom,... office, bath and a big bedroom-kitchenette apartment. By summer we expect to have at least the salesroom ready and be able to do business. We plan to specialize in our own stuff...and to handle such other things as actually belong to northwestern Wyoming: local post cards and photos, petrified wood, agates, jade, other minerals, cedar and other local woods,...Shoshone and Arapaho craft work. Joe wants to build a couple of enormous bull elk, sculpture in the round, as attention-catchers along the highway.

The store opened for business July 6, 1954, but such niceties as water, plumbing and living space had to wait until winter for finishing. Summer help did arrive when twelve-year-old Ric van der Schalie, son of Mary's cousin Annette, showed up. Not minding the rough living conditions, he helped sand down the models, and thrived on exploring the river where he caught squirrels in a live trap Joe had made for him. He listened to Joe's stories and wondered if they could possibly be true. To catch a bird, just put salt on its tail! Ric didn't try, but he sure wondered if it would work.

Mary and Joe planned to sell mostly their own works in the store as well as other items unique to northwest Wyoming.

Mary focused her attention on Ric. She took him with her on supply trips to Dubois, to visit Teton National Park, and even when she went to Riverton to have a tooth extracted. On the way back Mary kept saying that she was swallowing blood and feeling faint. Matter-of-factly, she instructed him to catch the wheel if she passed out. While she didn't, Ric was mighty impressed. He remembers her as gentle and kind and thought she was happy to have a kid around for awhile.

Later that fall the phone rang with the news that Miriam had lost her fight with breast cancer. She was the first of Mary's siblings to die. Mary and Joe drove to the Nebraska sand hill country for her funeral, and a reunion with Ernest Larsen and the Larsen children. For Mary it was an inspiring time, not a saddening experience. She felt surrounded by a sense of continuity and the immortality of life itself, both spiritually and physically. She shared her deeply felt beliefs about resurrection.

What a living reality it suddenly makes the thought 'the resurrection of the body.' If you don't conceitedly require the body to rise up as a human body; if you feel that all life is one, that a new form of life is just more of the same stream of life; resurrection isn't a dream or a vision or something that you leave for church. It's all about you, here and now.

'Everlasting life,' then, becomes a reality and not a hope. There is no real death. Death simply is a change from one form of life to another form of the same mystery. As long as we feel superior to other forms of life, death is a come-down. But when we feel confidently that other shapes of life are no different from us than our brothers and sisters, the prospect of death and change becomes simply interesting.

Mary shared her maturing theology with me the next summer, when I arrived to spend weeks clerking in the store. My college courses had turned my childhood religion on its ear and I came struggling to define my beliefs. From the Robin I knew of Mary's developing philosophy and I wanted to know more. The little I did to help, became insignificant compared with what I gleaned from discussions with Mary about her sense of what really mattered.

I joined the two of them in saying grace before meals, thanking God for the animal and plant life we were about to eat. She responded simply and forcefully to my questions, explaining her understanding of a love based world and how every meal is holy.

'Original sin is the necessity laid upon us all as individu-
als to prey upon other individuals in order to live, and for-
giveness is God's recognition of the fact of that necessity....
We can encounter without flinching the silent testimony of
the deer as we load his carcass into the car: 'This is my body
which is given for you. Take and eat it. This do in remem-
brance of me.' We have a right to it only if we have forgiven -
if we bear no grudges against anybody.... No wonder we
must ask for 'grace' before we take part in (a meal).

Well, I knew there was a lot of love flowing to and from her, and soaked up her ideas like ink in a blotter.

The Wind River Valley Artists Guild's National Art Exhibit was hung that year in the log schoolhouse next to the Dubois library. Mary immersed both of us in the preparations, while overseeing the library and keeping the store staffed. I learned to cook on their Coleman camping cookstove, and wash clothes in a hand crank machine set up behind the store building. One day we followed a dowser fellow around as he paced with his willow stick in back of the shop, looking for a water source. I returned home impressed by their very busy but simple lifestyle.

That summer of 1955 Joe was hard at work on a solitary gigantic elk - ninety-six inches high at the shoulder. He welded its structure out of steel pipe, mostly resurrected from bed frames left at town dumps. To create the one-hundred-inch spread of horns, he had to purchase a less hot acetylene torch to use in welding lightweight seismograph steel pipe into two amazing racks; each horn weighing one hundred pounds. When it became clear the beast would not be finished by cold weather Joe took time off to build an indoor stall for its winter quarters, with a doorway fifteen by eight feet to accept its large dimensions. After much experimenting, Joe contrived its hide out of fiberglass cloth and polyester resin, colored with dry pigment. On July 4, 1956 the noble elk took its place of honor in front of the store, where it successfully shocked passing tourists into stopping to see the largest elk in the Rockies. Sometimes they even stayed to purchase real western gifts or visit with the Backs.

Much as the Backs needed to make art pay their way, when needs arose in Dubois they did what they could to help out there,

Mary's Way

too. Sometimes the helping even gave them a little income. The summer after the elementary school burned, the school board knew they needed a building to serve the children in the far flung area around Dubois. Heavily bonded for the high school, the board had little money available for this project, so they told the contracting superintendent to just start building and see how far he could get.

He has hired all local labor, mostly old-timers, hard-bitten old eccentrics like Joe, and it's a minor miracle that he's built a team out of them. Three weeks ago Joe was at the schoolhouse for … a word with Bill Moriarty when Paul grabbed him for a hand, and that very afternoon Joe found himself mixing cement. Since then he's been working sixty-three hours a week - nine hours a day and seven days a week. The goal of course is September 4, opening day. They think they'll make it. Their morale is awfully high….

Now centered in their studio-store Mary and Joe's creative juices came to a boil again. Joe's small sculptures expanded to more complex combinations of figures. The latest in 1956 was a rider and a running horse roping a longhorn steer - their energy caught forever in the models coming out of the oven. He had recently contrived six humorous drawings that became post cards, (*See Sketch 11 A-F*) popular items in the

In 1956, Joe finished the largest elk in the Rockies – measuring eight feet high at the shoulder with a rack equally wide – which took up residence in front of the store.

The store, with its elk, was a sure attention-grabber for tourists.

store. Most of all, following the popularity of <u>How to Tie the Diamond Hitch</u> he turned to producing a book, <u>Horses, Hitches, and Rocky Trails</u>. Complete with Joe's yarns and drawings, it aimed to instruct the novice and armchair adventurer about packing into the back country. According to Joe, "It will be the <u>first</u> book ever written and illustrated, on how to pack a horse or mule. I left out how to 'do it' on elephants and zebras. I don't savvy them animals." Joe's handwritten text came to Mary to type into final form (with the understanding that she could alter Joe's unique grammar and spelling when it was incomprehensible).

Sketch Eleven A   *Joe's Post Cards*

Sketch Eleven B   **Joe's Post Cards**

She had dreamed up a set of Wyoming bird pins and pot ornaments to sell in the store. Her true to life yet tiny renditions of
Stellar's jay, magpie, mountain chickadee, bluebird, killdeer, red-
winged blackbird, and meadowlark really attracted attention. (See
illustrated catalog, pgs. 213-219) More than anything else, though,
that summer she wanted time to work on a large oil painting - five
feet by thirty inches - commissioned by a lawyer and his wife.
Reveling in the process of capturing the details of a Wyoming
mountainside in it, she had to drag herself away to work in the
store, fill orders, produce more stock, type Joe's book or keep up

Sketch Eleven C   **Joe's Post Cards**

Sketch Eleven D   **Joe's Post Cards**

with cooking and cleaning.

They never knew who would walk into the store: locals coming to talk, tourists drawn by the big elk, crafts people interested in making sales, old friends or family, or other artists intent on exchanging experiences. One September day two men creaked through the door, asking for coffee. While not unusual, when they started talking, Mary and Joe were astounded.

The older man said 'We stopped because we'd been hearing about you. I'm Tom Benton from Kansas City.' Wow! (Artist) Thomas Hart Benton! What a privilege! Anyway,

Sketch Eleven E   **Joe's Post Cards**

206   Mary's Way

the sequel to the cup of coffee was that he stayed ten days, renting a cabin from ...our nearest neighbor. He painted in Joe's studio with his friend.... They went on trips all over this country, by themselves and with Joe, and are planning to come back. Benton made a painting of Joe, bringing in some elk meat.

And best of all, he introduced us to the magic of the egg

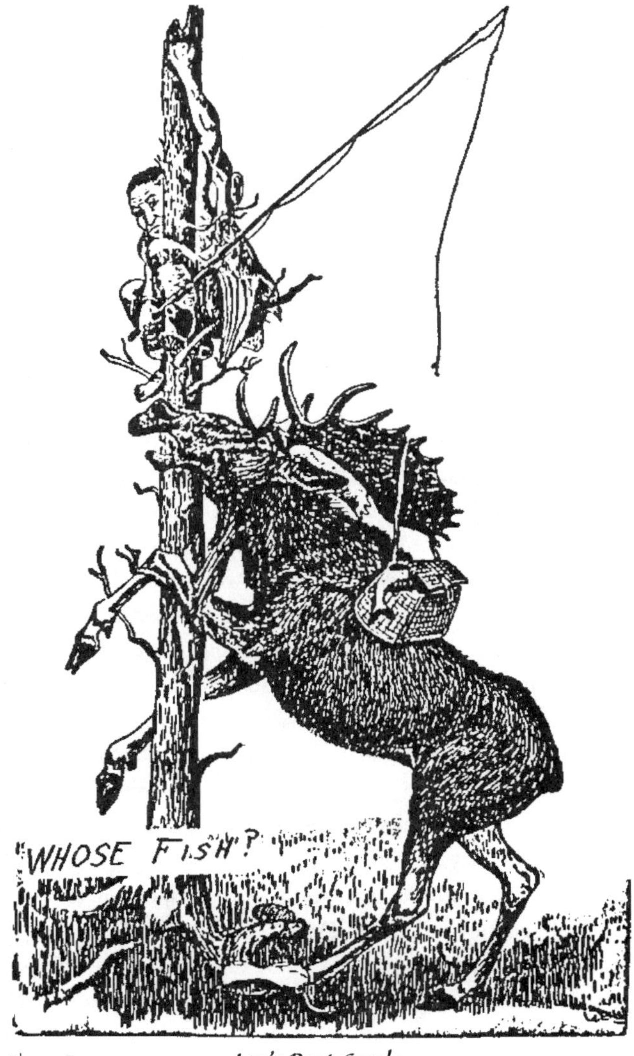

Sketch Eleven F   *Joe's Post Cards*

tempera painting technique. I'm off oil now - it's egg tempera for me! Ever since, I've been experimenting with it, and passing on what I've learned to my own painting classes. I can't keep away from it.... This is a mixture of egg yolk, dry powdered color and water, painted on a board primed with many sanded layers of glue and chalk. It sounds stiff and unresponsive, but its not; it's flexible and expressive. It's a very old technique which I read about long ago, but never tried. Tom Benton works entirely in that medium...(as does Ivan Albright).... I've been having a marvelous time using up hen's eggs.... It's more fun! For weeks I can hardly think of anything else.

Tom Benton's visit shook up Mary's painting world; as it shattered, she welcomed the new knowledge, anxious to learn its intricacies and pass them on to others. To her disappointment few students got as excited as she. The process involved multiple silky transparent glazes that allow the artist to overwork as much as desired. Yet to Mary, the techniques allowed her to paint very quickly, and she found herself finishing many more paintings than usual.

Then she heard about acrylic tempera - a plastic resembling buttermilk, that replaces the egg. Her brother Ed helped her locate the material which she enthusiastically tried out, although she worried how she could afford a good supply since it came only in hefty fifty gallon drums. At least eggs were easy to get, and she soon even had Joe's image captured in egg tempera.

While the shop did allow them to reach more people directly, making a living from their art still felt like an ongoing struggle. Nevertheless, Mary's reputation as an art teacher had spread. When the Lander Schools decided to add art to their curriculum, Mary got a call. "How would you like a full time job teaching art to seventh and eighth graders and other students as time permits?" What a question! At first it seemed impossible. As she and Joe considered how this would turn their lives upside down, they also realized it offered a financial cushion, too enticing to pass up.

Fall 1958 found Mary in Lander, ensconced as art teacher. Living weekdays with Mary Bain (who had nursed her following her bout with pneumonia so many years ago), she commuted to Dubois and Joe for weekends.

School is going all right. It is hard work for me. There are a lot of rewards, of which money is one not to be sneezed at. I don't discount the pleasure of watching the youngsters acquire confidence and become experimenters. I enjoy the fact that the art room is popular, that kids are constantly crowding it, and that mothers are dropping in quite often too. But I am good and tired every night, and find it hard to get work done on the two correspondence courses I have to take.... Weekends are wonderful, even if I do work like the devil.

One year of this was all they could stand. They found the separation just too hard, even though Mary did enjoy the teaching. When the Dubois principal called to interest her in teaching art to the two hundred seventy-five elementary and high school students for ten hours a week, she answered a quick "yes". For the next five years, she spent her afternoons encouraging the art spark in local children and adolescents. Because she had so much she wanted to accomplish, the part-time hours and subsequent scheduling problems proved very frustrating. At least Joe and Mary had a home life again, and she could help keep the sculpture orders moving.

While Mary taught, Joe worked on becoming an author-illustrator. Obstacles abounded, however! After hand delivering <u>Horses, Hitches and Rocky Trails</u> to Houghton Mifflin's representative in Denver, Joe had it returned. Another delivery to an Idaho publisher resulted in a contract, but not in terms Joe liked. <u>He</u> turned that down. Finally, Allen Swallow at Sage Books in Denver snapped up the manuscript and published the book June 15, 1959.

It was preceded by much writing and re-writing, drawing and re-drawing, typing and retyping, soliciting advice from friends, taking trips and interviewing editors, considering contracts, writing letters, working up mailing lists, and worrying. It was followed by sending out circulars, chewing fingernails over whether to buy a hundred copies to sell or not, wrapping books for mail-orders, reading reviews once in a while, selling books in our studio shop, and once even a royalty check..... We've sold seven hundred books from our own shop....

A hot item, the book took less than a year to go into its second printing. This success lit a fire under Joe. Ideas for books and illustrations poured out. Maybe there was a market for his devil-may-care humor!

As they sat talking about his idea for a book that he wanted to call <u>Mooching Moose and Mumbling Men</u>, the phone rang. It was Easter Sunday, 1961. Mary's nephew Ed relayed the shocking news that his mother, Dorothy, had died during the night. She had seemed so well, but arose from her sleep during the night, made a choking noise and fell over. No pain, but her life was gone. Mary had the Robin letter in hand intending to write in it. She asked Ed what to write. "Just say," said Ed, "that we are glad it's Easter." As Mary wrote, with sadness driving her pen, she sorted out her ideas about life and death.

Life is a body: a unity made of a great variety of diverse parts. Life can be pictured as an infinitely intricate sort of fuzzy tapestry wrapped closely about and part of the unliving Earth. It's to be pictured as a material body, rather than as a short-and-frantic-passage-from-the-cradle-to-the-grave. The body is made of every living thing – people and clothes-moths, puppies and trout and daffodils, snakes and cows and alfalfa, penicillium mold, typhoid bacteria, geraniums and seaweed, deer and peanuts and sweet peas. At any given point the tapestry may be thick and plushy, or tenuous and lacy. It reaches deep into black earth as far as the deepest tree roots – oh, much farther - to the deepest mines and high in the sky, as far as the lightest mold spore, the highest life-carrying satellite. It is a real body. And it is the body of Christ.

The body of life is immortal. Its parts are constantly changing shape. They grow and change. They 'die', but that is only the word used for their changing into other shapes, within the one whole body of Life, which is immortal. In all its parts it is constantly resurrected....

This whole body is activated by love. Sexual love is the creative force from generation to generation in every form of life. Motherly, fatherly, sisterly, brotherly, neighborly love is the conserving force in all forms of life at any given point and time. Nothing of it would exist without both these aspects of love.

Love, then, is a power. Love is a force. Love is not a sen-

timent, a character trait, a quality, a feeling. It is a power. It is the power of interdependence. It is, then, the power that holds living things together, that is responsible for the laws of society.... Perhaps it is love that makes electrons and atoms and molecules behave the way they do – plenty strong evidence of interdependence there. If that's so, then it's love that keeps the solar system on its track, and the stars in their courses.

213

1. **Lead Rider.** 14 inches high. Rider painted and horse branded and painted to order. Separate leather bridle and copper cheek-pieces. Shipping weight 18 pounds.

2. **Pack Horse.** 10½ inches high. Painted and branded to order. Pack outfit completely demountable, 10 separate pieces. Included is booklet, "How to Tie the Diamond Hitch" (No. 16). Shipping weight 14 pounds.

Joe and Mary Back   Dubois, Wyoming

4. Standing horse with elk meat. Horse painted and branded to order. Removable pack includes halter, pad, pack saddle, hind quarters of elk. 10½ inches high. Shipping weight 14 pounds.

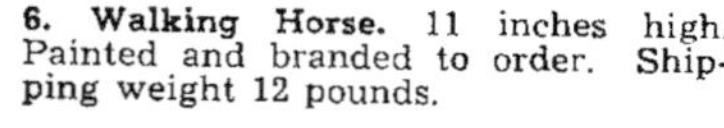

5. Trail Rider. Rider painted, horse painted and branded to order. Removable bridle with copper cheek pieces. 15 inches high. Shipping weight 20 pounds.

6. Walking Horse. 11 inches high. Painted and branded to order. Shipping weight 12 pounds.

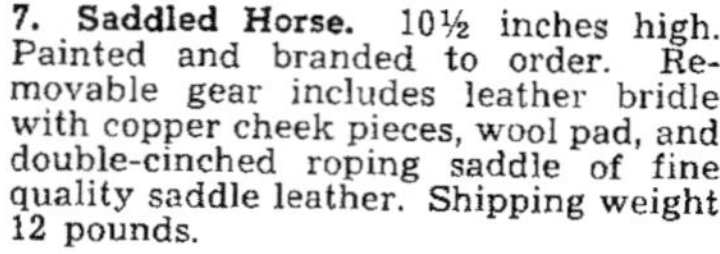

7. Saddled Horse. 10½ inches high. Painted and branded to order. Removable gear includes leather bridle with copper cheek pieces, wool pad, and double-cinched roping saddle of fine quality saddle leather. Shipping weight 12 pounds.

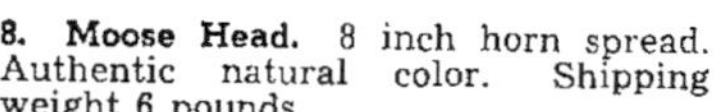

8. Moose Head. 8 inch horn spread. Authentic natural color. Shipping weight 6 pounds.

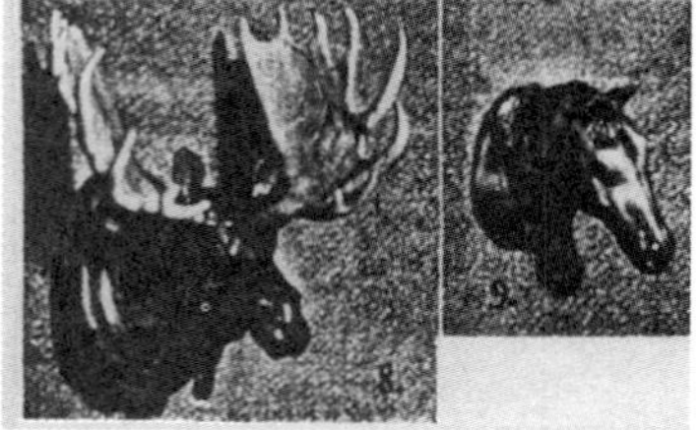

9. Horse Head. 5½ inches high. Painted to your order. Shipping weight 2 pounds.

Pack Train in Big Game Country. Includes numbers 1, 2, 4, 3, 5, this catalog.

10. Packing the Bronc. Length 24 inches, height 12 inches. All details complete and authentic. Painted and branded to your order, or finished in polished natural ebony color. Shipping weight 25 pounds.

11. (1) Curiosity. Brown cub and black investigate a hollow log. Length 11 inches.

(2) Calamity. Blackie gets stuck, Brownie tries to pull him out, rabbit escapes. Length 9 inches:

(3) Catastrophe. Brownie tries to pull out Blackie, rabbits laugh, Length, 13 inches. Shipping weight, set, 8 pounds,

12. Western Birds. Authentic colors and details. About 2½ inches long. Shipping weight, each, 6 ounces.

Lapel pins
a. Steller's Jay
b. Magpie
c. Mountain Chickadee
d. Mountain Bluebird
e. Killdeer
f. Redwing
g. Western Meadowlark

Pot Ornaments
h. Magpie
i. Killdeer
j. Western Meadowlark
k. Mountain Chickadee
l. Mountain Bluebird
m. Steller's Jay

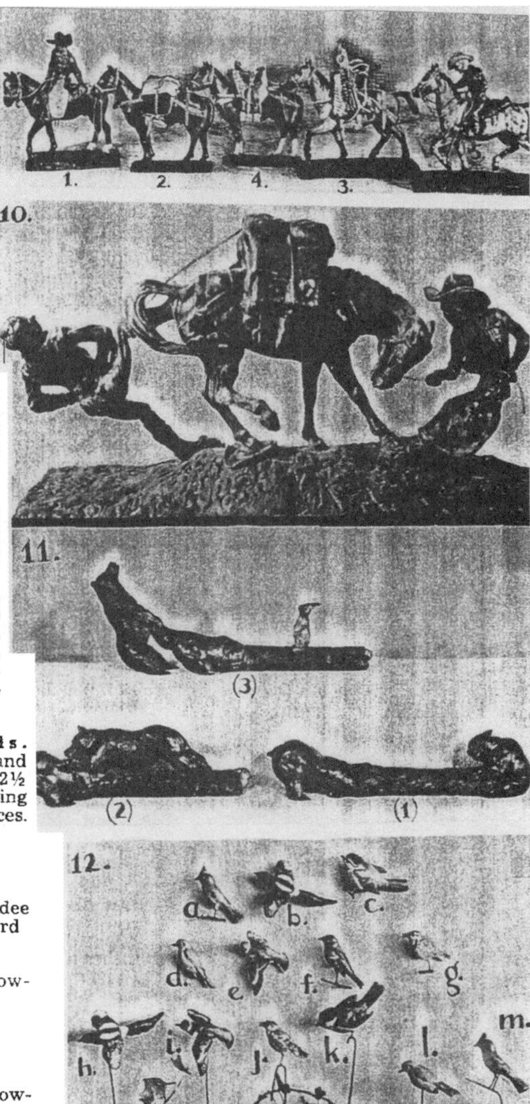

13. Keep Your Shirt On. Height 12 inches. Cowboy horseshoer and his mischievous pony. Finished in polished natural ebony color, or painted to order. Shipping weight 18 pounds.

14. Cowboy and saddle. 11 inches high. Polished ebony color, or painted to order. Shipping weight 5 pounds.

15. Close Harmony. Cowboy and his dog make music. 9 inches high. Blue levis and jacket; black and tan shepherd dog. Shipping weight 2 pounds.

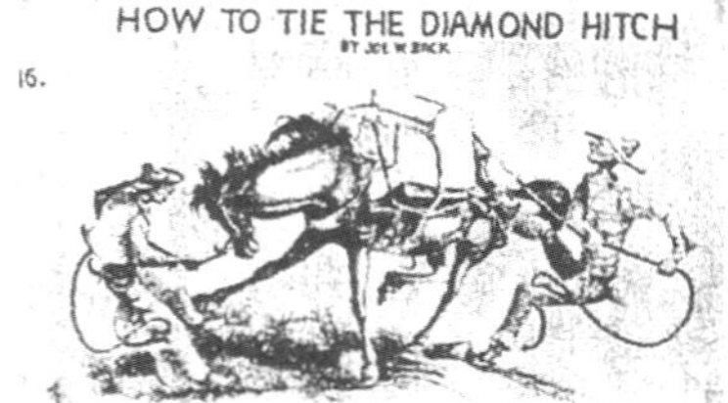

16. Booklet, **"How to Tie the Diamond Hitch."** Authentic information about the packer's art. Postpaid.

17. Grizzly Family. Mother Grizzly watches over two cubs. Polished natural ebony color only. 7 inches high. Shipping weight, pair, 10 pounds.

Mary's Way

18. Bull Moose. Stands 14 inches high to tips of horns. 8 inch spread. Authentic color and pattern. Shipping weight 10 pounds.

19. Mountain Sheep. Mature Bighorn ram. Stands 8 inches high. Authentic natural color. Shipping weight 5 pounds.

20. Antelope. Stands 12 inches high. Authentic natural color. Shipping weight 6 pounds.

21. Elk. 6-point Bull. Stands 14 inches high to tips of horns. Authentic natural color. Shipping weight 10 pounds.

22. Double Ram's Head Vase. Polished ebony color, or painted to order. 5½ inches high. Shipping weight 9 pounds.

23. Seated Cub Ash Tray. Polished ebony color, 3 inches high. Shipping weight 2 pounds.

24. Little Horse. 6½ inches high. Painted and branded to your order. Shipping weight 2 pounds.

25. Cub and Log Ash Tray. 3½ inches high. Polished ebony color. Shipping weight 2 pounds.

26. Howling Coyote, lying down. 4 inches high. Authentic natural color. Shipping weight 1 pound.

27. Barking Coyote, 4½ inches high. Authentic natural color. Shipping weight 1 pound.

28. Laughing Rabbit. 3 inches high. Authentic natural color. Shipping weight 4 ounces.

29. Howling Coyote, seated. 5 inches high. Authentic natural color. Shipping weight 1 pound.

30. Boxing Bear, 4½ inches high, natural brown, shipping weight 12 ounces.

31. Bear and Honey bookend. "Before." Natural Brown.

32. Bear and Honey bookend. "After." Natural brown. Shipping weight, pair, (31 and 32), 9 pounds.

33. Seated Cub. 3½ inches high, natural brown. Shipping weight 8 oz.

34. Standing Bear. 5½ inches high, natural brown, ship. wt. 1½ lbs.

35. "Ol' Dopey," caricature of a horse head, 7 inches high. Baldfaced roan. Shipping weight 3 pounds.

36. Head of Bighorn Ram. Height 8 inches. Authentic natural color. Shipping weight 6 pounds.

37. Antelope Head. 7 inches high. Authentic color. Shipping wt. 2 lbs.

38. Mule Deer Fawn. 4 inches high. Authentic natural color. Shipping weight 1½ pounds.

Mary's Way

JOE
and
MARY
BACK

JOE, painter and sculptor, is the designer of this series. Above, he is shown working on the clay original of number 10 "Packing the Bronc." For many years he has lived in the high mountain country of northwest Wyoming, where he has been a guide, packer, hunter, and a constant student of big game.

His ambition is to capture the spirit of the West as he knows it: incidents of the lives, and expressions of the feelings, of all the creatures who live here — mice, men, and moose, and sizes between.

Write or see Joe if you'd like some individual pieces custom-modeled — a portrait of your own horse, for example.

MARY, also an artist and student of the lives of animals, is designer of the bird models, number 12. The photo shows her working on a reproduction of Joe's original sculpture "Keep Your Shirt On," number 13. She takes care of the technical end of reproducing Joe's original's for sale. All the work is done by hand in Joe's or Mary's studio.

The Material is a new synthetic. Tough, strong, and durable, it combines the qualities of fine detail found in gypsum with the enduring strength and resiliency of furfural resin. Each piece is oven-cured at least 48 hours. In the oven it bakes to a rich dark color resembling both bronze and ebony, and acquires a metallic ring. We finish it either by polishing the natural dark surface, or by painting it to your order.

We Have No Manufacturing Secrets. We hope the originality and authenticity of our work will always be the basis of our reputation.

We Copyright the models for our protection.

We Welcome Visitors to our studios. They are located on Wind River, three miles east of Dubois, close to the Cathedral Cliffs of the Wind River Badlands. Drop in when you come by.

Joe and Mary Back   Dubois, Wyoming

Mary's Way

The Art of Living

❈ ❈ ❈ ❈ ❈

Mary felt very loved. Not just by Joe but by all the world around her. The Episcopal priest, Coach Wilson, had helped her as she sought to deepen her religious philosophy. She found in St. Thomas church a second home where she devoted much time and energy. Teaching Sunday School delighted her, particularly when she thought of ways to use her artistic skill. Every week she made a line drawing of a particular story for children to color.

My bible story drawings aren't so much…. They are very old-fashioned. It's not from the point of view of the good for the children, but just my own creative satisfaction. I get such a kick out of reading the Old Testament stories direct from the Bible, dreaming up the drawings, and putting them down in line drawings on duplicator stencils. I try for vividness, romantic appeal to children, as accurate a rendering of situation, action and costume as I can manage, a simple enough pattern so small children can color it without losing the picture, and a memory verse short enough to remember and expressive enough to tie in with the picture, and with some possible application to the children's own lives.

I've learned so much about the stories as I illustrate them: Lot's wife rigidly watching her burning home, while her teen-age girls try desperately to make her turn around; Jacob really wrestling with the angel (every picture I've seen just showed them kind of pushing each other around); the children bringing their offerings to Moses for building and equipping the Tabernacle; the family groups leaving for the long march into the desert under the night sky, with the pillar of fire up ahead; and Moses getting so angry he threw down the tablets of the law and BROKE them.

Before she knew it, she had become Sunday School Superintendent, while at the same time guiding the Art Guild as president and actively promoting the annual community Swedish smorgasbord (even creating a large, lively, detailed painting of the event). When not teaching, or working on the sculptures, or supervising the library, or baby-sitting the store in the summer, she helped Joe get his moose book manuscript ready. She chortled as she typed the collection of wild tales of Nosy the moose's interactions with humans. After Joe put the finishing touches on the nearly three dozen drawings, off it went to Sage Books who published it in 1963.

While mighty pleased with Joe's rising success as an author, Mary found herself struggling with her school teaching. During 1964 besides teaching, she became half-time school librarian, her mission to start-up a school library. When promised funds dwindled, and she could buy few books, she became disenchanted with the situation. The antics of junior high students also disheartened her.

Roughhousing, noise, misuse of books, must always be trying you out. A little wrestling, a little hitting, a little chasing around the stacks - these are apparently necessary to seventh grade boys, no matter how often they are thrown out for it. There are mischievous souls who love to tease by misplacing books, and there are some thefts.

Regretfully, she decided enough was enough, and she resigned her school positions. Now maybe she would have more energy for painting, although she knew they had gotten a year behind in sculpture orders. Having recently rediscovered an unfinished three- by three-foot canvas of her mother, Mary set to work finishing it. The hours just disappeared while she painted at the easel, trying to catch the likeness she remembered.

She had a new interest at church, too, that had evolved from her bible story drawings. She had been invited to bring her art right into the church services where she gave chalk talks - aimed at children but including the entire congregation. Standing up front, trim in her pant suit with her hair braids a tight halo around her head, she told a bible story in her glowing style. At the same time she chalked a picture capturing its essence, while everyone sat spellbound.

She started with blank paper. Deftly adding colors, she waited until the end to fill in the black defining lines and spaces. *"You can't see the picture without the black,"* she often reminded her audience as the added black made the scene come to life. The adults understood her dramatic demonstration of how life's dark moments help define the good times.

When Mary went to church, Joe tended store in the summer. His body was complaining. Arthritis of knees and hips had come silently but painfully, nearly crippling him. Nevertheless he just hobbled around, pushing himself to keep going on the projects that mattered to him. While store tending he sometimes worked on his latest idea for a book, <u>Suckers' Teeth</u>. Set around 1900, it called attention to the days when hunters nearly exterminated the elk; all because they wanted their two large ivory canine teeth as trophies. The book included a host of detailed pen and ink drawings poking fun at both humans and wild critters. Too often he would have to stop and visit with a customer. When he looked at all the animal model back orders waiting for action, he whistled. Shaking his head, he wondered how they would ever catch up.

In 1965 after Mary left her schoolteaching and <u>Suckers' Teeth</u> was published they talked and talked about how to improve their lives. The store had become a problem. In the summers it kept them under such tight rein that they chafed at its domineering ways. They needed freedom to live more fully. Two years earlier the doctor had become concerned about Mary's circulation, and warned her she needed to take time for more exercise. So most every day she took a walk, like she did one December day while puzzling over how to earn a living from their art yet also live. She called their dog Buttons and stepped out the back of the store. As she moved along she pretended her sister Frances was accompanying her.

Buttons is doing a wild dance on the end of her chain. Snap the catch and turn her loose.... She loves to run whenever we walk. Down our neighbor's meadow...nine horses are nipping yellow grass that shows above a light snow cover. Isn't that a deer beside them? It is! A proud young buck, sleek, high-headed, with a fair spread of horns.

Buttons starts for the animals, comes back abruptly at a call, bounces cheerfully down the dirt road. A rabbit jumping out of the frozen ruts sends her off on a quick foray into sagebrush and cactus on our left. She soon comes back and leads the way across the log bridge over Wind River. Three pairs of Barrow's goldeneye ducks burst up out of the water and circle whistling overhead.

Let's stop here and look. There by the roots of red birches, right on the rocky edge of the water, is the dipper who winters here, almost invisible in his gray blue outfit. Look! There he goes walking into the water, 'til his head's clear out of sight. Downstream from the rock-filled crib underfoot, you can see underwater a pattern of short white lines. They are peeled willow stems, dropped by the beaver who has a feeding platform inside the crib....

On both sides of the cattleguard at our gate wild rose bushes climb head high, now covered with bright red berries. Beyond are sprawly shoulder-high columns of grant wild rye and a raggedy field of picturesque weeds (like whitetop, rabbit brush, low sunflower, cocklebur, and clover) plus some grass. On the right are tall cottonwoods filling now with shadow.... Stand and listen to the cold and darkening woods. There are raucous sounds where magpies are settling to roost....

The sunset glow is bright over Windy Peak, and rosy on the snowy cone of Lava Mountain on the Continental Divide, 30 miles west. Dull red badlands rise to the north. Their shadowy ragged hulks loom over us. Watch your footing on the cattleguard. From the bridge the river is silvery pale. The goldeneyes have settled back on the water. The sunset glow is fading already. The brightest stars are showing.

A deep throbbing sound behind raises your neck hair, and you whirl around. You can't see him, but you know the great horned owl who lives in the cottonwoods is coming out for his night's hunt.

Buttons runs ahead, leading us home. The horses are

dark shapes in the meadow. The deer is invisible. Buttons stands quivering on the doorstep, tail wagging. 'Can I come in?' her eyes beg. 'Can I? Can I? It's Christmas!'

As Mary and Buttons pushed through the door, she may have startled Joe with her excitement. *"Let's move back across the river where I walked tonight,"* she may have urged. *"Why not build ourselves a studio-home in the woods close to the river."* They could get enough business without the store now; what with all the orders waiting production and Joe's books. Joe was probably ready for a decision It sounded good to him.

As the new river house took shape in 1966, Mary continued her daily jaunts. Following her on one such walk was not for the faint of heart. She set a fast pace, and zipped under, over or through barbed wire fences at a speed hard to duplicate. Where did she go? Along the river, of course, and its adjacent sloughs and springs. The woods differed from the thickets and the fence row attracted still other critters and plants. She checked the desert land away from the river, and the areas around the emerging house, yard and garden. Always intent on looking, she often brought back samples of plants or litter that she wanted to remember. She soon organized her walks into half-mile segments going in all directions from the new house.

She loved the Wind River and looked forward to living close to its wandering way. They set the house back, hoping to protect it from spring floods, as they both remembered the year Joe's bridge washed away downstream. Then of course, no one would forget what happened in June 1956.

The river had been coming up and up, and really began rampaging. There were two nights when few people slept, and lots of us were out filling sandbags and making impromptu dikes. The governor sent word to the highway crews to use all equipment and men, and sign on extra shifts, to build dikes and otherwise help. It was most exciting, and the highway crews actually turned the trick…. A few small bridges went out, but ours held. The beaver, of course, all lost their homes, and …wandered about disconsolately here and there.

The river was an enigma. Just when you thought you knew what to expect, it surprised you. Fed by many warm springs, the fifteen mile stretch of river near Joe and Mary never froze in winter; at least that's what people bragged, until one very frigid winter.

It was a once in a lifetime experience for me today when I walked all the way across Wind River on the ice…. At one place it looked as if it might be bridged over. I walked out carefully, my forward foot testing the ice at each step. There was not a single warning snap.

The bridge was ten feet or so wide, made of ice cakes piled across the channel, cemented with splashed frozen water and smoothed with yesterday's snow. The upper channel, about two feet wide, threw around little ice cakes the size of saucers that landed along its edges and against the bridge. It was building up levees on both icy edges and on the bridge….

The lower channel started hardly three inches wide, and all of Wind River tried to get through it. It snorted and bellowed and choked. It threw up long strings of water with drops on top. It was building levees with its vomit. I edged back as a drop bounced off my overshoe. The drop was not water - it was solid ice. (High Country News, Jan. 26, 1979)

This flowing lifeline attracted all sorts of birds and animals. Mary loved to spy on them, making quick sketches of such visitors as the trumpeter swans (*See sketch 12*). Dippers entranced her. These relatives of wrens came south from their summer mountain streams to winter in the Wind River. Their oily feathers trap a sheen of air bubbles, allowing them to walk under water on food hunts. Watching a pair interact one February morning she warmed to their antics.

Two dippers flying courting patterns…. Heard their hoarse twittering as I stood on the river edge beside the bridge…. They flew…under the near channel very fast and only a foot apart…and flew in a corkscrew spiral from bank to bank and upstream a couple of hundred yards, then a 180 degree turn and fast spiral flight back to the bridge, a turn under the floor…back through south channel twittering off out of sight…. Then back…and lighting a few feet apart on edge of ice…now began a second stage. The one I took to be

*the female stood quietly while the male took short flights
...over her, almost touching as he crossed each time.... At
the moment of almost touching the female crouched and
spread her wings. After five or six flights the birds
moved...into shallow water, standing knee deep on stones.
The pattern of short flights and crouch with spread wings
continued, with...a little splashing. After another five or six
flights the male took off out of sight upstream and the female
took a bath and groomed and polished her feathers. My
guess is they won't mate until...May, but they are enjoying
the preliminaries.*

One late fall day common mergansers (small ducks) attracted
her attention as she sat painting, her easel and canvas board set
up along the edge of the river.

*The early sun is low over my right shoulder, and shines
brightly against the undercut reddish bank. Beyond the*

Sketch Twelve   **Trumpeter Swans**

curve of river is a narrow band at the top of the painting, made of distant cottonwoods, badlands and cloudy sky. Near the bottom are two bright smudges of black and white on the water.

No one else could guess it, but I know those smudges represent a pair of common mergansers. I watched them there last week, the male shaking his feathers smooth close to me, looking down river at his mate just coming in for a landing.

I am warmly dressed. The air, though, is chilly on my fingers…. I am working as fast as I can, trying to get the triple quality of the nearby water - its dark transparency showing the rocks on the bottom, its solid mass shaping into hills with sinuous sparkly tops, and its reflective power repeating the shape of the mergansers. The landscape is shaping up, but I can't seem to fill in those black and white smudges. *(See Sketch 13)*

Incredible. A whir of wings behind me becomes four mergansers, lighting on the water - three females, one male. I drop my brush and grab sketchpad and pencil. The fish ducks are not so obliging as to take last week's poses, but they do give me fresh reference for action and pattern.

How glaring white the breast, flanks and wings of the male. Like the flash of a welder. How dense the black of his head and neck, with a sheen of iridescent green. How brilliant his red beak and orange feet.

Sketch Thirteen
Mergansers

His wives are quite different, more snaky-looking heads and necks, rusty-red with ragged crests and white throats, bodies white below and gray above, wings black and gray. Apparently quarreling, they stand up in the water, fly at each other, then drop down into the current and swim circles around each other. They relax, give themselves to the current and ride away from me, bobbing up and down over the waves of the rapids. Then they take to the air as suddenly as they dropped down. They fly round the bend, parallel to the water in a level-headed, arrowy way.

Wow. I'm sweating. I shed my jacket, and go back to my palette to try to mix just the right colors before I forget. (High Country News, Dec. 12, 1980)

Mary loved nothing better than to dawdle along the river banks, for what she saw there reinforced her emerging theology.

Resurrection was the miracle under my eyes this afternoon as I stepped on the soft old corpse of an enormous cottonwood, its body against the shore, its mouldering limbs reaching out into the stream. It cut off from the rioting current a little backwater, deep and black. It fed the roots of a small thicket of rusty and raspberry-red willows, whose long scarlet roots dangled on down into the water below. The

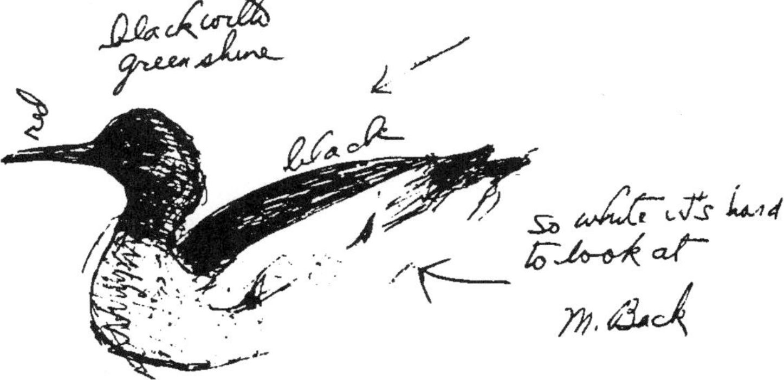

roots had caught and held a variety of small limbs, leaves, and other trash, further curtaining off the tiny backwater. Soft cushions of moss were spotted over the punky old limbs. Grass and iris were tangled among the willow roots, on the surface of the big old body. A school of tiny trout flashed in the mossy shelter of the backwater. Resurrection indeed! And the end is not yet. A tiny cottonwood sprout was start-ing, too....

As they worked to complete the cabin, news came of further family losses. Frank's husband Mo died of cancer. The remaining family ties resurged in importance. When Milton and his wife Marion visited, he helped build bathroom cabinets in the new house and then the Coopers and Backs just dropped everything and went on a twenty-day camping trip, reveling in each others' company. The next year Frank joined Mary in Dubois and they drove the rutted dirt road into the eastern edge of the Wind River Mountains to attend the Audubon Camp at Trail Lake Ranch. Those days spent close to Frank, wrapped in the mountains, close to wildlife, stirred Mary's soul. Ideas for paintings and thoughts supporting her views about the oneness of life jostled each other in her brain. Returning from a hike, perhaps she enthused to her sis-ter -

All life is equal, being interdependent and a part of one body. This is the same equality as propounded in the Declaration of Independence, that all men are created equal. Forms of life are different in all respects of appearance and reactions but all forms are equal before the love of God. The things we learned in Sunday School are all truths: all living things are children of the same father, and with an equal claim upon Love. What is false is the vertical setup of life forms that we get taught at school, with one-celled animals at the bottom and man on top....

The only 'betterness' is in respect to love. God being love, only that individual is 'better' which contains more love, or more God. As most of us know, by this criterion many a dog is 'better' than many a human. Every form of life contains some of love, or God, else it could not reproduce itself or care for its kind. God in any form of life is equally God.

As she observed the life around her she came to understand
how everything was tied together, both the good and the bad.
Human interference, like spraying pesticide to get rid of tent caterpillars, could have unexpected effects, she explained in a letter to
me.

> Four springs ago I discovered a big tent caterpillar nest
> on my gooseberry bush, and went for a can of spray to get rid
> of it. As I headed toward the door, with the can in my hand,
> a robin flew toward me with a sprig of sage in her mouth,
> and lighted above the door. I quietly backed off and replaced
> the spray, thinking, 'I bet it's those caterpillars brought the

Mary drawing

robin.' Sure enough, she built a nest on the antelope horns above the front door, laid eggs, and raised a brood, feeding them on the tent caterpillars, which just about lasted until the babies flew. Next year there were no tent caterpillars, but the robins came and raised another brood just the same; and also a third year. Last spring they were back again. Mother Robin had just finished laying her clutch, when one day she disappeared. Perhaps a weasel got her, or a cat, or a hawk. At any rate, though we mourned her, we were happy that we'd enjoyed three seasons of robins, thanks to avoiding pesticides just once.

Mary and Joe settled happily into the new cabin, attracting much bird attention to their feeders set out next to the kitchen window in the grove of cottonwood trees. For awhile, king of the feeders was a little one-legged nuthatch who patrolled his territory, striving to keep all other birds away. If Mary were to award prizes to her favorites, they would go to the rosy finches who came to her feeder in the winter. These "rosies" brightened her winter days as they flocked around. They never came in the summer, for then they carried out family life on mountain tops above 12,000 feet.

Our valley represents mild weather for them - 'south for the winter', though for some of them it is literally north, for some of them live in the Wind River Range directly south of us. They are little dark sparrows with yellow bills and beautiful light pink feathers making a pattern across wings and rump when they fly - it disappears when they light. The ones I have here all have neat light gray caps. The rest of the pattern varies, for my flock of fifteen contains three species who have found their way to my windowsill from areas actually thousands of miles apart.

The black rosy finch...lives in the Wind River Mountains, the high Absarokas, and the Tetons. Naturally, most of the flock are blacks. The gray-crowned rosy (a misnomer if ever I heard one, for all three species have gray crowns) nests on Mt. Assiniboine and other high peaks in British Columbia and Alberta, and there are a male and female of this species in my flock! They are bright cinnamon brown where the blacks are almost black. The male is brighter than the female, but the female is bossiest.

And there is one Hepburn rosy, whose summer home is the high mountains of Alaska, and the top of Mt. Rainier and Mt. St. Helen's.... How did it ever find its way here?

When the weather is mild, they mostly disappear - go up the slopes of the mountains, I suppose, to see how close they can come to their summer homes. But as soon as it gets either cold or stormy or both, they crowd around. It was cold this morning, about six above zero, and there were all fifteen of them at earliest daylight completely covering the windowsill, like shingles.... When the weather is cold, they spread out their breast feathers and sit right down on their feet, creeping around like so many mice. I had thought them strictly seed-eaters; but one day when it was below zero, I just thought some suet would give them warmth, and nailed down some hunks. They loved it!

Mary loved these winsome visitors so much, she decided to visit them on their nesting grounds. For nearly twenty years she backpacked with friends each June, hiking high into the tops of nearby mountains where she hoped to find females nesting. Since the nests were simply holes in rocks, finding any involved becoming an ornithological sleuth. Most years they found pairs of rosy

Mary on a Rosy Finch nest search with John Anderson in 1982.

finches, but no nests. Several years she came close. For example she wrote in 1972 -

> *Made camp on Arrow Mountain at last clump of Arrowline spruces. We used a six foot snowdrift for water. A very snug comfy camp. After tea at sunrise climbed Arrow Mountain before breakfast.... Packed above trees to midridge between Arrow and Circle, near ridge of curiously eroded pale tan rocks (Big Horn Dolomite) where we saw a male black rosy finch on a pinnacle and heard him sing.... Went across a draw to the nearest timberline spruces...made camp on slope so steep we found barely room for two level beds....*
>
> *(Observations): three bull elk far off, two cows passed camp at noon, hairy marmot on divide,...coyote trotting across meadow below camp, rock chuck and golden mantel ground squirrel.*
>
> *Spent morning above a rock formation...in territory of pair of rosy finches, pair of mountain bluebirds and pair of rock wrens. A female black rosy finch gleaned for fifteen minutes or so at edge of drift in recess in rock formation, then flew into a crevice and disappeared - did not reappear in half hour I watched. Surmise she was brooding eggs. Rock wren worked hard for two hours to 'sing us away'. We felt sorry for him. His fatigue was evident. When we left...we felt sure he told his wife, 'I sure sent them away with a bug in their ears! I told them a thing or two'....*

One cold December day a forest ranger happened on someone crawling up the rocky slope above Dinwoody Creek. Investigating, he discovered Mary. Her clear blue eyes lit up as she exclaimed happily that she was just out looking for rosy finch nests. Water ran from her eyes from the cold wind, but she continued on her way intent on seeing what she could find.

Keeping track of the bird world became an ongoing passion. As an avid bird counter, she led the Dubois annual Audubon Christmas bird count (one of hundreds taken each year across the United States). She assigned volunteers to different areas to survey for bird numbers. Then at dark they would all stomp off the snow and go to the Backs for a carry-in dinner. After swapping stories and eating in the wood stove warm cabin they compiled the count. She knew the birds in the valley intimately and fiercely questioned any odd sightings; rejoicing when many varieties were reported.

She also took yearly tallies of the spring migrators and breeding birds. If an unusual bird showed up in the area, Mary would know about it. While bird numbers were important, nothing excited her more than just watching bird behavior in action, even such commoners as magpies and ravens.

Thirty-eight magpies flying west at sunrise…. The magpie flight intrigues me. It seems foreign to their rancor, rakish, garrulous habit. It seems solemn and liturgical in nature, always about the same, silent, sweeping, just above the tree tops. Reminds me of a sophisticated sharpie barfly, caught somehow in a high church Episcopalian service of Holy Communion….

Twenty-plus ravens near the dump…. Most of them were sitting on a sunny slope soaking up sun. Some had wings half-spread, but six were stunting by the red badlands cliff…. The steady west wind against its face must make beautiful up drafts which the ravens were riding, up, down, around, only a few inches from the rocks sometimes. Ragged plumage on some made them look like torn scraps of tar paper. One grabbed a hunk of snow as he took off from just about the top of the ridge - a hard piece maybe three or four inches long. It didn't seem to bother his balance. Up there above the ridge, wings spread but not flying, he bent his head over to his foot and took a bite of snow. Some grandstander!

Over the years Mary got quite a reputation as someone who cared about the wild. Dubois folks knew. If someone found an injured animal or bird, take it to Mary. She would try to nurse it back to health. When a rescued bird died, she often put it in her freezer until she could sketch or paint it. An injured great horned owl resisted help so furiously, that she had to give up. Later she found just a few owl feathers and guessed a coyote had owl for supper.

One of the first invalids <u>was</u> a young coyote, found when only a couple of months old. Named by Mary, 'Feather' remained a skittish guest.

>*He is far from tame, though now six months old…. He would like to be tame, but, says he, he has too much sense. He's not at all fierce, only timid. He'll hold his ground until I am very close; then I can see his wrists begin to tremble as his resolution falters; then he dashes for his hidey-hole. He's apparently healthy as can be, his fur in beautiful shape, and he's as graceful a young silvery dog as you'd ever see. With every man's hand against him, we dare not turn him loose. Yet our only excuse for keeping him penned is that we want to study him. So we're making drawings and paintings of him as we find time.*

An April day brought an eared grebe (a small water bird) with an injured foot. He arrived carried carefully in a cardboard box. This overnight visitor bathed in a pan of water and ate ten pieces of raw trout, before Mary and Joe released him at Ring Lake the next day. *"He certainly looks joyful,"* laughed Mary as he charged off swimming with both feet. Such visitors as baby birds took round-the-clock attention. A young flicker lived in protective custody for two weeks before taking off on its own.

Freed of the store, they sought inspiration in the landscape. They took regular trips off season to Trail Lake Ranch, having agreed to monitor conditions there for the owners. They came to anticipate these drives knowing they would probably get a good look at mountain sheep along the way. One December day after they had crawled along the rutted, potholed road they happened on a group of bighorn sheep. During the winter, sheep often moved down out of the Wind River Mountains to congregate on the lowlands along the river there. This day gave them an inside view of sheep relationships.

>*Saw…about 70 bighorn sheep, including at least a dozen rams. All were with their harems, in little bunches of six to ten, except one bachelor ram…we saw go swaggering uphill to a bunch with a bigger darker ram…. The challenged ram moved deliberately out from his girls, stood shoulder to shoulder beside the challenger, turned his head slowly and gave him the cold and fishy eye. The challenger tried to step on past in the direction of the girls. The herd boss bent his head and gave the challenger a slow push in the*

*ribs that almost unbalanced him. He literally backed off,
then turned and went off the way he had come. Looked like
a display of the rules of the game.*

After they added a camper to their truck, they started taking mini-trips. At first they tried to take one day a week to paint in the mountains somewhere. When that proved too hard to arrange, they compromised on journeying to some scenic spot one evening a week. Enjoying these tantalizing tidbits of mountain exploring so much, they talked of a real trip. British Columbia had always intrigued them. When persistent invitations came from friends there, they finally decided, "Why not!" Off they went for a three week odyssey. Mary returned with the fall imagery fresh in her mind.

*Birches - slender ladies in see-through blouses of yellow
spangles....*

*The Rockies near Columbia Lake are wearing tattered fir
knitwear pulled over hard grey bones....*

The next summer they hightailed it to Alaska and the Yukon; another dream trip finally realized. She giggled over the red headed picket pins hoarding bread. *"One stuffed his cheeks so full they hung like misplaced breasts under his jaws."* She delighted in sampling the tundra flora.

While Joe's body continued to rebel and made walking a major undertaking, Mary tried, when she could, to get up into the mountains on her own two feet. Of the trips she took, highlights included a journey to a petrified forest and a four-day retreat into the mountains with church associates. Those who accompanied her described their hikes with Mary as being equivalent to a semester of college. Every casual word she uttered so nonchalantly reflected her deep knowledge of a wide variety of disciplines: biology, theology, botany, ecology, anthropology, archeology ...and on and on. Especially her understanding of animals and their ways amazed her companions.

At age 69 she joined nine younger folks in a trek crossing wild country, from Dubois to Cody. This two-hundred-mile car trip, they accomplished in six days as they hiked fifty miles cross country through roadless rugged terrain. Led by the Episcopal priest Burdette Stampley who had become a good friend, they hiked at the staggering rate of eight miles a day, Mary reported.

Everyone carried a backpack weighing 30 to 40 pounds, everyone rejoicing day by day as the packs got lighter by the transfer of food from packs into people.

The route was over the Absaroka Divide, some of the highest, wildest, and cliffiest country in the Rockies. None of us will forget the excitement of climbing up past the snow cornice at Cougar Pass, 11,364 feet, with the whole craggy world suddenly dropping away underfoot. It was fun to see that we exhibited the hysteria and disorganization supposed to go with oxygen starvation, and to see how we sobered up as we climbed down the slide-rock slopes into the exquisite (and oxygenated) valley...of Secret Basin. We vividly remember the seventeen tight switchbacks chiseled into the cliff between Pierpont Pass and Clark's Creek Meadow.

There was a lot of wading in fast cold water.... I fell into the Shoshone with my pack on - a very wet experience. I had to call for help. Needle Mountain is an event. More than 12,000 feet high, thousands of feet of sheer cliffs above the Shoshone River, it is a challenging beauty and a great obstacle to trail builders. Three miles of narrow pathway have been blasted and hacked out, high up the canyon wall. (It) provided us with an unforgettable last camp - a tiny grassy spot behind a cliff-edge hundreds of feet above the river. Too

Sketch Fourteen   *Mary Falling In*

<table>
<tr><td>Sketch Fifteen</td><td>Burdette Considers Routes</td></tr>
</table>

small to pitch tents, it did allow for nine sleeping bags side by side, like sardines under the moon, and a tenth in a little niche higher up the rocks - you had to be careful about turning over, not to roll off the edge. (See Sketches 14-16)

Both Mary and Joe believed fiercely in the importance of wilderness, rich with wildlife and having few human markings. After Frank and Mo gave them membership in the Wilderness Society, they became fast friends with its leader, Olaus Murie (and his wife) who lived just over Togwotee Pass. The Backs supported the idea whenever they could. When lumber interests batted down wilderness proposals, Mary wrote letters to newspapers explaining her support for Wyoming lands beyond human control, even though she knew she'd get nasty letters back.

With a wilderness bill bottled up in Congress in 1962, she had lobbied like crazy, hoping to be heard.

The local big sawmill sold out two years ago to a new outfit from Oregon.... The manager (a darn nice guy, too) told us the part that induced them to move here from Oregon was the Teton Wilderness!... Makes a chill run up my back to think of that last-stand wilderness at the headwaters of the Yellowstone getting lumbered-over and all roaded up.

Some years later she assisted Senator McGee in doing a conservation survey of the watershed at the head of the Wind River. When hearings were scheduled about proposed wilderness areas - such as the Glacier Wilderness - Mary joined those speaking in

Sketch Sixteen   *Looking at the Map*

favor of the most sweeping proposals. Her outrage over misuse of the wild, peaked over a moose killing incident. A local rancher killed at least 18 moose, most of them pregnant cows, claiming they damaged his hay.

He was arrested, got out on bail, and managed to evade trial on one pretext after another for almost three years. Last fall the farce was completed, when his final appeal went to the state Supreme Court.... They acquitted him, on grounds of the basic right of self defense! (He is a millionaire; could there be any connection?) Aftermath of that was that the game department sold permits for 142 moose on the upper Wind River. Hardly anybody got any. Feeling ran so high about the game department selling so many licenses for nonexistent moose, that there was talk about even getting up a suit for using the mails for fraud! For years there've been three moose wintering in our cottonwood bottoms, but none this winter.

When a local ranger told them he had counted 19 in the upper valley, they hoped the moose were recovering. Life and death - moose and man. Suddenly one of Mary's most dependable supporters was gone. Cancer took beloved Milton's life in August 1971, just a few months after my mother, his wife Marion, died in an auto accident. Mary had rushed to the east coast to share some time with him, special hours that she treasured. After Milton and Marion's ashes were spread in a forest near their home, Mary liked to think of them, resurrected - part of ongoing life there. They might be gone from their bodies, but they remained very much alive for her.

Whatever survives at the death of the body must be whatever is of God in us, and that has to be our capacity to love.... Love, being God, cannot die. What is heaven and where is it? Well, by definition heaven is where God is. And that is saying, heaven is where love is. Here or hereafter, now or millenniums away. We have to think in other dimensions than the four that we are familiar with: length, width, thickness and time. Love is not a matter of geography, or history, or outer space. Love is greater than any or all of these, it is found within them and outside of them, and the presence of love makes heaven.

Joe and Mary had health problems, too. Joe had hip replacement surgery, which to their dismay didn't hold. Then his esophagus acted up, making him feel like his innards were burning up. Mary anguished with him, trying to help her partner when the pain spasms left him angry and hurting. Then, without warning, Mary had a heart attack. Somehow they both survived, leaning on each other and their good Dubois friends. That summer they also had a new member of the family who became Mary's companion as she recuperated.

Clark, a baby Clark's nutcracker, had come to live with them when found abandoned in May, 1973. A chunky gray bird with white patched black wings, he became quite a personality. In his early weeks he had thrived on hamburger and water; learning to fly short jaunts from the kitchen table to the bookcase. When released outdoors, he flew off, only to return a few hours later - making himself known by flying right through the open kitchen window. Some days he had bounced from trauma to trauma; first getting attacked by robins and then crashing into a closed window. He loved to join Joe and Mary for a picnic supper by the river, where he indulged in trout, flies, corn and cheese.

While Mary enjoyed his company, she admitted Clark *"was foolish about Joe"* - riding on his shoulders, pulling nails out of his pockets.... *"Clark stayed and visited all afternoon...sat on my shoulder, whispered into my ear"* she wrote. Then, on August 9 he disappeared. My but they missed him, but they knew he needed to join his own kind. Two days later he returned, silent and wary, and talked softly to Mary. Before he left for good, he kept them laughing at his antics - hogging peanuts, going crazy over hamburger, and fawning over Joe.

Before long Mary surprised herself at how well and strong she felt. The Episcopal priest, Burdette Stampley, welcomed her back at church where he admired her ability to minister to those around her. "She accepts and cares for people most of us have difficulty caring for, she often acts as a reconciler when two people have hurt each other, she has the unique ability <u>always</u> to see good in everyone, she stands ready to be helpful to anyone at any time. In short, Mary Back is <u>THE</u> most loving person I have every met." He wrote these words when he recommended Mary for the 1977 Diana Award for community service. The criteria to be met by the three local nominees included that "each had unselfishly given of herself to a remarkable degree in some area of service which benefits others. Each was a woman who exemplified in her daily life the wholesome and inspiring qualities of love, faith, and courage." The Dubois winner would be entered in statewide competition.

Stampley recognized her as a truly remarkable human being and thought it about time people paid attention to her quiet accomplishments. "Through many ways she has enabled this community to appreciate our mountains, to see things we would not have seen without her, and to listen to her gently expressed, but very knowledgeable point of view about our responsibility to generations as yet unborn.... Mary Back has taught me much, much more about God, religion, and the meaning of the Gospel than did three years of intensive seminary training. Without a doubt knowing Mary and sharing priceless conversations about the most important things in the world...have been the most exciting things in my life in Dubois.... Two things about her contributions are especially noteworthy - her art and her teaching. Mary's art is a style that is completely original... in its capacity to be realistic and yet capture the special beauty in the world which Mary sees through her eyes alone. In her teaching of art she encourages what she practices. She always tells her students that everyone has their own style. She teaches them to develop their own originality without copying anyone else's."

Mary had sat down with Stampley and shared the sad as well as the glad times of her life, drawing a lifeline showing its ups and downs. (*See Sketch 17*) Her understanding of love had taken a roller coaster ride. When her infant Martha died in childbirth, she did not understand how God could be loving and allow this child's death. The passage of her years in Wyoming allowed her to rediscover that in fact, God <u>is</u> Love. She came to understand that the ups and downs are all part of life. When she affirmed life, she observed it consisted of opposites: well being and sickness; joy and pain; success and failure; discovery, adventure, and fear; motion, emotion, quietness and peace.

When Mary was honored as the Dubois winner of the Diana Award for 1977 and then went on to win the State Award, she couldn't believe it. After all, she just did what needed to be done; what anyone would do. Once again she was very thankful for all the love she observed around her.

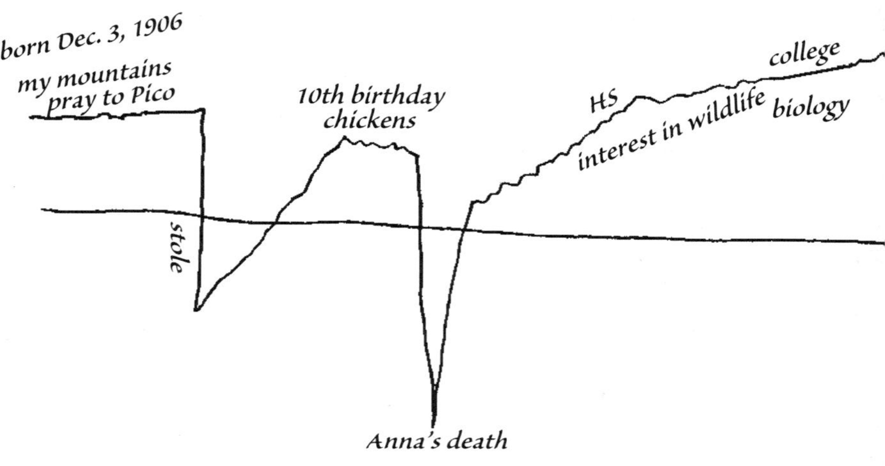

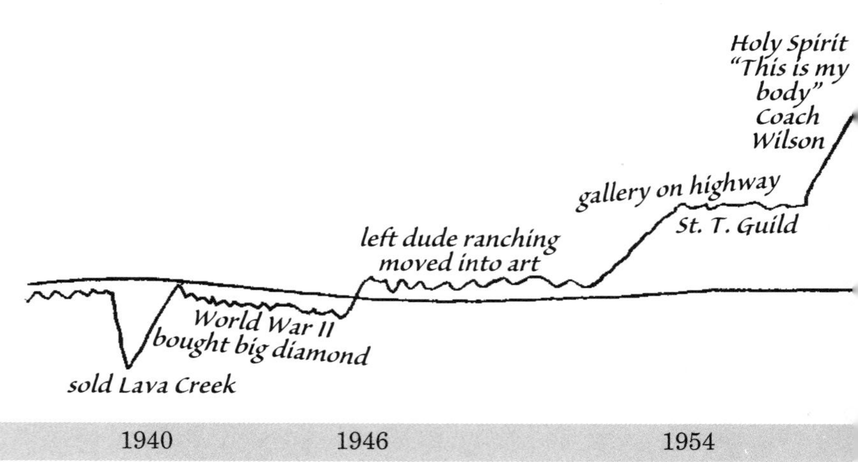

Sketch Seventeen
Mary's Lifeline

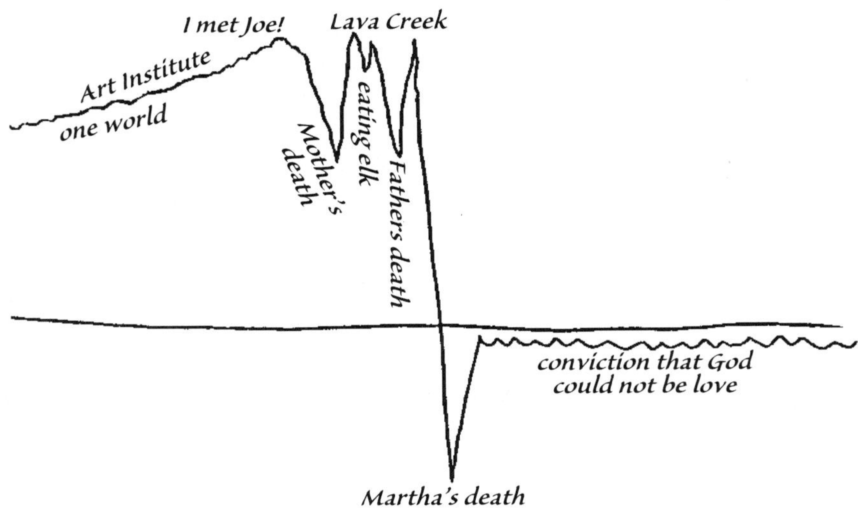

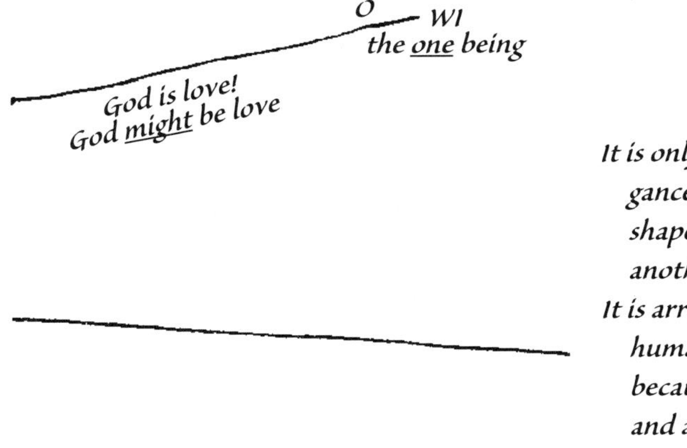

It is only human arrogance that says one shape is better than another shape.

It is arrogance that says humans are superior because of knowledge and ability to reason. Knowledge is not a good. Knowledge is a tool - may be good, may be evil. The only good is love.

Living Art

❖ ❖ ❖ ❖ ❖

Life was wonderful. Freed of the store responsibility, living by the river in their studio, opportunities to use their art came knocking at their door. Accustomed as they were to delivering animal models to customers, they now received new reasons to take to the road in the interest of art. Would they both come teach sculpture and painting in Pinedale for a week? "O.K." How about a two "man" show at Casper College? Could they round up enough of their paintings for an exhibit? "Well, yes."

In addition, new projects were brewing at their studio. Mary's daily walks had provoked her into writing a book about the natural history of the ecological niches she investigated. Entitled <u>Seven Half Miles from Home, Notes of a Wind River Naturalist,</u> she based it in the pile of journals she had kept since the very first walk. While she struggled to turn her notes into readable prose, she learned that a new book about Fremont County would use a reproduction of one of her paintings. This special painting showed the Burlinghams, the first pioneer family, arriving in the upper Wind River Valley in 1888. With Ramshorn Peak towering in the back, her good friend Frankie Moriarty, (then a child of ten) skipped across the canvas, while others in her family clambered out of their covered wagon. Mary was all smiles when she heard about it.

Joe was a-buzz with an idea! He was seriously thinking of getting out of the plastic impregnated sculpture business altogether.

His idol, Charlie Russell, the western artist who created the best paintings Joe knew anything about, also had produced some mighty fine bronze sculptures of cowboys and animals. "Boy, would I like to try my hand with bronze," he admitted to Mary. The more they thought about the idea, the more it seemed this was the time to take the risks to make Joe's dream happen.

Getting involved with bronze work was a major undertaking.

Shifting to bronze…requires either a financial angel or a whole lot of savings. Ours has been the savings routine. It takes in the neighborhood of $8,000 to make a start in bronze. You can do it for less if you do all the work yourself, but it means using all your creative time for a long while learning the process, including vast amounts of mistakes. We decided to go the foundry route. The first really good statuary bronze outfit we found out about is in Prescott, Arizona. We've made three trips there already: one to leave the originals with them, one to work on the wax shells which are the in-between step in the lost wax process, and the third to pick up five finished bronzes.

We are now trying out a much closer place in Loveland, Colorado, have made those first two trips and are about to leave tomorrow to get the first bronzes from them. The pieces are so expensive that it is necessary to get to know a whole new circle of people who have money enough to buy them, and we haven't learned that technique yet. We did sell one piece for $1500 to….Paul Corbett of Barrington, Illinois. He stopped in at the Prescott foundry, saw the wax of it, and phoned Joe.

When Mr. Corbett's check came in payment, they were so nervous about dealing with so much money, that they had his credit rating checked, and discovered he was a bank president in Chicago! Later Mr. Corbett donated the sculpture to the Whitney

Joe's bronze "Keep Your Shirt On"

Gallery of Western Art in Cody.

In the next fourteen years Joe's fingers delighted in crafting the clay originals that then became table top size bronze replicas. The subjects included cowboys, dudes, horses, moose and bears and often glimmered with Joe's humor. For example, one depicted a moose cornering a hunter up a tree; another showed a bear and hunter with a guide taking a photo. Solo and group renditions of horses revealed Joe's incredibly good sense of their anatomy. They exude fluid grace as they canter or frolic; all glowing with the dark beauty of bronze. Joe was amazed how well the bronzes sold, as each of the few copies made from an original were priced $1,000 or more. When some of the first bronzes sold out, they even had more copies made.

Joe's new sculptures certainly caught people's attention,

Joe sculpting

"Treed"

and one day he got a call from folks in Douglas about creating a bronze to commemorate Douglas's bicentennial. Pleased as punch, he created a cowboy riding a bucking horse and cast it in bronze. In 1976, "Jerky Bill on Poison Spider" was dedicated and this thrusting man-horse dynamo became the center piece of the lobby of the new Converse County Courthouse in Douglas. Then Joe set off to create more of his own bronzes. As much as possible they combined foundry trips with visits to other artists and exhibits at museums reached along the long route. The last bronze came from the foundry in 1985.

To Mary's joy, the Dubois folks who had incorporated the new local history museum came looking for her help. They wanted a mural depicting the history of Dubois. Could she help? Could she! As she planned and painted, she also made sure she had time to backpack in the mountains and learn how to use an electric chain saw to cut their firewood supply. While the bronzes kept Joe's creative

"Horse and Hunter"

juices percolating, his arthritis made moving around harder every year. He had finally put all his tools on wheels to make it possible for him to keep puttering on home care projects. Nevertheless, she needed to help out as much as she could.

The book she'd put so much care into made the rounds of publishers; a frustrating many-year process. Finally, success came when Johnson Books agreed to publish it - if shortened by 100 pages. Somehow she managed that most difficult of tasks - cutting the words she had agonized over in the first place. Still, the very essence of the book remained - her sense of the oneness of life. She wrote in the book:

The great joy of a study like this is conscious immersion in the body of life; swimming in it, on an equal basis with the other forms of life who are all part of it, too; learning that in life as well as death we humans are all part of the same body as all the rest of living things. (page 14)

Pleased with the book, and astounded with how it sold, Mary

"Stop! My Hat's Gone"

"Git Over, Sunnybitch"

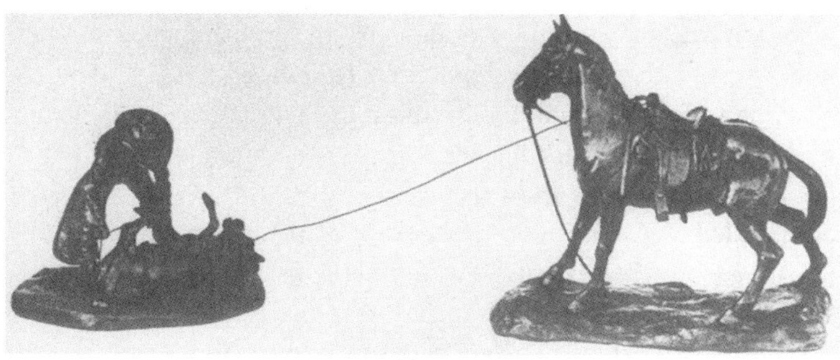

"Calf Roper"

could now spend more time polishing her religious thinking. At Sunday School she bounced her ideas off other parishioners and the minister, growing ever more certain about the power of God.

Plugging into that power is practicing the presence of God. Sit down in the woods near the river and meditatively consider one simple grass plant as if you were it. After a little practice you can feel your green cells stretching up in long narrow blades; you can feel the sun and the breeze; you can feel your slender white roots reaching down into the soil....

(One day) I met a mouse in my clothes closet. I looked down at him, and he looked at me. He has eyes like mine, a brain built on the same plan, lungs and kidneys like mine, and a family to protect.

After putting myself in the place of a mouse, it's no trick at all to put myself in the place of another human, any human. Why, I am practically identical whether he or she is near or far, of a different race or my own, of a different time or right now, a friend or an enemy. He or she is me. I am him or her. We are God's children together.

To me, this is really practicing the presence of God, who is love.

At church she saw the process in action. The more she put into its activities, the more she got in return. People seemed to relate to her simply stated beliefs.

Increasingly, she felt inspired to put her religious ideas and biblical stories into her art.

Her view that all life has one pulse she put into paint in such oils as 'Take...Eat This is My Body'. She depicts the Christian ceremony of communion with the blood and body of Jesus intermingling with a bull elk and a mule deer buck; with ripe fruits and field crops; with fresh bread and a fat Hereford.

She took Jesus and his disciples and painted them as if they lived today. After painting 'Jesus in the Temple' she explained, "*I put Jesus in blue jeans and a t-shirt by way of saying Jesus was a curious minded boy of his time - and our time too.*" In 'Young Isaac" she portrayed him fishing in a river that looks remarkably like the Wind River. Other paintings included 'John Baptizing' and 'Hold it Straight Jesus'. This painting of Joseph, Jesus and Mary shows a sawdust covered Joseph sawing a board while Jesus holds it and

Mary cleans up. When Mary entered it in the Wyoming religious art festival it won a first prize blue ribbon.

Exhibiting works at the Wind River National Show and the Audubon Wildlife Show brought much satisfaction, as did a one-woman show of her own. Most exciting of all, though, was the 1982 event held by Central Wyoming College, that recognized Joe and Mary's artistry by awarding them Medallions of Honor. Mary grew quite flustered when they received the letter telling of these awards. Oh, my! How wonderful, but - all that attention. Joe had just had another hip replacement operation and was still mending. The college wanted to also exhibit some of their art and memorabilia and someone would need to organize and transport them. How ever would they manage?

They liked the idea of being artists in residence for three days, interacting with college students and the public. So they went. Friends and neighbors gathered round and did what needed to be done to make it possible. A furniture store agreed to loan Joe a lounge chair for his motel room, as his leg couldn't handle getting in and out of a regular bed. That late September day they arrived at the Riverton campus - Joe in a new flannel shirt, hobbling; Mary beaming in a checkered pant suit, her white hair freshly braided crowning her head. They no sooner checked into their motel room, when someone knocked on the door. To their utter amazement, when they opened it, there was Mary's sister Frank and their cousin Mary Ellen.

Living art couldn't be beat! The days of ceremony (with Mary's first ever corsage), workshops and visiting just whirled by. Joe demonstrated the use of clay and wax in starting bronzes; Mary talked about the Wind River ecology, using paintings and drawings to enrich the presentation; Joe captivated his listeners as he talked about storytelling and writing, and Mary led a workshop where she and aspiring artists experimented with capturing sagebrush in paint. The visiting couldn't have been better. Before he returned home, Joe found his body would let him sleep in a bed again.

Life did seem pretty good. Paintings, bronzes and books brought in a steady income and they just dealt with their signs of aging as best they could. Gone were the days when they had to pay debts with paintings or sculptures, as they now even had funds stashed away in savings. Perhaps their greatest wealth, however,

Looking over the memory quilt

lay hidden around them in their friends and neighbors.

It took the Back's fiftieth wedding anniversary in 1983 to impress on Mary and Joe just how many fans they had. Twila and Stan Blakeman, younger friends who operated the local campground, organized the party which Mary insisted should take place at the Back's studio home. When Twila worried the crowd would overwhelm the small house, Mary said, rather offhandedly, *"Well if too many come, some of them will just have to leave."* She never expected much of anyone would come.

A human river of folks flowed through the house that February day. Visitors greeted Joe and Mary, squeezed past the bedroom to view the memory books and quilt, past the refreshment table, and out the kitchen door, where they wondered how they ended up outside. People from all over the U.S. sent memorabilia for the memory books and 138 squares for the quilt.

Twila had scheduled a party, just a few days before the big event, to put the quilt together and tie it - even though they were four squares short. When she heard from one of Mary's artist

friends who had a square to add, Twila reluctantly agreed to delay the quilt tying a couple of days. During that time the three additional squares arrived in the mail. Astounded, she chuckled, "Somebody up there is working on this quilt too!"

Mary and Joe were totally dumbfounded by the books and quilt. After looking at every detail of the quilt's squares, Mary put it on their bed. She swore she could feel the love that went into those squares as she drifted off to sleep. She slept under the quilt for the rest of her life.

The scrapbooks overwhelmed them. Mary probably read every precious word to Joe, drinking in the thoughts and memories. Quotes from folks like Helen Sabatka, who thanked Mary for encouraging her to paint as it had given her a lifetime of joy, must have brought smiles. Young friends Ron and Jan Brunk's words must have brought chortles. When they married, Mary and Joe had given them advice which the couple now gave back to them. Tell each other each morning how beautiful or handsome the other is - whether they look it or not. And each evening tell each other 'I love you' whether you feel like it or not.

Sculptor and cowboy friend Vic Lemmon's thoughts warmed them. "In double harness for 50 years and I can still see the sparkle of deep feeling you have for each other. I sure wouldn't be sculpturing if it wasn't for your giving and you do that for everyone and enjoy doing it. There aren't too many who savvy like you." Mary Finley spoke for the many children who had been inspired by Mary's chalk talks. The bible stories had come alive for her she said, and beyond that, Mary's art classes had given the youngster the courage to be creative in her own way.

Others, like Chuck Larsen, reminded Mary how much her philosophy of life meant to them. He enclosed a copy of a medallion he had seen at an art gallery at Cardinal Strick College in Milwaukee. This spoke to him of Mary.

AGAIN and AGAIN
The miracle takes place
the amazing transformation.
In which air turns into leaves
and the earth becomes roots.
In which the sun fills the seed
Bursting
New Life
Breaks through in the
Transformation of
death.

Poems from many gifted friends enriched the books. One from Pete Condis brought a flood of memories.

❈ ❈ Mary's Bird Will Live Forever ❈ ❈

We called Mary up, early one morning,
A bird flew into our window without any warning.

It died instantly with the sudden impact,
Without losing a feather on it's beautiful back.

It's a Golden Crown Kinglet said Mary with a sigh.
Oh why on earth did it have to die.

Mary took it home in her tender hands,
She's a wonderful person who loves this land.

She came back in a couple of weeks,
With a loving smile and a glow on her cheeks.

She handed us a picture she made,
A Golden Crown Kinglet resting on a limb in the shade.

This bird now rests on our living room wall,
It will live forever, winter, summer and fall.

God Bless Joe and Mary and give them long life.
For he's a perfect husband and she's a wonderful wife.

I'm sorry this poem has to come to an end,
For we could write forever about our very dear friends.

Tory and Meredith Taylor captured Mary and Joe in rich, thoughtful, imagery. "If we were to assign a symbol or emblem to each of you, Mary's would be a feather, and Joe's would be a torch. The feather for Mary would represent her work with Audubon and her knowledge of birds and nature. Of greater significance it would stand for the gift she has for making all people feel they are a special part of God's wonderful world. In Thomas Berger's <u>Little Big Man</u>, Chief Old Lodge Skins said, 'To see you again causes my heart to soar like a hawk.' We cannot think of a better way to describe seeing Mary.

"Joe's symbol would be a torch or wand passed by runners in a relay race. In the masterpiece, <u>Horses, Hitches, and Rocky Trails,</u> he dedicates an entire chapter to taking care of the mountains and our responsibility to respect all living things. It is a responsibility, obligation and privilege handed down from one generation to the next. Joe - the torch has been passed."

As Joe and Mary soaked up the love in the scrapbooks and quilt, they had no way to know that in the coming year, 1984, their whole world would fall apart. Mary had a series of heart attacks. She thought her life as Mary Back had ended. The first sent her to the hospital.

> *I wasted a whole week there, just because I didn't expect to get well. I thought it perfectly sure that my time had come. I wasn't hopeless or scared, just thought realistically that this was the only time I'd have this experience, and I'd better pay attention.... I didn't get better. Then early Sunday morning March 18 I died.... Of course this is not the first time this has happened.... I wish I could contribute some mystifying details about what it's like to be 'out-of-the-body'*

but for me it's a complete blank. I woke up to a sunny Sunday midday, and to a circle of smiling faces....

Dr. Fleming told me what happened. 'I thought we lost you Saturday night. Your heart stopped, your lungs quit, your blood pressure went down to nothing. We got the oxygen tube and the breathing machine in place. Then we flattened you on a board and massaged your heart hard. Are you positive you've no chest pains? It's easy to crack ribs with that hard massage.' All of a sudden there was a great light shining, and I knew I was going to get well.

Sketch Eighteen A
Tillie Mote

Following two more heart attacks after she returned home, a flight to Denver in a tiny ambulance plane enabled a four-way bypass operation that gave her a renewal. If that wasn't enough sickness, Joe then developed a major intestinal blockage, followed by a heart attack. Again, somehow they survived. Mary felt God had given them the message that they still had missions to accomplish.

Joe didn't bounce back well this time, however.

Sketch Eighteen B
Tillie Mote

His eyesight had deteriorated so much that he couldn't sculpt, paint, or write easily. Even the publication of Mary's book didn't jolt him out of the depression that swamped him. He couldn't follow the advice he had inserted at the end of <u>Horses, Hitches and Rocky Trails</u>, "When you come to the end of your rope, tie a knot in it and hang on." Disconsolate, one afternoon he hobbled outside, aimed his pistol at his heart and pulled the trigger. When Mary came running she found him still very much alive. The bullet

Sketch Eighteen C

George Mote

had bounced off a rib. Joe groaned, "See, I can't do anything right!"

Later that summer my husband and I came visiting and got to talking to Joe about what it had been like to homestead so many years ago near Douglas. After going to see a homesteading video in the high school auditorium, Joe returned home spluttering, they had it all wrong! Well, I asked, "Why don't you tape your recollections and tell how it really was?" With tape recorder in hand he started doing just that. Before he finished, ideas for a book surged forth. He talked with Vic Lemmon about doing a book of guiding-hunting yarns. As they gabbed about the idea, a greater one emerged. Why not do the book together? Since Johnson Publishing showed an interest, Joe talked his manuscript onto a tape, and Mary transcribed it onto paper for him. When published in 1986, <u>The Old Guide Remembers, The Young Guide Finds Out</u> had Joe's fans storming Wyoming bookstores for copies.

Pleased with Joe's recovery, Mary spent her days sketching and painting at the easel in the living room with light flooding over her shoulders, when not typing for Joe. After rockhound friends brought her a piece of serpentine, she tried her hand at sculpting Joe's head. She left the back of his skull unfinished following the Indian warning that a completed work meant death for the person. She would do all she could to protect her Joe!

Sketching was a favorite activity whenever folks came to visit or when she went to church or Dubois meetings. When she stopped to think about it, she guessed she had sketched more people in more places than she could even remember. (*See Sketches 18 A-C*) All she needed was a pencil or crayon, some kind of paper, and a few minutes. At one art guild dinner Mary joined other artists in a "quick draw" event. She sat at the back of the room where she could look out the

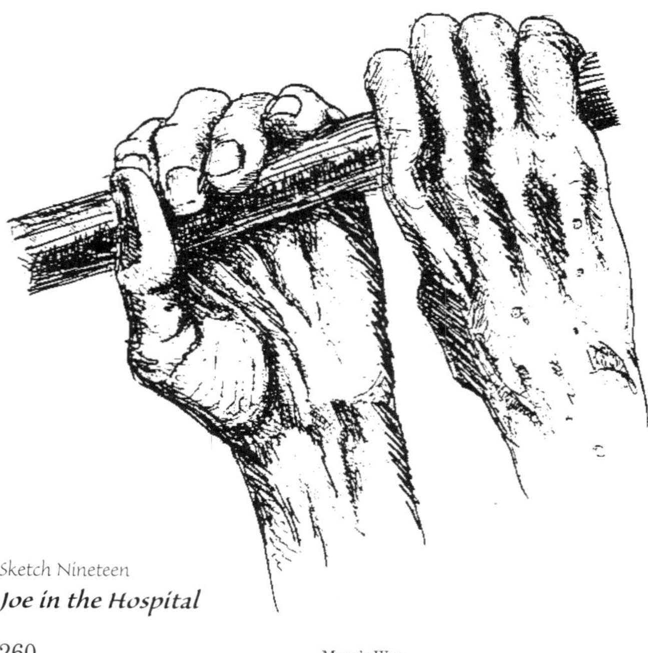

Sketch Nineteen
Joe in the Hospital

back door to see her Irish setter pup, and quickly caught the dog's likeness in a pastel drawing.

Everywhere she went her journal accompanied her. Ever since she began those daily walks so many years ago, she'd taken to making notes. Now she wrote not just about her walks but also other details of her life. She scribbled notes and sketched at meetings, often capturing the likeness of somebody sitting near her. She wrote lesson plans, listed official counts of birds seen for Audubon reports, kept art sales records, and made shopping lists. When either of them ended up in the hospital, Mary kept a record of all the details, complete with sketches. (*See Sketch 19*)

While she found she needed almost daily naps to recharge her batteries, she relished her walks along the Wind River. More than that, she had become a guide at the Dubois Museum in the summer. This meant leading visitors out into the Wyoming landscape to see firsthand the unity of life that thrived even in apparently barren desert-like land. She made sure she got home in time to help Joe with his latest book project: a novel.

He had pulled together memories from his homesteading days and written a story about the friction created when cars appeared on the western scene. Calling it <u>The Model T and the Lazy Board</u>, he suggested that Mary do the illustrations. She had worked up a bunch of sketches when Joe complained that he just didn't feel at all well. Following a trip to the doctor who took biopsies, the report came back . He had bladder cancer. Afraid his time was running out, she finished a dozen sketches and one completed drawing before the operation. While he survived, Joe's body had just had enough. He drifted downhill and died on September 7, 1986. She reported, *"I was holding his hand, but I don't believe he knew me that last day."*

Even though she recognized that Joe needed to move on to his next stage of life, she ached with his loss. It helped to have a memorial service and arrange for good friends, Vic Lemmon and Stan Blakeman and others, to ride his ashes into the wild land northwest of Dubois where Joe had so loved to explore.

The day after the service she conducted a climb in the badlands for 22 college students on a natural history Audubon tour. When the tour guide had asked for her help and learned about Joe's death, she apologized for bothering Mary. *"Now wait a minute,"* Mary replied, *"I think I would enjoy having a group of young people hike with me. I really would be honored."*

And so the group of twenty-year-olds hurried after her, short-winded behind her lean, easy-going, eighty-year-old frame, as she picked her way through the thickets along the Wind River.

They stayed to chop firewood, cook on her wood stove, and talk about how she and Joe had built their own self-sufficient home. They admired the solar greenhouse she had created with help from Audubon friends, that allowed her to have year-round tomatoes. They learned about Mary's belief that the earth is a living organism.

One of the students, Lauren Mofford from Maine, even stayed on with Mary, keeping her company for two weeks. Mary was thankful, *"I needed her."* She also mused, *"You know life is rich and it takes both the light and dark threads to weave a tapestry!"* And so she carried on without Joe beside her, but knowing his ashes would boost life in the mountains just up the valley. While Mary had to go on, it was hard. She wrote in 1987,

> *The loss of Joe was like an amputation, a cutting off of half of me. I survived the operation, but the bigger job is learning to function as a cripple…. I am aware that my new career, at least for some time, has got to be 'Learning How to Live without Joe'….*

Having that book to work on as a memorial to Joe, carried Mary along through some of the difficult days of living without him. She took great care as she created ten drawings to accompany the text, knowing they needed to be as perfect as Joe would have wanted them. This assignment was quite a challenge as she experimented with adding more spice and humor to the drawings than she would normally have done.

Fortunately, Mary did not live alone. Seamus, her vibrant Irish setter, lived on with her. That dog had quite a reputation. One day as Mary entertained guests, she went to get a pecan pie she had readied and set on the table. To her shock, she discovered Seamus had inhaled the contents, leaving just the pie crust behind. Never a dull moment with Seamus as a housemate! She found herself caught up in painting and drawing the beautiful dog, and even made a small sculpture before Seamus died a few years later.

As she tried to get accustomed to life without Joe, she found herself surrounded by her caring friends and neighbors who seemed always ready to give a hand. Then she got a big surprise.

DUBOIS' LONG-TIME RESIDENT ARTIST and educator Mary Back contemplates the booty she garnered last Friday at a special awards banquet honoring artists who have made significant contributions to the arts in Wyoming. The raku totem at her side was created by Cheyenne artist Terry Kreuzer Hagstrom. The images on the amphora-like sculpture relate to Mary's work as a painter and educator in the arts. The *Frontier* reprints the proclamation signed by Governor Mike Sullivan in its entirety. We can think of no higher honor to commemorate Mary's achievements than to print it verbatim, so that all of Dubois may know of her accomplishments.

Frontier photo/Linda Putman

PROCLAMATION

WHEREAS, *it is recognized that artistic and cultural experiences contribute greatly to the lives of Wyoming's residents; and*

WHEREAS, *since 1947 when she began teaching extension classes in art for the University of Wyoming, ranching wives, mothers, storekeepers, cowboys, lumberjacks, school teachers, tourists, and youngsters have benefitted from outstanding and dedicated work as an art teacher; and*

WHEREAS, *before moving to Wyoming in 1933, Mary Back worked as a staff artist for the biology department of her college in Berea, Kentucky, was an apprentice in the workshops of the Chicago Academy of Sciences, and was the first curator of a natural history museum in the forest belt outside of Chicago; and*

WHEREAS, *her interest, support and promotion of the arts in Wyoming has continued through her numerous volunteer activities including her work with the International Wind River Art Show, which is the direct result of her years of teaching in Fremont County; and*

WHEREAS, *when the Wind River Artists' Guild was formed, Mary was president for the first three years, and she continues to work, paint, exhibit, and help with the annual show held in Dubois in August; and*

WHEREAS, *recognizing Mary's work over the years and her contributions toward enhancing all forms of art and inspiring students to work in their own particular styles, she, along with her husband, Joe, was awarded Central Wyoming College's Medallion of Honor in 1982;*

NOW, THEREFORE, I, MIKE SULLIVAN, *Governor of the State of Wyoming, bestow the 1987 Governor's Award for the Arts for Service to the Arts to*

MARY BACK

recognizing her as a leader within the arts field, locally and statewide, as well as recognizing her ongoing, tireless efforts in promoting the arts in Wyoming.

IN WITNESS WHEREOF, *I have hereunto set my hand and caused the Great Seal of the State of Wyoming to be affixed this twenty-eighth day of January, 1987.*

(SEAL)   *s/Mike Sullivan*
Kathy Karpan   *Governor*
Secretary of State

United States Senate
Assistant Republican Leader
WASHINGTON, D.C. 20510

March 31, 1987

Mrs. Mary Back
P.O. Box 827
Dubois, Wyoming 82513

Dear Mary:

What a delight to learn that you were honored with a special award given to Wyoming artists! I can think of no one more deserving of the honor -- and obviously the Wyoming Council on the Arts shares that view!

You have exhibited so much talent, warmth, heart, and love over the years -- your work has touched the hearts of so many people in our state, throughout the entire region and the nation.

I am so pleased that our fine new Governor, Mike Sullivan, presented that award to you. You are such a remarkable and talented lady. Your Wyoming friends and your friends throughout the world are so very, very proud of you for all that you have accomplished. I hope that things are going well for you.

Ann joins in sending our love.

Most sincerely,

Alan K. Simpson
United States Senator

AKS/lsh

Without telling her, the Wind River Valley Art Guild submitted her name to receive one of the annual awards made to Wyoming artists - the Governor's Award for Service to the Arts, and Excellence in the Arts. On February 20, 1987 she found herself in Cheyenne at a special banquet, where Governor Mike Sullivan honored her for forty years of service to Wyoming as a professional artist and arts educator. She received both a citation and a raku totem created by Cheyenne artist Terry Kreuzer Hagstrom. A month later she pulled a letter from the U.S. Senate from her mailbox. Opening it, she marveled at the note from Wyoming Senator Alan Simpson (*See letter, pg. 265*). Mary could hardly believe all this was happening to her but she didn't have too much time to think about it before she became a world traveler.

Her sister Frank had pestered her about taking some trips. Finally, Mary agreed. First she returned to Berea for her sixtieth college reunion, where she actually tried her hand at poetry writing again. Then she and Frank flew off to Russia for a tour. She returned from that trip shaky and ready to take life easy. She enjoyed going to the Dubois Senior Center for her noon meals and welcomed her nephew Chuck Larsen back for another visit. His wife had recently died, and he and Mary needed each other. He enjoyed chopping wood for her and marveled at the simple life she chose to live. They both celebrated the publishing of Joe's last book, <u>The Model T and the Lazy Board</u> (in 1988).

She kept thinking there was something more God wanted her to accomplish; why else would he have given her more time? The year before Joe died she decided one thing she really wanted to accomplish had to do with working more seriously on her theology. Through the church she enrolled in the four-year extension course 'Education for the Ministry' from the School of Theology of the University of the South in Sewanee, Tennessee. The study enthralled her and she immersed herself in the required readings and then sought other references, too. She soon sparkled with a surge of ideas.

> *We grow our own souls, if souls may be defined as whatever of divinity is in us. We are born with a potential for love, but as yet no capacity. The potential is turned into capacity by practice and training.... If our process of education does*

not train us in the techniques of building love into life, then they have done nothing....

Secondhand or reused love is the aspect of love with which most of us are concerned, most of the time. This includes instinctive mother love, the physical aspects of sex, the handed down body of moral and ethical principles....

Primal, or divine love, is another matter.

As to primal, or divine love, there is an infinite quantity available; the universe is awash with it. But how to lay hold of it, how to incorporate it into our systems? We breathe it in, we breathe it out, but that's not the way to build it into our bodies. I submit that the saints are those who have found out how. Great humility, prayer and fasting, 'practicing the presence of God' are among the techniques. I submit that the 'saints' (and any one of us in our saintlier moments...) are responsible for catching hold of God, or love, and building more love into life....

When she completed the program, Sylvia Crouter, who had mentored her progress, could only salute her oldest student, and marvel at her intensity of purpose at age 83.

The Back's art business had done so well, that now Mary found it possible to donate to a wide variety of causes, although the Wind River Valley Art Guild remained uppermost in her thoughts as the group struggled to purchase property and build an art center. She painted a little, but found her energy and desire diminished. Joe's studio had been made into an apartment which she rented, glad to have someone close by in case she needed help. Walking the banks of the Wind River to keep in touch with the landscape, she was content; unaware that she would soon face an immense challenge, a fire.

Awaking from a nap, she smelled smoke. Assuming a picnic campfire by the river must still be smoldering, she stepped outside only to discover the fire had spread toward her cabin and was nibbling its way up the back wall. While no harm came to Mary and the local fire department saved the house, the smoke damage was devastating. The stored bronzes survived unscathed, but many paintings, drawings, and years of memorabilia became tarnished with soot. Friends gathered, and former mentor Sylvia, tucked

Mary into a guest house on her ranch where she would stay for several months before she could return to live in the river house again.

The fire nearly finished her artistic energy. Living art was no longer a driving force. She focused instead on the art of living, one day at a time, husbanding her limited energy, still caught up in the wonders of nature all around her home, nestled so close to the Wind River. After Seamus died she thought she would not get another dog. Then a shaggy mutt showed up at her door and hung around persistently. Finally, she took to calling him Moose and decided, well, maybe she and this sad-looking mongrel really made a good pair. And a belated love affair blossomed.

During the last few years of Mary's life as Mary Back, she struggled with her body as it struggled, first with cancer and then with strokes that put her into the hospital. Mary's artist friend Mary Ellen Honsaker, arranged for a temporary home for Moose. When she went to pick up Moose to take him to visit Mary in the hospital, Mary Ellen discovered his foster parents were not caring for him. What to do? As she and Mary's good friend Twila Blakeman sought another home for Moose, Mary died. At about the same time Mary Ellen found Moose sitting in her car, as if aware that his loving lady had finally left him. Somehow, he knew.

On May 28, 1991 at the age of 86, Mary became something more than Mary Back. Many who had felt her touch mourned her death and found it hard to believe it was time to let her go. While she donated her body to medical science for research and study, her essence remained with her friends. Younger friend, Lyndie Anne Duff, shared her thoughts about Mary in a poem she shared at Mary's memorial service.

❀ ❀ For Mary, Wyoming Painter ❀ ❀
and Friends

She sings sagebrush and cowbone psalms
Among saffron-dusted desert flowers;
Of redrock's brooding form, those
Lives (a thousand thousand) of the
Silver-dappled river, and
Rhapsodies of many-storied stone, then
Gilt-winged flickers caught in flight;
A quality of desert dust, time-bearing
Water smelling leaves, the cottonwoods and
Willows wrung from mist.

In all drift of inlanding gulls, green, grey and gold, she
sums gracefully the essence of the light - dark-lined - and
Too, the river in the spring: milky,
Glacier-fed, in shadow, in the lee of
Aspen, smoky spruce - the hush of early
Morning split but gently mended by
The killdeer's cry - yet sighs the sad
Collision of it all with humankind, and we
Too are gathered in her light, and brought
to see and feel, by osmosis, her great gift
For life: given oranges upon a yellow cloth
A jar of honey, amber sunlight, silver moon
She gives us God

Epilogue: Living On

❖ ❖ ❖ ❖ ❖

Following her interlude with medical research, Mary's ashes returned to Dubois in a brown plastic box. The container sat for several years on a shelf at St. Thomas church while Twila and Stan Blakeman (executors of her estate) pondered a final resting place. When I inquired about the ashes, we all agreed she really should return to the landscape somewhere. Maybe with Joe's ashes? The more we talked, the more we liked the idea. This, however, would not happen easily. Joe had been spread on the top of a trail-less peak, Terrace Mountain, northwest of Dubois; miles from any road. I daydreamed about a pilgrimage of family and friends who would return Mary to Joe, and life atop the mountain.

Summer 1998 approached, bringing a reunion of the descendants of Mary's brothers and sisters in Bozeman, Montana. A call to Joe's guide friend, Vic Lemmon, got the idea percolating. Before I knew it, a combined horse pack trip and foot trek had taken shape. Four Dubois men would ride horseback and carry Mary's ashes and all our supplies, while my husband Sandy and I with two of our adult children would hike the fifteen or so miles, spread over three days.

"Make sure you bring bear mace. That's grizzly country," Vic warned. Although I was not keen to meet a bear, I felt sure Mary would enjoy having one as a neighbor.

On an overcast July day our procession left the trailhead. Four riders led the way, followed by one extra horse, four loaded pack horses, four dogs and we four hikers. Vic Lemmon and Stan Blakeman had distributed Joe's ashes and now served as essential guides to locate his resting place again. Local veterinarian, Robin Waldron, organized our food and would supervise our cooking. We moved easily through tall, stately evergreens with flowers on all sides.

The horses soon moved out of sight, leaving us to stroll through a rainbow of wildflower colors. My daughter Bonnie and I chanted a litany of the blooms we recognized -

"Columbine... cinquefoil... wild geranium... spirea... stonecrop... desert buckwheat... bell flowers... lupine... scarlet gilia... asters... paintbrush... larkspur... yarrow..."

Others, unknown to us, we absorbed quietly. Preoccupied with the beauty surrounding us, I stopped wondering about any nearby grizzlies. I thought about Mary and how she would love the meadows. She would know the names of all these brothers and sisters we were passing; why they grew where they did; and which were natives and which were foreigners.

After crossing the south fork of the Buffalo River and moving upland, we camped in meadows at the base of Terrace Mountain. From my tent, my eyes filled with the meadow flowers, and Angle Mountain towering beyond showing off its tree studded sides and rocky cliffs and slides. Further west, the Tetons rose in snowy splendor. Ten-thousand-foot Terrace Mountain awaited behind us, out of sight. Sage blooms tickled my nose, while my ears tuned to the gray jays' strident calls, and the soft dings of the belled horses as they fed close by. A thunderstorm growled and circled, finally dumping rain that blanketed us into the evening. As the sky cleared in the west, we dried out around bonfires, under the spell of the darkening starlit sky with a sliver of a moon overhead. Tomorrow Mary would again be part of all this.

The next day, with no trails to follow, riders, hikers and dogs clambered upward from the 6,000 foot valley through the vertically climbing meadow behind our camp. The slopes we followed all morning were scramble steep, alternating patches of forest with meadows glowing brighter as we gained altitude. We sang out new names - "blue bells... forget-me-nots... yellow paintbrush... phlox..." When Sandy called our attention to bear scat recently deposited, our song changed to "Hey, bear," called inquiringly to ask permission of any nearby grizzlies to travel unmolested through their territory.

The riders dismounted and walked often to help their horses better manage the climb, and to reconnoiter the route. The challenge was to avoid the cliffs between us and the ash spreading site near the top. We moved ever more slowly as we neared 10,000 feet – one foot after the other – mesmerized by the changing flowerscape: blue lupine fields, wild geranium pink fields, yellow fields, multi-colored meadow. I imagined the thrust of rock underneath us, that carried the core of the earth higher and higher. Beyond, views spread out in all directions, the rough land caught in intermittent interplay of sun and cloud shadow. Up over a final ridge and we had arrived. Vic pointed across the sloping bloom-filled meadow to a treed point of land jutting over the valley far below. "Joe's there", he affirmed.

Just then a herd of several hundred elk crested an adjacent ridge. Looking around, I knew this lookout would make a perfect home for Mary, too. She would appreciate the elk, as well as the nearby flowers, trees, snowy fields, and bear, while the other mountains and valleys spread in a wavy landscape north, south, east and west. Suddenly lightening flashed, thunder grumbled

The top of Terrace Mountain

Ruth Mary scattering Mary's ashes

ominously off to the southwest, and inky black clouds unleashed sheets of rain. The storm appeared headed for us atop exposed Terrace Mountain. We would have to spread the ashes but forget the service we had hoped to conduct, coinciding with one being held back at St. Thomas church in Dubois. We needed to get down to lower slopes quickly.

The meadow became Mary's bed as each of us scattered handfuls of whitish-gray ash. Caught by the breeze, the particles moved like ghosts, drifting briefly before touching down to rest on the ground. Once more Mary was part of the tapestry of life, her family of living things. As the ashes settled, Joe and Mary seemed reunited in a renaissance of life.

Mary would describe this as her resurrection. For as she liked to say - *"There is no death. It is impossible to take life… Dust to dust, earth to earth, ashes to ashes is significant if we re-read it life to life… Life becomes more life. In life as well as death, we humans are all part of the same body as all the rest of living things."*

Then we moved - horses, hikers, dogs - rushing to get off the mountaintop. Before we crossed the first ridge, the rain started. By the time we reached sheltering trees, thunder clapped, lightening bolted nearby and the rain turned to downpour, then hail.

Mary's Way

Much as I pushed myself, everyone soon moved out of sight. Peering through the downpour I could just make out my tall son Glenn, standing like a beacon on the ridge line and I headed for this way marker thankfully, with my heart pounding loud in my ears. While we hustled moving down the mountain, my initial fear turned to delight in the wetness, even as my shoes filled to overflowing with water. Navajos believe a mountain covered with rain signifies the supernatural is in control. Being in the midst of this storm felt sacred and exhilarating. Both fire works, and water works had come to celebrate Mary's return to life.

The next day on our hike back to the road, our family stopped along the north fork of the Buffalo River, which drains Terrace Mountain, to hold our planned service. We felt close to Mary and memories of her crowded around as we rejoiced in her return to the earth. For me, she was the aunt for whom I was named. She was a close observer of the world around her in both prose and paint. She was a teacher, whether in a one-room schoolhouse, driving around rural Wyoming inspiring budding artists or hiking into the mountains with friends. She was a devoted church participant and religious thinker. She accepted enthusiastically the challenges that life brought her: becoming carpenter, builder, dude rancher, airplane mechanic, librarian, or technician when she needed to. She came to understand that even sad times, such as the death of Martha, were all part of God's love.

After the loss of their only child, the Backs apparently never tried to have other children. They kept their concerns about this to themselves; not sharing the sorrow the loss of Martha brought to their lives. Since young people sought them out, Joe and Mary nourished others instead, becoming foster parents to many. Mary's brothers, sisters and cousins shared their children with her, knowing she and Joe had so much to offer their offspring. The Robin letter that tied us all together was just one indicator of the family love that supported our far-flung families so buoyantly. Frank's daughter Carolyn shared her understanding of what was going on in her 50th anniversary letter. "Love is what has always surrounded us, an extended family separated by geography but tied together with a remarkable sense of closeness." Those of us who spent time with the Backs found ourselves immersed in Mary's love and Joe's stubborn humor; enriched and changed for the better. Two of her grandnieces continue the artistic tradition, struggling to work as painters in Boston and Baltimore.

Mary and Joe are alive indeed in Dubois, and it doesn't take much effort to find them. Mary's gentle persistence left a flourishing art guild and a vital community library that carry on because of the nurturing attention she paid them. They left their $400,000 estate to the Wind River Valley Art Guild and St. Thomas church, including all paintings, sculptures and even their home.

Glimpses of the Backs can be seen in the fine new building which houses the guild on the banks of the Wind River. Even their cuckoo clock is there in the Joe Back library, while the Mary Back classroom attracts hopeful artists. To Twila Blakeman, Mary is a living presence who is with her daily. Memories spill easily. Mostly she remembers the way Mary relished all life, creating something beautiful out of every opportunity. There was the day Twila arrived late for a date with Mary. Before she could apologize, she realized Mary had been so caught up watching the wildlife around her, that she never missed Twila!

Stop at any store in town, and someone will probably have a story. John Finley, sculptor, and painter of scrimshaw, recalls Mary as his third grade art teacher who many years later got him to agree to help lead the art guild. Joellyn Story attended a bible study group with Mary. When Jo just couldn't figure out how to define God, Mary made it seem easy, "Well Jo, it's simple," she said. "God is Love!" In Welty's General Store one of Joe's small pack trains still catches people's attention where it stands in repose on a counter.

What you hear again and again is how Mary helped people challenge their boundaries.

She inspired local cowboy Tom Connell, who grew up sketching and painting in a family who didn't think much of his efforts. Her fearless support, gave him the courage to really believe in himself as an artist. He went on to make a name for himself in Wyoming art circles. Allyene Palmer sees Mary as the champion who gave her the nerve to find herself as a person with possibilities. She remembers growing up in a home on the wrong side of the river where she was only encouraged to wash dishes. When Mary urged her to join her painting classes, Allyene discovered she could do other things. While she enjoyed the classes, she told Mary what she really wanted to do was paint with words. Gently, but firmly, Mary made sure she joined a writing group in Riverton; and even picked her up and took her there! Today she is a published poet, working on her Ph.D. in philosophy.

For Lyndie Anne Duff, Joe and Mary became parent figures who rescued her from a dismal life. Born in San Francisco in 1940, she grew up "a little wild dandelion" with busy artist parents. When she reached Dubois, depressed and purposeless, Burdette Stampley and Mary reached out to her. Mary's positive and caring nature pulled Lyndie out of her depression. Before she knew what had happened she found herself at church with Mary, walking with her along the Wind River, and at home with Joe and Mary in their riverside studio. With Lyndie's return to life, she became a devoted disciple of Mary's way. Today, she is a church deacon, having undertaken training to minister to others. Along with reaching out to prisoners needing befriending in the Rawlins prison, she cares for her ill husband and remembers Mary.

At the memorial service held in Mary's memory after her death, Lyndie penned eloquent words describing the meaning of Mary.

"Mary is like living Bread - she is salty and deep like the sea. We speak of Mary in the present because Mary will always be with those who love her and, through her book, with others. She is our mother. She is warm and nourishing. She gives meaning to life. Her presence among us creates a sense of family. She draws us to her and pours herself out to all who touch her life, but she never paused long enough to realize what she was doing. She has the gift of discerning the holy in all life around her, and makes us stop, look, listen and appreciate because she does. She accepts and thanks God for everything no matter how inconvenient it might seem.

"Mary's creativity, a natural expression of her abundant love, seems such a spontaneous response to goodness and beauty in God's world that we can't help but celebrate life with her, as though every day were a birthday, and every sunrise another Easter. When she teaches, she is as patient with herself as she is with us. Humility, which comes from a word meaning earth, describes Mary well. Salt of the earth. Simple and straightforward, stubborn sometimes too, like trees have to be to grow up in the stony New

England soil. But like God, she loves so much. Mary is always slow to anger, and quick to serve the Christ in others that others might not notice.

"Jesus also said, 'Come to me, ye who are heavy-laden.' So Mary never turns anyone away, nor does she take it on herself to judge the just or unjust. She stands at the gate of God's house even now, to welcome us. Surely her smile and her arms still reach out to us. She invites us all into the life of God by the way she lived. It's like when Jesus said 'Come,' and it's hard to resist. Mary personifies the call to come to God's feast and be fed. She is infinitely patient where we might lose our ability to bear with one another's human frailties.

"We think of I Corinthians 13:4 - 'Love is patient and kind; love is not jealous or boastful; it is not irritable or resentful; it does not rejoice at wrong but rejoices in the right. Love bears all things, believes all things, hopes all things, endures all things'.

"Mary is Love."

Mary's Way

SOURCES

Mary Back Robin letters, 1947-1990
  WILSON COOPER, 248 TREVARNO ROAD, LIVERMORE, CA 9550

Mary Back letters to Frances and Merrill McGawn
  CAROLYN McGAWN MORRIS, 5527 SCHMIDT ROAD, ELKHORN, WI 53121

Mary Back letters to Milton Cooper
Mary Back Robin letters, 1935-1946
Mary Back Long Trail Journal, 1930
Nature stories written for the Trailside Museum
Mary Back Journal about Joe
  RUTH MARY LAMB, BOX 1395, BOLTON LANDING, NY 12814

Assorted Mary Back letters to family
Journals of Mary Back's walks
Assorted news clippings and articles
Assorted photographs of Mary and Joe Back
Unpublished stories by Joe Back
Paintings, drawings and animal model technical devices
  WIND RIVER VALLEY ARTISTS GUILD, PO BOX 26, DUBOIS, WY 82513

Other memorabilia
  TWILA BLAKEMAN, DUBOIS, WY 82513

Nursery rhymes, illustrated by Mary Back
  JOANNA SPENCE, P.O. BOX 878, TREMONT, IL 61568